Critical Essays on
W. D. Howells,
1866-1920

Critical Essays on
W. D. Howells,
1866 - 1920

Edwin H. Cady
& Norma W. Cady

G. K. Hall & Co. • Boston, Massachusetts

Library of Congress Cataloging in Publication Data
Main entry under title:

Critical essays on W.D. Howells.

(Critical essays on American literature)
Includes index.
1. Howells, William Dean, 1837–1920—Criticism and
interpretation—Addresses, essays, lectures. I. Cady,
Edwin Harrison. II. Cady, Norma W. III. Series.
PS2034.C7 1983   818'.409   83–6089
ISBN 0–8161–8651–0

This publication is printed on permanent/durable acid-free paper
MANUFACTURED IN THE UNITED STATES OF AMERICA

CRITICAL ESSAYS ON AMERICAN LITERATURE

This series seeks to publish the most important reprinted criticism on writers and topics in American literature along with, in various volumes, original essays, interviews, bibliographies, letters, manuscript sections and other materials brought to public attention for the first time. In this first of two volumes by Edwin H. Cady and Norma W. Cady, the editors have assembled over seventy essays published during the lifetime of William Dean Howells. Among the selections are articles and reviews by such contemporaneous writers as Henry Adams, Henry James, Hamlin Garland, Stephen Crane, George Bernard Shaw, Mark Twain, W. E. B. Du Bois, and George Washington Cable as well as comment by such modern critics as Van Wyck Brooks, H. L. Mencken, and Wilson Follett. We are honored to add this collection to the series, and we are confident that it will make a permanent contribution to American literary study.

James Nagel, GENERAL EDITOR

Northeastern University

CONTENTS

INTRODUCTION

While Howells lived he was a prominent feature on the American literary landscape in each of six decades. Since his death in 1920, criticism and literary history have never quite decided what to make of him. It has become commonplace to quote Henry James's consoling message to Howells at 75, "Your really beautiful time will come." It is also commonplace to remark that though James's beautiful time came long ago Howells's has not. One of the reasons why Howells's time has not come is that the public continues to reflect the controversial critical reception of the man, his work, his ideas, and his points of view.

He wrote so much so well in so many modes that nobody professes to have read it all. Nobody fully knows him. Worse, much of what has passed for criticism rests on little or no reading. Among Howells's bitterest enemies patterns of ignorance too often stand plain. Asked how many novels of Howells he has read, William Roscoe Thayer confessed, "Only one." In his memoirs, Van Wyck Brooks wrote that during the period when he destroyed Howells's reputation, he had read perhaps one Howells novel. Brooks suggests in *The Opinions of Oliver Allston* that he came to appreciate the reach and power of Howells's fiction only when he read it at about age forty-five. Regardless of when Brooks did read Howells, no hypothesis short of original invincible ignorance can explain the contrast between the villain of *The Ordeal of Mark Twain* and the hero of *Howells: His Life and World*. The matter of Theodore Dreiser and Howells[1] calls for consideration.

The ways of the world being what they are, it need be no surprise that friends and critics played Howells false. Life, some people say readily, is unfair. The problem of Howells is more complex than that, however. He is difficult to grasp. He deliberately created glittering surfaces beneath which a hammock-reader need not glance; but for the serious reader he built layers of meaning as deep beneath the surface as he could reach. His longevity and the progressive acceleration of change around Howells kept him, like us, always in a process of adjustment. His extraordinary powers of work accumulated a mountain of documents. The number, the significance, the wide range of

xii   Critical Essays on W. D. Howells

his personal contacts bewilder the observer. He knew, with few important exceptions, the American authors born from the first through the eighth decades of the nineteenth century; his overseas acquaintance was broad. Authors he admired, especially the young, he cultivated and promoted. He was the friend of three Presidents of the United States; of labor leaders and millionaires; of rebels, social critics, and mere reformers; of many of the best minds of his time. He played a part in movements: for the abolition of slavery and the advancement of racial equality; for the emancipation, education, enfranchisement and equality of women; against capital punishment, against imperialism and militarism; against class division, against exploitation, privilege, and snobbery; for democracy, socialism, peace, and world government. As a critic, he backed unpopular authors, many of them progenitors of the Modern: Turgenev and a host of Continental realists; DeForest, Howe, Garland; Dunbar, Crane, Cahan, Norris, and Chesnutt; Dickinson, Jewett, Freeman, Murfree, and many of their sisters; Tolstoi, Dostoevski, Hardy, Ibsen, James A. Herne, and Shaw; the New Poets. He developed an independent ethics to hold his reality principles together.

It is not strange that he churned up tall dusts of controversy. Critical commentary in his time became wildly variable, often contradictory. The collection of comment here registers a history of conflict. What it proves, perhaps above all else, is that most of his contemporaries could grasp him no more exactly than their posterity.

I

In 1860, when Howells burst onto the national scene as a "Western" poet, he seemed an instant celebrity. Lowell praised Howells's part of *Poems of Two Friends* for its art and its western authenticity. The Bohemians of New York's *Saturday Press* singled out the same poems as evidence of a sort of genius. Perhaps it has been too little understood that antislavery politics played a part in the welcome young Howells received in Boston, Cambridge, and Concord. His family newspaper was "the voice" of Congressman Joshua Giddings and Senator Benjamin F. Wade, radical and strategically outspoken Ohio abolitionists. The Columbus, Ohio, paper on which Howells worked was the voice of Salmon P. Chase's political machine, and Howells had therefore won the prize of writing a campaign biography of Lincoln.

With the war coming on, however, not even a Western phenomenon could find an Eastern market for his novel in manuscript or his literary services. As a consolation prize he took a share of the Republican "spoils of victory" and left to hold the U.S. Consulate in Venice for the duration. He virtually disappeared from the literary scene until the war was over. But that was a small loss. In Venice he learned to read, write, and speak Italian. He mastered Italian art and literary tradition from Dante through Goldoni and into the contemporary. He developed an antiromantic, ironic power of vision which would connect him to the *avant garde* of his generation.

On Howells's return, he materialized as a triple phenomenon. He was Western and radically Republican at the dawn of the Ohio Period in American public life. He knew modern Italian politics and literature and traditional culture. He had sharpened his journalistic skills. E. L. Godkin admired Howells and hired him for *The Nation.* In a matter of weeks, however, James T. Fields tapped him to become assistant editor of *The Atlantic Monthly,* the flagship of American intellectual and literary magazines. New England sounded and the rest of the country resonated to a shock of recognition: a Western phenomenon had become a force within, perhaps the heir apparent to, *The Atlantic.*

In Cambridge, Howells found himself welcome in Longfellow's Dante Club, in the bosom of the family of Henry James, Sr., and in The Club, a dining association of the galaxy of Harvard faculty and other Cambridge wits of his brilliant generation. In Boston society he was welcome at the dinner tables of the friends of Fields and Lowell and Holmes. Among other duties at the *Atlantic* Howells was responsible for reviews and for recruiting, nationally, the "new people," the authors of his generation in every section.

Perhaps it is less than fair to say (though of course it was then suggested) that Howells's *Atlantic* advantages skewed criticism favorably. *Venetian Life* (1866) won rave reviews from Charles Eliot Norton (*Nation*) and George William Curtis (*Harper's*). Lowell, who had "discovered" Howells, found a subtle way to call his young friend a "master" in the *North American Review.* The book would stay in print for the rest of the author's long life, and it is likely that it has never been out of print. In turn, Henry James, whom Howells "discovered," called him a "master" for his next volume: *Italian Journeys* (1867).

Their Wedding Journey (1871) which began *Atlantic* serialization simultaneously with Howells's succession to the editorship of *The Atlantic,* also made its debut to choruses of praise. Yet its longevity, the history of its favor with American readers, may be no less impressive than that of *Venetian Life.* Generations of the newly wed left on honeymoons with *Their Wedding Journey* in their luggage. Henry Adams, who predicted that phenomenon, helped make his prophecy self-fulfilling by presenting the book to Clover Hooper, his own bride.

A Chance Acquaintance widened Howells's favor with audiences; but it was with *A Foregone Conclusion* that he first achieved the dimension of a "modern classic." Critics would recognize the fact

early, remember it for the rest of the author's life, and use the book
for a touchstone by which to test the quality of later work as well as
the degree of its advancement beyond the first received standard of
excellence in Howells. Henry James set the point in two reviews, and
even George Saintsbury, the dean of English critics, registered his
surprise at finding *A Foregone Conclusion* really quite good. Howells
had arrived upon the serious critical scene to stay.[2]

II

With its issue of November 1881 *Scribner's Monthly Magazine*,
which had published under that title for eleven years, changed its name
to the *Century Illustrated Monthly Magazine*, vol. 23, New Series, vol. 1.
The new editor, Richard Watson Gilder, trumpeted his claim to
connect vitally with the past while effecting a new departure. He
stressed his theme that for *Scribner's* "the practical recognition of the
merits of the magazine in Great Britain has been as surprising as it
has been gratifying. We have received from the English the most
generous treatment—from the press, the publishers, the book-sellers,
and the people, and it is a great pleasure to greet them as a constituent
part of the audience which we address in this article." He continued,
harping on the notes that the *Century* would be fresh, imaginative,
international, and, above all, well illustrated—lavishly, giftedly, beautifully *illustrated*. It would cater to a British audience. It is not hard to
imagine that one part of Gilder's audience which shared none of his
pleasure consisted of the publishers, editors, and regular contributors
of the comparatively stuffy, seldom illustrated British magazines whose
market Gilder proposed to invade more aggressively.

The first *Century* made good on Gilder's word. Its first page contained only an elegantly engraved portrait of George Eliot, accompanied in the body of the text by a laudatory article from the pen
of an English critic, Frederic W. H. Myers. Other British authors and
critics figured large in *Century*'s first volume: Andrew Lang on "Matthew
Arnold" (with portrait); James Bryce on "Lord Beaconsfield"; Edmund
Gosse on "The Early Writings of Robert Browning" (with portrait);
Mary Cowden-Clarke on "Leigh Hunt" (with portrait): Arthur Pen-
rhyn Stanley on "Frederick W. Robertson" (with portrait). Dobson
and Gosse had poems. British books were pleasantly reviewed: Gilder
came in hard.

Naturally, American authors were not less celebrated. Again fol-
lowing the "Index" to *Century*, "New Series, Vol. I," there appeared
George E. Waring, Jr. on "George W. Cable" (with portrait); Edward
Eggleston on "Josiah Gilbert Holland" (with portrait)—Holland, first

editor of *Scribner's*, had died before he could launch the *Century*; Thomas Sargent Perry, "William Dean Howells" (with portrait). Not counting treatments of James A. Garfield and David Webster, the score in "New Series, Vol. I" for major articles on authors was British five, Americans three.

In volume two, the series of author studies went on. Emma Lazarus did "The Personality of Emerson"; Edmund Clarence Stedman did "James Russell Lowell"; C. Kegan Paul did "Cardinal John Henry Newman"; Gosse did "Dante Gabriel Rossetti"; John Burroughs did "Henry D. Thoreau"; Howells did "Mark Twain." Through the end of volume two, through October 1882, all seemed well, though the score had shifted to Americans four, British two. But when, in November 1882, opening volume three, Howells did "Henry James, Jr.," all hell broke loose in England, spreading swiftly to the U.S.A. where a British brouhaha about American authors was meat for even the semi-literate media.

Magazines of the day generally made copies available to news outlets well in advance of their official dates of publication. Gilder's English competitors had clearly decided to give him what for. To make an example they leaped at a tactical opening provided by Howells's praise of James's advance in novelistic technique over the craft of such predecessors as Thackeray and Dickens. All they needed was a faulty syllogism:

> Major premise: Howells and James are identical.
> Minor premise: Howells exalts James above the
>   classic masters of fiction.
> Conclusion: Howells and James exalt themselves
>   over Thackeray and Dickens

Though any schoolboy could tell them that there is a howling flaw in the major premise, they no doubt knew it and certainly they did not care. They saw that any hack could leap from a false syllogism to raise the traditional British cry against Yankee brag, presumption, ingratitude, and spread-eagle mendacity. They saw a hope that such a campaign might blunt Gilder's new invasion.

For the public caning of W. D. Howells, hacks were chosen by two of the best-known organs of British literary discipline. Both hacks hid long behind the British tradition of anonymous reviewing. Now we know[3] that one was Mrs. Margaret Oliphant Oliphant, who gave her all for *Blackwood's Edinburgh Magazine*, of dreadful fame. The *London Quarterly Magazine*'s hack was Louis John Jennings.

With, no doubt, a clubman's inside information, Howells's friend Edmund Gosse wrote in advance, begging Howells to issue a statement praising Thackeray and Dickens to forestall the oncoming assault. To give Howells a foretaste of what was approaching, Gosse penned a little pasquinade:

> Motto For The American Critic
> Ho! the old school: Thackeray, Dickens:
> Throw them out to feed the chickens.—
> Ho! the new school: James and ———
> Lay the flattery on with trowels.
> (Doggerel by a candid friend.)

Howells, at work in Switzerland, had to ask in reply for a copy of his James piece to see what in the world he had said to raise such a storm.

He of course never retracted. How could he? That in the hands of Henry James fiction had become an art finer than the art of Dickens or Thackeray is so self-evident that a critic who bothered to mention it now would seem silly. The assault did not check Gilder; perhaps notoriety helped the *Century*. But the long-term effects on Howells's criticism, especially his campaigns in "The Editor's Study" from 1886 forward, effects even on his fiction, were to be profound.[4] From 1883 forward, the perfidious British assault and its repercussions would echo somewhere, in the foreground, in the background, of almost everything critical written or drawn in caricature of Howells. What sent Howells to war may be so plainly read in Oliphant and Jennings that it needs no explication.

III

Howells publicly said nothing for the moment about the British onslaught, swallowing wrath. It may be true that his resignation from the *Atlantic* editorship had left him more open to critical "correction" than before. Howells had enjoyed critical favor, no matter whether he benefitted from critics' fear. Though the case of Mayo W. Hazeltine's review of *The Lady of the Aroostook* had been extraordinary, he did "pronounce" it "the most virile, healthful and estimable achievement in recent American fiction." Better than any critic since, Hazeltine picked up the true point of *The Lady* as a variation on the theme of the international novel. Given the fatuous "Anglomania" which possessed the monied classes of the United States during the last third of the century, the ironic thrust of Howells's novel (like much of Henry James's work) stabbed at the social inanity, easily turned to psychic immorality, expressed in American cultural provinciality. Mrs. Oliphant would catch the same point and try to turn it upon Howells. Hazeltine, however, seems the more wonderful in that many a later, hostile critic was to treat *The Lady of the Aroostook*, misread, as a perfect instance by which to prove that Howells's fiction was no more than pale mauve, violet-scented nullity.

Thomas Sargent Perry's essay covered wider ground than any previous comment. "William Dean Howells" in the March 1882 *Century* stands at the head of critical efforts to judge his work in full. Howells, of course, knew that the *Century* was tooting its own tin horn. Decades of political journalism and magazine editing had not left him innocent about the ways of public relations. Having used Perry as a critic for years on the *Atlantic*, Howells knew how incisive he could be. Howells also knew that the note of personal affection on which Perry's essay ends was real. This, then, was the best that could be said for him to that point. It might have been chilling had he not known that privately he had long before entered upon a new and deeper phase of his expressive life.

Reviewers had fidgeted over intimations that in *The Undiscovered Country* and in the relative failures, for Howells, of *Dr. Breen's Practice* and *A Woman's Reason*, something new had risen to trouble the hammocky ease with which they were accustomed to enjoy comedies of manners. The fourth installment of *A Modern Instance* appeared in the same *Century* number with Perry's essay. Even before its serialization was complete, Howells's public, and the critics, could see that they had to deal with a new, rather disturbing author. Full critical realization of the new phenomenon awaited, however, *The Rise of Silas Lapham*, serialized in the *Century* between November 1884 and August 1885. Then they registered the shock.

IV

The ideological thrust of Howells's early work needs careful study. Though it was real, it upset relatively few critics, perhaps because when they saw it they did not think it important. After 1885, however, Howells was to be engaged in ideological fight, warring and being warred upon by critics, for the rest of his life. The big critical guns first fired in reaction to *Lapham*. Three critiques take on particular importance: two are by solid, well-informed critics, both personally Howells's friends; a third represents that vulgate criticism, not sectarian so much as mindless, with which Howells had long to struggle.

Horace E. Scudder saw precisely that *The Rise of Silas Lapham* testified to growth in its author. He felt the strength in the author's discovery "of the higher value to be found in a creation which discloses morals, as well as manners." It was "the difference," Scudder thought, "between the permanent and the transient in art." Scudder read the novel in 1885 more accurately than many a later and, at least to us, more visible critic. He also sensed the effect in Howells which has put off many a later critic: the artistic means seem too refined, "we complain that the author of [Lapham's] being, instead of preserving him as a rustic piece of Vermont limestone with the soil clinging to it, has insisted on our seeing into the possibilities of a fine marble statue which reside in the bulk." Nevertheless, Scudder concluded, we can "thank our stars" that "we are dealing with a real piece of literature, which will surely not lose its charm when the distinctions of Nankeen Square and Beacon Street have become merely antiquarian nonsense." And so matters stand now: Scudder wrote superb Howells criticism.

No less able than Scudder, no less well acquainted with Howells personally, Hamilton Wright Mabie felt an ulterior and ideological motive in his response to *The Rise of Silas Lapham*. To express himself he chose an outlet famous for heavyweight theological disputation, the old Calvinistic *Andover Review*. Mabie built his plan of attack with a deadliness of design worthy of Jonathan Edwards. *Lapham* is Howells's "best" and "most characteristic work," the finest sort of achievement possible in its mode. It represents an admirable advance upon the author's earlier novels while keeping faithful to their line of progress. In short, he says at the point of attack: "it will be conceded that the sum total of excellence which even a reader who dissents from its underlying conception and method discovers in this story is . . . such as to entitle it to very high praise, and to give added permanence and expansion to a literary reputation which, from the standpoint of popularity at least, stood in small need of these things." Nevertheless, he continued, the novel is "unsatisfactory . . . deficient in power, in reality, and in the vitalizing atmosphere of imagination."

The single, central damnation of Howells's masterwork was to Mabie, that it is not romantic. It is "cold," he said. It is satiric and dispassionate, even faintly cynical. It has no "unforced faith in the worth, the dignity, and the significance for art of human experience in its whole range. . . ." That Mabie attached special meanings to these words becomes evident in his condemnation of dirty Zola: Howells has, at least, "a refined realism." But what he does not have is faith in superhuman significance; and without it he can have neither imagination nor love: "It is certainly a mental or moral disease . . ." which betrays men like Howells and Henry James to the "weakness" of their vision. "It is very significant that realism either fails to grasp life firmly and present it powerfully, or else seizes upon its ignoble aspects; its vigor is mainly on the side of moral pathology."

Mabie understood intellectual difference with a sharpness worthy of Arthur O. Lovejoy. The issue, he sees, "goes to the very bottom of our conceptions of life and art. . . . The new realism is not dissent from a particular method; it is fundamental skepticism of the essential reality of the old ends and subjects of art." The faith Mabie means is either theism or something platonic: "the conception that life is at bottom a revelation; that human growth under all conditions has a spiritual law back of it: that human relations of all kinds have spiritual types behind them; and that the discovery of these universal facts, and the clear, noble embodiment of them in various forms, is the office of genius and the end of art." But realism "is, in a word, practical atheism applied to art."

As infidelity, realism has misread the meaning, misjudged the future of modern science, Mabie contends. "What is needed now, in fiction as in poetry, is a revitalization of the imagination and a return to implicit and triumphant faith in it." That achieved, artists to come "will be realists as all the great artists have been," each one a soul "who held resolutely to the fact because of the law behind it, who saw that the Real and the Ideal are one in the divine order of the universe, and whose clear glance into the appearance of things made him the more loyal to the Whole, the Good, and the True." Perhaps Mabie was right, or perhaps he was an Emersonian epigone, the representative of a genteel tradition. In any case, he saw a part of the issue[5] clearly, and he handled it intellectually as responsibly as he knew how. Those facts made him a formidable opponent, and issues he raised have re-appeared many times in the annals of the war of the critics over Howells.

That the participants in the broad international movement toward realism, including the Americans, were generally agnostics is historically demonstrable. An agnostic, however, is not an atheist. And Mabie had thrown dangerous words at Howells. Among other implications, "weakness," "coldness," disease," "mental and moral pathology," even "atheism" often stood in the Victorian system of signs as code words for sexual depravity and its consequences. It was, however, one thing to have them appear in the rather elite forms appropriate to the *Andover Review*. It was something else to have them bandied as scandal in the popular press of the Midwestern Bible Belt or in a semiofficial pub-lication aimed at the Catholic faithful of great city parishes.

V

No intent to reflect on matters of religion lurks behind the selection here of "Novel-Writing As A Science" from the *Catholic World*. Though the essay is patently, unflinchingly what it is, it is not so bad as the knowing misrepresentations in *Life*, a Harvard humor magazine which escaped into the "real world." "R. P." 's advantage over the same sort of thing everlastingly in the New Orleans *Picayune* or over the divagations of Maurice Thompson, the Hoosier archer, is that "R. P." comes straight and economical, well-packaged.

In June 1886, Thompson delivered a paper before the Women's Club of Indianapolis modestly entitled "The Analysts Analyzed." It was picked up by literary gossip journals and developed into an intellectually squalid affair about which Howells said nothing public. The poet laureate of Crawfordsville, Indiana, Thompson had been usefully befriended by Howells as *Atlantic* editor. Now Thompson turned upon him with diffuse charges of vulgarity, indecency, malice, infidelity, and want of patriotism. Doubtless to his surprise, Thompson got cudgelled for his pains by Chicago as well as New York critics. He spent much of the next ten years making matters worse by protesting his admiration for Howells while "explaining," and achieved his revenge by writing *Alice of Old Vincennes* (1900). To document the affair here would take more space than Thompson deserves. Without the Hoosier patriotism, W. R. Thayer was to set forth Thompson's main arguments with a legal cogency not then common in Crawfordsville.

The point is that a lowbrow version of the Realism War seeded itself widely, extending historically at least as far as Sinclair Lewis, another corn-belt esthete. Meanwhile, "R. P." and his ilk covered the city beat. The fact that "R. P." as a controversialist would have horrified any Roman Catholic intellectual could have meant no more to "R. P." or his journal than it would have to Thompson, to *Life*, or to Anglican Bishop Wilberforce when he supposed he could squelch Thomas Huxley by enquiring in which branch of his family Mr. Huxley traced his descent from that ape. At the level of the public mind where scandal is "hard news," the idea of intellectual integrity is always in hard luck. "R. P." thought he knew that "Mr. Howells . . . not very long ago wrote that he and Mr. Henry James, Jr., were the only novelists who understood their business."

Historically, "R. P." may have been the first who suggested the staggering notion that Howells had a "Puritan mind." "R. P." 's eyes saw by the light of prejudicial stereotypes. To him Howells seemed not genteel enough. But the glaring issue was Darwinism. For "R. P." in that battle no damning slur was too bad: "degradation," "decadence," "godless." Not, perhaps, knowing the word, he meant *regressive*: "It is the progress from man to the apes, from the apes to the worms, from the worms to bacteria, from bacteria to—mud. It is the descent to dirt."

VI

Meanwhile, not noticing that lightning had struck, Howells and the world of letters went on about their business. The Washington correspondent of the London *Mail and Express* leaped to interview an international celebrity on 10 April 1886. He scored several journalistic scoops in talking to Howells, notably the information that *Indian Summer* had been written before *The Rise of Silas Lapham*: not all criticism and literary history have yet entirely adjusted themselves to that revelation. The English reporter caught the mood of confident power with which Howells had freshly plunged into the Realism War with "The Editor's Study." Once again it was a new Howells, aggressive and happy, as he described his mood privately, in "banging the babes of Romance about." His innings had come.

He was in the same mood at Lake George in July of 1887, perhaps warmed by the recent praise of Henry James, the more precious because it climaxed with an expression of great interest in his further development. James's reservations, delicately phrased, Howells already knew. At Lake George the New York *Tribune* reporter sketched a masculine type full of wit, creatively active, strong and bold. For Howells personally it was the last such buoyant summer of his life. Tragedy, domestic and intellectual, stood ready to strike; and it was to be "a black time" with him after that for years to come. Because he had courage and strength, his daughter's terrible descent to painful death and the consequent shattering of his wife's nerves tried him *in extremis*. Though he did not break, he felt a tragic sense of life growing within him.

Hand in hand with tragedy walked his renewed sense of social concern. That concern tightened and darkened his fiction, and it brought him to an action for conscience' sake which might have destroyed him professionally. The only person of major public consequence, the only American man of letters who would plead publicly that clemency be extended to the unjustly condemned Haymarket Anarchists, Howells came near to seeing his reputation lynched informally together with the legally lynched Anarchists. Friends, including old radicals and reformers, shunned him. Others betrayed him. His publisher admonished him. The "November's Come" column of *Life* for 3 November 1887, insolently pairing its fleer at Howells with its unspeakable cartoon, expressed the ruling mood of the United States of Lyncherdom. Howells might have been willing to forgive the *Catholic World* for the sake of the word he got of generous support from the *Pilot*, an official newspaper of the Roman Catholic Archdiocese of Boston, justly concerned for the morale of its largely "foreign" people and ready to speak a good word for Mr. Howells the pariah. Another dissonant, rather Modern, note had been added to the chord which critics heard as "Howells."

Some critics, happily, hastened to make it up to him. Thus Laurence Hutton reviewed *Annie Kilburn* in *Harper's Monthly* and Anna Laurens

Dawes contradicted Mabie in the *Andover Review*. And a great breakout came with the unforeseen public success of *A Hazard of New Fortunes*. That vindication had indispensable help from critics. Curtis, who had declined to help the Anarchists, cleverly argued from "The Editor's Easy Chair" for the fundamental soundness of the critical campaign being waged "in the neighboring tribunal, the Study." Then he proceeded to argue the merits of an item on "the calendar of new cases of fiction," that of "A Hazard of New Fortunes, by Howells, W. D." on which no verdict could be expected from "the Study." Garland, whose critical tact resembled boiler plate in comparison to Curtis's silk, nevertheless had a fresh metaphor to express in "Mr. Howells's Latest Novels." The leader, he said, "the innovator in literature is a sort of Arnold Winkelried; and though he receives the lances of the confronting host, he feels that he has a dauntless band behind him, small though it may be." In conclusion Garland grew almost specific: only the historical perspective afforded by time will let critics do "full justice . . . to the group of young writers now rising in America . . . of whom Mr. Howells is the champion and the unquestioned leader." It was an interesting notion with which to enter upon an abruptly new order of things in American life and letters, the Nineties.

VII

In considering that famous decade, as Donald Pizer says in the best of anthologies from it,[6] it is essential to see "The Centrality of Howells." At once, accordingly, the Realism War came to a sort of climax with the publication of hastily gathered pieces from a part of Howells's "Editor's Study" columns into *Criticism and Fiction*. Horace Scudder thought "Mr. Howells's Literary Creed" exaggerated. Brander Matthews, though he thought Howells sometimes unfortunately "more forcible than suave," exulted that "he has done not a little toward destroying the tradition of deference toward British criticism," which was in itself "a survival of colonialism."

Released from his contract with the Harpers to free-lance, a condition briefly punctuated by his adventure with the *Cosmopolitan*, Howells made heads swim with the flow, the variety, the revolutionary shifts of his creativity. From 1890 through 1900 he published, not counting farces, new editions, or volumes edited and introduced, twenty-three books. Among them were fourteen novels, six of those major and each radically different from the others. Each of the single volumes of criticism, poetry, and gathered essays was in its way important. And he opened a new vein of autobiography, producing three books, each distinct, of permanent significance. Criticism has not yet comprehended that flash-flood of creativity.

The reviewers and the critics tried, of course. Howells then was always news. Criticism, however, instead of mastering what it had thought a well-known subject, flurried in confusion. To shift the figure, from early years Howells had presented to critics a moving target. Now he appeared in multiple guises, all moving, developing. Nobody managed to track them well enough to calculate a configuration. Radical and realist, he became the patron of Garland's onrushing newnesses: and of Dunbar and Crane, Cahan and Chesnutt, Norris. The friend of socialists and rebels, he began also to appear as a chronicler of older, simpler times—his boyhood West and, in contrast, the golden days of Cambridge with its Fireside Poets and legendary scholars. He moved to New York and found Ibsen to place beside Tolstoi and Zola, scaring all the Thompsons, enraging all the Thayers of the age.

Laurence Hutton, because he understood *An Imperative Duty* and approved its ironic attack on racism in the heyday of the Jim Crow movement, otherwise astonishingly called it "the strongest piece of work Mr. Howells has done since the appearance of 'A Foregone Conclusion.'" When, on New Year's Day 1892, Howells wished to release formal announcement of his long awaited move to New York and his hopes for the *Cosmopolitan*, Garland, one of Boston's more conspicuously radical young men, won the assignment to reveal in the Boston *Evening Transcript* that now: "Unquestionably Mr. Howells will be a greater power than ever in the radical wing of American literature . . ." That brought forth John Burroughs to proclaim "Mr. Howells's Agreement With Whitman." Charles Dudley Warner, succeeding Howells in "The Editor's Study," made his peace with a shrewd comment which defied the old idealizers (including himself). Speaking of the embezzler's midwinter flight to Canada in *The Quality of Mercy*, Warner said that the single episode "would make the reputation of a new writer." More than conceding, Warner wrote eagerly: "The author does not explain. He simply narrates with a singular fidelity to the common aspects of life, and yet the power of all this is an apprehension of the unseen and the spiritual that makes this flight a high achievement of the artist."

For a "Real Conversation" with Mr. Howells the New York realist, S. S. McClure gave Boyesen 4000 words to be used to adorn the premiere of McClure's new magazine. It was almost the best, certainly the easiest of Howells interviews; and Boyesen probably fulfilled his assignment in climaxing upon the next to the last remark: ". . . I shall persist in regarding you henceforth as *the* novelist *par excellence* of New York." Howells was permitted the last word, perfectly in character: "Ah, you don't expect me to live up to *that* bit of taffy!" Perhaps Boyesen provides as well as any interviewer the right chance to speak to the question, if there is any, of the interview as a critical essay. A prominent interview counts more tellingly for reputation than almost any piece in a sober intellectual quarterly. Inevitably, an interviewer brings assumptions to the occasion. More often than not, the interviewer has prepared a plan of questions which might readily translate into an outline introduced by a lead sentence already planned. Only the interlocutor of rare sensitivity and integrity can shake free. The interviewing ears hear and eyes see through filters of predilection. After it is over, she or he must write it up, fitting it to the shape of what the writer understands. Therefore the interview must tell its reader what the interviewer thinks, and therefore an interview with an author is a species of critical essay, good or bad. Howells the old journalist, as mentally quick interviewers saw, understood their business as well as they. He could provide "good copy" when he wished and controlled interviews well. His personal charm was not famous for nothing. Early on in New York he got and gave more interviews than at any other time in his life.

The most significant, of course, is the interview Stephen Crane did for the *New York Times* in 1894. Crane then thought himself to belong to Howells's school as one of Garland's new writers: and the younger man was on a footing with the older man which permitted Crane to josh with Howells. A couple of years later he wrote a letter to Howells saying: "I always thank God that I can have the strongest admiration for the work of a man who has been so much to me personally for I can imagine the terrors of being indelibly indebted to the Chump in Art—even to the Semi-Chump in Art." No doubt Crane, whose street-smartness fascinated Howells, had explained "Chump" and "Semi-Chump" and they had laughed together.

Crane's interview records perhaps the most exact and effective of all the definitions of realism Howells formulated. Who really said it? Did Crane inspire Howells to a new height of self-definition? Did Crane invent to explain? Or, as seems most probable, was it a joint production of genius (a word in which Howells insisted on not believing) striking an epiphany off genius? As Howells told Crane, realism had lost its fight for the public taste. The realists would have to wait. But in the light of such adventures as marked Howells's new start in New York, it did not matter that William Roscoe Thayer pronounced sentence upon him in Boston. Thayer's "The New Story-Tellers and The Doom of Realism" was only another episode of the familiar Realism War. It changed nothing that Henry C. Vedder rose to the attack or that Boyesen counter-attacked with "The Great Realists and The Empty Story-Tellers." That war was old. Newness gripped Howells during the 1890s, within and without. The public situation Edward Marshall, Stephen Crane's friend and a superb newspaper man, comprehended exactly in "A Great American Writer." A critic had remarked to Marshall, he said, that: "'There is no middle ground with Howells—people think him either a master or an ass.'" Marshall continued: "Everybody in America knows something about Howells and likes or dislikes him. There is none to whom he is unknown." He was hot news for the papers.

VIII

In art and argument, Howells's imagination dwelt ever more deeply during the period on fateful questions about American life and the American psyche. The questions, increasingly complex, looked to a profound issue: could American democracy survive modern industrial and urban crises? It remains the issue with us to this moment. For Howells it translated into specific questions, of course: labor and capital; poverty and progress; affluence and ethics; racism, ethnicity, feminism. Like Freud's contemporaries throughout the West, Howells was searching into the mysteries of the psyche, turning his realism of vision inward. The critics stumbled behind as they could—in bewilderment. Clifton Johnson, interviewing, liked the "Sense and Sentiment" of Howells's feminism. But Harry Thurston Peck, professor, poet, and elegant man about town foreshadowed to self-destruction, could simply not at first care for the Westerner's artistic physiognomy.

Perhaps Peck, a New England Brahmin by breeding, becomes historically important as standing at the head of the long line of male "intellectuals" not able to care for Howells. There is something typical about Peck's query regarding *My Literary Passions*: "who is especially concerned to know that Mr. Howells, at the time when he first heard of Don Quixote, was engaged in shelling peas?" It could be argued that Howells had told a revealing anecdote about his origins and that Peck's reaction bespeaks urban snobbery. Events like Howells's turn toward Ibsen or the published proffer to Howells of George Bernard Shaw's friendship left no evident impression upon Professor Peck. What struck Peck as a sick melancholy in "Mr. Howells As A Poet" became for the moment a principle in "intellectual" reaction against Howells.

Henry James might consider his old friend an incurable optimist: in New York during the so-called "Gay Nineties" they thought otherwise. The anonymous writer on "Mr. Howells's Views" felt so exercised he could not get the title right of the first gathering of the radical essays Howells wrote prolifically from 1893 through the following decade and beyond. His mind rejecting the grasp of reality asserted by *Impressions and Experiences*, the critic, in a significant unconscious slip, insisted that it was *Impressions and Opinions*. It may not have been Peck, but the article's language, its way with a sentence, and its style of mind suggest the Professor. The New York pieces might well have been called "Sensations of a Sick Soul," says the review: "On the whole, the reader turns away from Mr. Howells's impressions of our civilization doubting their insight and sanity. They are too bad to be true, and have . . . a certain malign, narcotic influence, difficult to describe and ill to feel." In the language of William James's *Varieties of Religious Experience*, the critic's sensibilities sound like those of one of the "tender-minded," shrinking from reality. Knowledge of the facts would have astonished certain later schools of Howells criticism.

A decade earlier Boston had accused him of moral disease. But that had been worlds ago in the life of a culture obedient to Henry Adams's law of the constant acceleration of change and in the life of an artist unfolding with extreme intensity. Earlier they had convicted him of disbelief in ideality. Now in New York they condemned him in effect for not being Theodore Roosevelt, happy amidst conflict, triumphant in strenuous hope, making glad the tender-minded. But another of Adams's laws applied to the question of Howells: multiplicity. John D. Barry, also one of Crane's friends, understood *The Landlord at Lion's Head* better than almost any critic who wrote during the first half of the next century.

Barry did fall into a misapprehension which was rapidly assuming the status of a "fact"—that Howells "had sprung from New England stock, and he fitted into the life of Boston as if he always had belonged to it." Both statements were wrong. Howells's father, born in Wales, had come to the Ohio frontier in boyhood. His Dean grandfather was an Irishman who eloped with a Pennsylvania Dutch girl sprung from a family long on the frontier. Howells and "Proper Boston" never got on well together. Annie R. M. Logan caught the real point when she remarked that, before New York, Howells had written "a series" of novels which might be entitled " 'Boston Under the Scalpel,' or 'Boston Torn to Tatters,' or 'The True Inwardness of Boston.' " Concerning *The Landlord*, however, Barry knew whereof he spoke. Compare it to *A Foregone Conclusion*, he pointed out, and you can measure the development of the author: *The Landlord* reveals the "matured mind, the sobered thought, and—it is hard to say it—the pessimism." Barry, however, sympathized with the reality principle he saw: "long experience . . . long searching into the human heart," had revealed tragic truth to Howells. "The struggle between evil and good, ending so often with the triumph of evil—this is the spectacle that so perplexes and so fascinates him. . . . In other words, during the past few years his work has deepened, has approached more closely the springs of human action."

Affectionate, grateful tributes from readers who loved Howells for

what he did and stood for also appeared, of course. The American
Fabian, discussing "Mr. Howells' Socialism" could hardly have been
more complimentary. It did not think him sick for telling the truth
about "the characteristics of a plutocratic city" or "the fierce battle
for bread," and it quoted from Harry Thurston Peck in a mood altogether different. The American Fabian represents perhaps a score of
radical and communitarian magazines which took pains to express
appreciation of Howells. When he went on a lecture tour in 1899,
Gerald Stanley Lee welcomed the shyest of authors warmly: "We want
to hear Mr. Howells in America to-day because he particularly belongs
to us and because we particularly belong to him and because we are
both proud of it. . . . He is part of our literary climate. We breathe
Howells—most of us. It never occurs to people to hold an Anniversary
for Oxygen." Newspaper comment on the tour ran the spectrum of
possible comment according to Edward Marshall's principle. Reporters
who thought Howells an ass revived memories of Mrs. Oliphant Oliphant.
Those who thought him a master found words, sometimes extravagant,
with which to hymn their praises, even affection. The quarrel had
become permanent.

IX

Although round calendrical figures have no biographical meaning,
Howells's career took a great turn with the wheeling centuries. While
he was out lecturing, Harper and Brothers, the great firm with whose
fortunes his had been joined for the past fifteen years, declared bank-
ruptcy. In the reorganization, however, it transpired that the revived
firm regarded Howells as a major asset previously poorly utilized.
His annual contract was renewed, giving him the great old "Editor's
Easy Chair" literary column with carte blanche to say whatever else
he wished in the firm's other magazines. It was made clear that he was
more than welcome to the pages of Harper's Monthly or Weekly or
Bazar (sic) or The North American Review. He was urged to take an
office at Franklin Square and recruit authors, as he had recruited for
the Atlantic.

It was for the time being an arrangement advantageous to Howells
in security and power. In the long view, however, it surely hurt him.
He had reached out and found, helped, and spoken profoundly to
members of the great literary generation which was born in the
seventies and came of age in the nineties. He reached the next great
literary generation, born in the eighties and coming of age after the
turn of the century, hardly at all. In general, they could not meet him,
did not know him, and seldom read him. In 1900 Howells became 63.
He was outliving his generation, and the power in his audience to

read him as a contemporary was withering up. The young mainly, no matter how irrationally, hated, misunderstood, misinterpreted, and attacked him. To them he stood for the established against which they must rebel. They neither knew nor cared that Howells and that same Establishment had long been at war. To adopt the Freudian metaphor, he became to them the horrid Old Man whom they must kill before he castrated or captured them.

It was bad luck that among the greatest luminaries of the generation of the seventies the two who were especially his—Crane and Norris—died young. The third star, Dreiser, was alienated by typically eccentric conduct. As the German critic Halfmann first dared to point out, Dreiser's purported "first interview" blended fakery with plagiarism from *My Literary Passions*. He had not talked to Howells at all and compounded the offense by titling his fraud "The Real Howells." That being true, the likelihood appears that nothing Dreiser ever said about Howells is to be credited in the absence of evidence external to Dreiser. Where is the document to show that Howells ever made an appointment with Dreiser? Lacking such evidence, Dreiser's "second interview" with Howells becomes as suspect as the "first." Having lied about Howells and plagiarized him, Dreiser sealed the alienation by writing an impossible letter, at once fawning and arrogant. Not to get a reply let Dreiser feel it right to hate Howells and go on lying about him the rest of Dreiser's life. Nobody survived, then, from the generation of the seventies who could play for the generation of the eighties the role of liaison to Howells in which Garland served many of those from the seventies. Nobody, however, pays indemnities on bad luck, either.

The misfortune of Howells's not falling silent soon enough also exasperated the rebels who would become that Modernity toward which Howells continued to work. An ignorant contempt toward all things American for which Van Wyck Brooks later attempted repeatedly to account possessed the rising generation. "Puritanism," as they reinvented it, fantasizing a multitude of deformities and disabilities alleged to flow from it, explained to their satisfaction why no American culture had ever been. Before them was nothing—or, if there was, they did not wish to hear about it. They saw their historic charge to be a mission to sweep a rotten past away and build an American culture from bedrock. The *locus classicus* analyzing "the Modern" in all its modes of sensibility is still Frederick J. Hoffman, *The Twenties: American Writing in the Postwar Decade* (New York, 1955); and of course Hoffman needed to reach deeply into the previous decade in order to ground his explications.

Collegians called the first decade of the century "the oughty-oughts": if your class was 1903, "oughty-three," then you had been in

college in 1900—"oughty-ought." Though waning, Howells remained a
force pretty well through the "oughties." It might easily be shown that
much of his force served the oncoming movement. But if he had looked
for gratitude instead of faithfully working according to his personal
vision, he would have had fair cause for bitterness. Harriet Preston
Waters managed to be half fair in summation of his career, treated in
the past tense. But she concluded in a sneering bathos. E. S. Chamberlayne had the grace to imagine that perhaps Howells had matured
beyond the reach of the still "immature" attitudes of his countrymen.
Chamberlayne saw into a part of *The Son of Royal Langbrith* rather well.
A critic of 1905 can be forgiven for not having been able to know that
the novel is unmistakably proto-Freudian; but it perhaps confirms the
immaturity which he feared in himself that he could wonder whether
the author intended the tragic side of the novel.

X

At last it became, so to speak, a game of critical ping-pong, with
flailing opponents gradually driving Howells's supporters out of com-
petition. The opposition did not care how it played: it could be argued
that it preferred to foul so long as it could smash. Life is not "fair,"
and the young cannot be fair toward idols its guts tell it must be
shattered. Down went Howells.

He went down, of course, mainly with those who were to become
posterity. Clemens wrote one of the best of his few good literary critiques
in appreciation of his old friend's style in 1906. Like James, Clemens
all his mature life delighted in Howells's command of style; but Clemens
took time to say precisely what he most admired and why. To move
from Clemens to Van Wyck Brooks's "Mr. Howells at Seventy-Two" in
1909 would astonish a reader who knew the history illuminated by
earlier critical documents but who did not know the documents to come
in the early Brooks's war against all inherited American culture. Brooks
began, "Mr. William Dean Howells has never surprised anybody, thrilled
anybody, shocked anybody."

It was much easier to say such a thing if one did not know anything.
Perhaps more effectively than any other prophet of the Modern, Brooks
laid waste Howells's reputation. But that was in his early period. When,
transformed, Brooks wrote the *Makers and Finders* series of best-sellers
to celebrate American literary culture, he came again to Howells. Then
he did not know quite what to do with the ruin he had made. Transformed again, Brooks in his late period would confess that in the early
period he had not read the literature he had damned. Neither had his
contemporaries, he testified. When he read Howells, Brooks was surprised if not thrilled; he should have been shocked. Eventually he would

write the worshipful study, *Howells: His Life and World*. For Brooks, if not his world, the matter of W. D. Howells came full circle.

Howells's world, as the press reported, celebrated him superbly at the moment of his seventy-fifth birthday in 1912. The testimonies gathered by William Stanley Braithwaite for the *Boston Evening Transcript* and its special number matched those collected by Col. Harvey, now "Harper & Bros.," for the spectacular birthday dinner and the special number of *Harper's Weekly*. The better for the honoree's literary reputation had he promptly, romantically died. The great "Letter" from Henry James struck a note for which Edith Wyatt's "A National Contribution" could only provide a harmonic.

After that, if with pauses on the way, things went downhill with Howells. Since he had neglected to say "*nunc dimittis*," the new criticism said, in the Roman way, "*fuit*": he was; he is dead. Such is the thrust of John A. Macy in *The Spirit of American Literature*, 1913, perhaps the first literary history written from the point of view of the new school. Howells and James, says Macy, admired European realism but could not connect to it: they could not tell the truth. What Howells lacks is *passion*: seldom "does he come to grips with a terrible motive or heart-tearing ecstasy." Is Howells not, therefore, "a feminine, delicate, slightly romantic genius . . . a sketcher, a very delicate farceur, a war correspondent who has never been in range of bullets?"

In 1917 there appeared the first book-length study: *William Dean Howells: A Study of the Achievement of a Literary Artist*. Its author, Alexander Harvey, appears to have gone mad after his fashion. He began to write a passionate if idiosyncratic tribute to his subject; well past midpoint he heard about Sigmund Freud and thought he was converted. Instead of suppressing his book or at least rewriting it, Harvey pivoted at a point more than two-thirds of the way through. There he recanted, abjured, denied everything he had said. The resultant travesty of criticism Harvey topped off with a comic, exhibitionistic "index." Happily for the subject, Harvey's performance struck Howells's sense of humor. He had always held "judicial" criticism to be nonsense. The book is impossible to excerpt.

In the face of such a carnival of folly, an attempt at sober criticism like that of Helen and Wilson Follett could do nothing. But when whirl was king, conditions were right for the H. L. Mencken of *The Smart Set*. He could say what he pleased: Alexander Harvey is "a placid conformist"; Howells is a "journey-man," the contriver "of a long row of uninspired books, with no more ideas in them than so many volumes of the *Ladies' Home Journal*. . . ." Howells "really has nothing to say . . . he seems blissfully ignorant that life is a serious business, and full of mystery . . . he is an Agnes Repplier in pantaloons." The liberated undergraduates, however perennial, never stopped snickering.

Survivors from the generation of the seventies or earlier, like the on-coming first generation of Howells scholars, could try to stem the tide. After Howells's death in 1920 there would be superb tributes, most not published until after 1920, from artists of international stature. Booth Tarkington, writing of "Mr. Howells" in *Harper's Monthly* for August 1920 said, in peroration:

> "The gentlest of spirits," and the wisest; thus he will be remem-
> bered. Yet there was no softness in his gentleness. His gentleness
> was the human kindness of a powerful iconoclast who began the over-
> turning of the false gods. He lived to see the fragments derided and
> his destructive work well on to completion; but, more than this, his
> iconoclasm was not anarchic; he pulled down a poor thing, not merely
> to pull down; he did it to set up a better. He remembered that when
> half-gods go the gods should arrive, and he had the gods with him.

For the "twenty years between the wars," the years of the Modern, however, nothing availed for Howells. They made him one of the idols to smash. Not until their prestige also waned, not until twenty years after Mencken wrote, would the question of Howells begin to open again.

Since Professor Ulrich Halfmann is the only editor of *Interviews With William Dean Howells*, the editors are grateful to him for per-mission to see and use his prepublication texts of interviews he has either newly found or seen more recently than we. We also gratefully acknowl-edge permission to reproduce texts from the following holders of copy-right: The Atlantic Monthly Co. for Helen and Wilson Follett, "Con-temporary American Novelists: William Dean Howells"; Doubleday, Inc., for John A. Macy, "Howells," *The Spirit of American Literature*, New York, 1913; Professor William White Howells, for the heirs of William Dean Howells, for "In Honor of Mr. Howells," *Harper's Weekly*, 9 March 1912, II; Professor R. Wilson for *The North American Review*, for Henry James, "A Letter to Mr. Howells," April 1912; and for Edith Wyatt, "A National Contribution," September 1912; Random House and Alfred A. Knopf, Inc., for H. L. Mencken, "Howells," *Prejudices: First Series*, New York, 1919.

Notes

1. See Ulrich Halfmann, "Dreiser and Howells: New Light on Their Relation-ship," *Amerikastudien*, 20, No. 1 (1975):73–85. Prof. Halfmann generously gave the benefit of every doubt to Dreiser.

2. There have been two previous collections of critical commentary on Howells, both published in 1962, both attempting to represent the full spectrum as it seemed twenty years ago: Edwin H. Cady and David L. Frazier, *The War of the Critics over*

William Dean Howells (Evanston, Ill.: Row, Peterson); and Kenneth E. Eble, *Howells: A Century of Criticism* (Dallas: Southern Methodist University Press). Neither had enough space.

In Howells studies the basic source remains William M. Gibson and George Arms, *A Bibliography of William Dean Howells* (New York: New York Public Library, 1948). Though much has enriched, nothing has displaced it. Three other compilations have prime importance. In their order of appearance they are: *Interviews with William Dean Howells*, ed. Ulrich Halfmann, *American Literary Realism*, (Arlington: University of Texas, 1973). Clayton L. Eichelberger, *Published Comment on William Dean Howells Through 1920: A Research Bibliography* (Boston: G. K. Hall, 1976); and Clayton L. Eichelberger, *Harper's Lost Reviews: The Literary Notes by Laurence Hutton, John Kendrick Bangs, and Others* (Millwood, N. Y.: KTO Press, 1976). Three collections of letters provide indispensable help, though when even the last is done it will leave much yet to print, especially in the presentation of some sixty or more significant literary correspondences. The collections are: Mildred Howells, *Life in Letters of William Dean Howells*, 2 vols. (New York: Doubleday, Doran, 1928); Henry Nash Smith and William M. Gibson, *Mark Twain-Howells Letters. The Correspondence of Samuel L. Clemens and William D. Howells, 1872–1910*, 2 vols. (Cambridge: Harvard University Press, 1960). And, of the six volumes projected, four are currently available of *W. D. Howells: Selected Letters* (Boston: Twayne Publishers). Edited by various hands, among whom Christoph Lohmann emerges as chief, the volumes are: 1: 1852–1872; 2: 1873–1881; 3: 1882–1891; 4: 1892–1901. In general, each of the sixteen volumes thus far published of the Indiana Edition of *A Selected Edition of W. D. Howells* is richly informative in its editorial apparatus. There are two major biographies: Edwin H. Cady, *The Road to Realism: The Early Years of William Dean Howells, 1837–1885*, and *The Realist at War: The Mature Years of William Dean Howells, 1885–1920* (Syracuse: Syracuse University Press, 1956 and 1958); Kenneth S. Lynn, *William Dean Howells: An American Life* (New York: Harcourt Brace Jovanovitch, 1971). It is also perhaps worth mention that the materials reproduced in this volume tend to find themselves in a three-sided conversation with those in Edwin H. Cady, ed., *W. D. Howells as Critic* (London: Routledge & Kegan Paul, 1973); and those in a volume at press with the working title of *W. D. Howells: Radical Essays*.

3. For first working out this problem I am grateful to Professor James Gray, now of Austin College, Austin, Texas.

4. For broader discussion of this event, see, *inter alia*, Edwin H. Cady, *The Realist at War . . .* , esp. pp. 1–55: and Cady, *W. D. Howells as Critic*.

5. The issues in all their bearings, so far as the author could see them, have been canvassed in Edwin H. Cady, *The Light of Common Day: Realism in American Fiction* (Bloomington: Indiana University Press, 1971).

6. *American Thought and Writing: The 1890's* (Boston, 1972), pp. 34–109.

1866-1882

[Review of *Venetian Life*]

James Russell Lowell*

Those of our readers who watch with any interest the favorable omens of our literature from time to time must have had their eyes drawn to short poems, remarkable for subtilty of sentiment and delicacy of expression, and bearing the hitherto unfamiliar name of Mr. Howells. Such verses are not common anywhere; as the work of a young man they are very uncommon. Youthful poets commonly begin by trying on various manners before they settle upon any single one that is prominently their own. But what especially interested us in Mr. Howells was, that his writings were from the very first not merely tentative and preliminary, but had somewhat of the conscious security of matured *style*. This is something which most poets arrive at through much tribulation. It is something which has nothing to do with the measure of their intellectual powers or of their moral insight, but is the one quality which essentially distinguishes the artist from the mere man of genius. Among the English poets of the last generation, Keats is the only one who early showed unmistakable signs of it, and developed it more and more fully until his untimely death. Wordsworth, though in most respects a far profounder man, attained it only now and then, indeed only once perfectly,—in his "Laodamia." Now, though it be undoubtedly true from one point of view that what a man has to say is of more importance than how he says it, and that modern criticism especially is more apt to be guided by its moral and even political sympathies than by aesthetic principles, it remains as true as ever that only those things have been said finally which have been said perfectly, and that this finished utterance is peculiarly the office of poetry, or of what, for want of some word as comprehensive as the German *Dichtung*, we are forced to call imaginative literature. Indeed, it may be said that, in whatever kind of writing, it is style alone that is able to hold the attention of the world long. Let

*Reprinted from the *North American Review*, 103 (October 1866), 610–13.

a man be never so rich in thought, if he is clumsy in the expression of it, his sinking, like that of an old Spanish treasureship, will be hastened by the very weight of his bullion, and perhaps, after the lapse of a century, some lucky diver fishes up his ingots and makes a fortune out of him.

That Mr. Howells gave unequivocal indications of possessing this fine quality interested us in his modest preludings. Marked, as they no doubt were, by some uncertainty of aim and indefiniteness of thought, that "stinting," as Chaucer calls it, of the nightingale "ere he beginneth sing," there was nothing in them of the presumption and extravagance which young authors are so apt to mistake for originality and vigor. Sentiment predominated over reflection, as was fitting in youth; but there was a refinement, an instinctive reserve of phrase, and a felicity of epithet, only too rare in modern, and especially in American writing. He was evidently a man more eager to make something good than to make a sensation,—one of those authors more rare than ever in our day of hand-to-mouth cleverness, who has a conscious ideal of excellence, and, as we hope, the patience that will at length reach it. We made occasion to find out something about him, and what we learned served to increase our interest. This delicacy, it appeared, was a product of the rough-and-ready West, this finish the natural gift of a young man with no advantage of college-training, who, passing from the compositor's desk to the editorship of a local newspaper, had been his own faculty of the humanities. But there are some men who are born cultivated. A singular fruit, we thought, of our shaggy democracy,—as interesting a phenomenon in that regard as it has been our fortune to encounter. Where is the rudeness of a new community, the pushing vulgarity of an imperfect civilization, the licentious contempt of forms that marks our unchartered freedom, and all the other terrible things which have so long been the bugaboos of European refinement? Here was a natural product, as perfectly natural as the deliberate attempt of "Walt Whitman" to answer the demand of native and foreign misconception was perfectly artificial. Our institutions do not, then, irretrievably doom us to coarseness and to impatience of that restraining precedent which alone makes true culture possible and true art attainable. Unless we are mistaken, there is something in such an example as that of Mr. Howells which is a better argument for the American social and political system than any empirical theories that can be constructed against it.

We know of no single word which will so fitly characterize Mr. Howells's new volume about Venice as "delightful." The artist has studied his subject for four years, and at last presents us with a series of pictures having all the charm of tone and the minute fidelity to nature which were the praise of the Dutch school of painters, but with a higher sentiment, a more refined humor, and an airy elegance that recalls the better moods of Watteau. We do not remember any Italian studies so faithful or the result of such continuous opportunity, unless it be the *Roba di Roma* of Mr. Story, and what may be found scattered in the works of Henri Beyle. But Mr. Story's volumes recorded only the chance observations of a quick and familiar eye in the intervals of a profession to which one must be busily devoted who would rise to the acknowledged eminence occupied by their author; and Beyle's mind, though singularly acute and penetrating, had too much of the hardness of a man of the world and of Parisian cynicism to be alto- gether agreeable. Mr. Howells, during four years of that consular leisure which only Venice could make tolerable, devoted himself to the minute study of the superb prison to which he was doomed, and his book is his "Prigioni." Venice has been the university in which he has fairly earned the degree of Master. There is, perhaps, no European city, not even Bruges, not even Rome herself, which, not yet in ruins, is so wholly of the past, at once alive and turned to marble, like the Prince of the Black Islands in the story. And what gives it a peculiar fascination is that its antiquity, though venerable, is yet modern, and, so to speak, continuous; while that of Rome belongs half to a former world and half to this, and is broken irretrivably in two. The glory of Venice, too, was the achievement of her own genius, not an inheritance; and, great no longer, she is more truly than any other city the monument of her own greatness. She is something wholly apart, and the silence of her watery streets accords perfectly with the spiritual mood which makes us feel as if we were passing through a city of dream. Fancy now an imaginative young man from Ohio, where the log-hut was but yesterday turned to almost less enduring brick and mortar, set down suddenly in the midst of all this almost immemorial permanence of grandeur. We cannot think of any one on whom the impression would be so strangely deep, or whose eyes would be so quickened by the constantly recurring shock of unfamiliar objects. Most men are poor observers, because they are cheated into a delusion of intimacy with the things so long and so immediately about them; but surely we may hope for something like seeing from fresh eyes, and those too a poet's, when they open suddenly on a marvel so utterly alien to their daily vision and so perdurably novel as Venice. Nor does Mr. Howells disappoint our expectation. We have here something like a full-length portrait of the Lady of the Lagoons.

We have been struck in this volume, as elsewhere in writings of the same author, with the charm of *tone* that pervades it. It is so constant as to bear witness, not only to a real gift, but to the thoughtful cultiva- tion of it. Here and there Mr. Howells yields to the temptation of *execution,* to which persons specially felicitous in language are liable, and pushes his experiments of expression to the verge of being unidio- matic, in his desire to squeeze the last drop of significance from words;

but this is seldom, and generally we receive that unconscious pleasure in reading him which comes of naturalness, the last and highest triumph of good writing. Mr. Howells, of all men, does not need to be told that, as wine of the highest flavor and most delicate *bouquet* is made from juice pressed out by the unaided weight of the grapes, so in expression we are in danger of getting something like acridness if we crush in with the first sprightly runnings the skins and kernels of words in our vain hope to win more than we ought of their color and meaning. But, as we have said, this is rather a temptation to which he now and then shows himself liable, than a fault for which he can often be blamed. If a mind open to all poetic impressions, a sensibility too sincere ever to fall into maudlin sentimentality, a style flexible and sweet without weakness, and a humor which, like the bed of a stream, is the support of deep feeling, and shows waveringly through it in spots of full sunshine,—if such qualities can make a truly delightful book, then Mr. Howells has made one in the volume before us. And we give him warning that much will be expected of one who at his years has already shown himself capable of so much.

[Review of *Their Wedding Journey*]

Henry Adams*

An interesting question presents itself to the cautious critic who reads this little book, and who does not care to commit himself and his reputation for sound judgment irretrievably to the strength of such a gossamer-like web: it is whether the book will live. Why should it not live? If extreme and almost photographic truth to nature, and remarkable delicacy and lightness of touch, can give permanent life to a story, why should this one not be read with curiosity and enjoyment a hundred or two hundred years hence? Our descendants will find nowhere so faithful and so pleasing a picture of our American existence, and no writer is likely to rival Mr. Howells in this idealization of the commonplace. The vein which Mr. Howells has struck is hardly a deep one. His dexterity in following it, and in drawing out its slightest resources, seems at times almost marvellous, a perpetual succession of feats of sleight-of-hand, all the more remarkable because the critical reader alone will understand how difficult such feats are, and how much tact and wit is needed to escape a mortifying failure. Mr. Howells has a delicacy of touch which does not belong to man. One can scarcely resist the im-

*Reprinted from the *North American Review*, 114 (April 1872), 444–45.

pression that he has had feminine aid and counsel, and that the traitor to her sex has taken delight in revealing the secret of her own attractions, so far at least as she knows it; for Mr. Howells, like the rest of mankind, after all his care and study, can only acknowledge his masculine incompetence to comprehend the female character. The book is essentially a lovers' book. It deserves to be among the first of the gifts which follow or precede the marriage offer. It has, we believe, had a marked success in this way, as a sort of lovers' Murray or Appleton; and if it can throw over the average bridal couple some reflection of its own refinement and taste, it will prove itself a valuable assistant to American civilization.

[Review of *A Foregone Conclusion*]

Henry James*

Those who, a couple of years ago, read "A Chance Acquaintance" will find much interest in learning how the author has justified the liberal fame awarded that performance. Having tried other literary forms with remarkable success, Mr. Howells finally proved himself an accomplished story-teller, and the critic lurking in even the kindliest reader will be glad to ascertain whether this consummation was due chiefly to chance or to skill. "A Chance Acquaintance" was indeed not only a very charming book, but a peculiarly happy hit; the fancy of people at large was vastly tickled by the situation it depicted; the hero and heroine were speedily promoted to the distinction of types, and you became likely to overhear discussions as to the probability of their main adventures wherever men and women were socially assembled. Kitty Ellison and her weak-kneed lover, we find, are still objects of current allusion, and it would be premature, even if it were possible, wholly to supersede them; but even if Mr. Howells was not again to hit just that nail, he was welcome to drive in another beside it and to supply the happy creations we have mentioned with successors who should divide our admiration. We had little doubt ourselves that he would on this occasion reach whatever mark he had aimed at; for, with all respect to the good fortune of his former novel, it seemed to us very maliciously contrived to play its part. It would have been a question in our minds, indeed, whether it was not even too delicate a piece of work for general circulation,—whether it had not too literary a quality to please that great majority of people who prefer to swallow their literature without

*Reprinted from the *North American Review* 120 (January 1875), 207–14.

tasting. But the best things in this line hit the happy medium, and it seems to have turned out, experimentally, that Mr. Howells managed at once to give his book a loose enough texture to let the more simply-judging kind fancy they were looking at a vivid fragment of social history itself, and yet to infuse it with a lurking artfulness which should endear it to the initiated. It rarely happens that what is called a popular success is achieved by such delicate means; with so little forcing of the tone or mounting of the high horse. People at large do not flock every day to look at a sober cabinet-picture. Mr. Howells continues to practise the cabinet-picture manner, though in his present work he has introduced certain broader touches. He has returned to the ground of his first literary achievements, and introduced us again to that charming half-merry, half-melancholy Venice which most Americans know better through his pages than through any others. He did this, in a measure, we think, at his risk; partly because there was a chance of disturbing an impression which, in so far as he was the author of it, had had time to grow very tranquil and mellow; and partly because there has come to be a not unfounded mistrust of the Italian element in light literature. Italy has been made to supply so much of the easy picturesqueness, the crude local color of poetry and the drama, that a use of this expedient is vaguely regarded as a sort of unlawful shortcut to success,— one of those coarsely mechanical moves at chess which, if you will, are strictly within the rules of the game, but which offer an antagonist strong provocation to fold up the board. Italians have been, from Mrs. Radcliffe down, among the stock-properties of romance; their associations are melodramatic, their very names are supposed to go a great way toward getting you into a credulous humor, and they are treated, as we may say, as bits of coloring-matter, which if placed in solution in the clear water of uninspired prose are warranted to suffuse it instantaneously with the most delectable hues. The growing refinement of the romancer's art has led this to be considered a rather gross device, calculated only to delude the simplest imaginations, and we may say that the presumption is now directly against an Italian in a novel, until he has pulled off his slouched hat and mantle and shown us features and limbs that an Anglo-Saxon would acknowledge. Mr. Howells's temerity has gone so far as to offer us a priest of the suspected race—a priest with a dead-pale complexion, a blue chin, a dreamy eye, and a name in *elli*. The burden of proof is upon him that we shall believe in him, but he casts it off triumphantly at an early stage of the narrative, and we confess that our faith in Don Ippolito becomes at last really poignant and importunate.

"A Venetian priest in love with an American girl,—there's richness, as Mr. Squeers said!"—such was the formula by which we were first gossipingly made acquainted with the subject of "A Foregone Conclu-

sion." An amiable American widow, travelling in Italy with her daughter, lingers on in Venice into the deeper picturesqueness of the early
summer. With that intellectual thriftiness that characterizes many of
her class (though indeed in Mrs. Vervain it is perhaps only a graceful
anomaly the more), she desires to provide the young girl with instruction in Italian, and requests the consul of her native land (characteristically again) to point her out a teacher. The consul finds himself
interested in a young ecclesiastic, with an odd mechanical turn, who
has come to bespeak the consular patronage for some fanciful device
in gunnery, and whose only wealth is a little store of English, or rather
Irish, phrases, imparted by a fellow-priest from Dublin. Having been
obliged to give the poor fellow the cold shoulder as an inventor, he is
prompt in offering him a friendly hand as an Italian master, and Don
Ippolito is introduced to Miss Vervain. Miss Vervain is charming, and
the young priest discovers it to his cost. He falls in love with her, offers
himself, is greeted with the inevitable horror provoked by such a proposition from such a source, feels the deep displeasure he must have caused,
but finds he is only the more in love, resists, protests, rebels, takes it all
terribly hard, becomes intolerably miserable, and falls fatally ill, while
the young girl and her mother hurry away from Venice. Such is a rapid
outline of Mr. Howells's story, which, it will be seen, is simple in the
extreme,—is an air played on a single string, but an air exquisitely modu-
lated. Though the author has not broken ground widely, he has sunk
his shaft deep. The little drama goes on altogether between four persons, chiefly, indeed, between two,—but on its limited scale it is singularly complete, and the interest gains sensibly from compression. Mr.
Howells's touch is almost that of a miniature-painter; every stroke in
"A Foregone Conclusion" plays its definite part, though sometimes the
eye needs to linger a moment to perceive it. It is not often that a young
lady in a novel is the resultant of so many fine intentions as the figure
of Florida Vervain. The interest of the matter depends greatly, of course,
on the quality of the two persons thus dramatically confronted, and here
the author has shown a deep imaginative force. Florida Vervain and
her lover form, as a couple, a more effective combination even than
Kitty Ellison and Mr. Arbuton; for Florida, in a wholly different line,
is as good—or all but as good—as the sweetheart of that sadly incapable
suitor; and Don Ippolito is not only a finer fellow than the gentleman
from Boston, but he is more acutely felt, we think, and better understood on the author's part. Don Ippolito is a real creation,—a most vivid,
complete, and appealing one; of how many touches and retouches, how
many caressing, enhancing strokes he is made up, each reader must observe for himself. He is in every situation a distinct personal image, and
we never lose the sense of the author's seeing him in his habit as he
lived,—"moving up and down the room with his sliding step, like some

tall, gaunt, unhappy girl,"—and verging upon that quasi-hallucination with regard to him which is the law of the really creative fancy. His childish mildness, his courtesy, his innocence, which provokes a smile, but never a laugh, his meagre experience, his general helplessness, are rendered with an unerring hand: there is no crookedness in the drawing, from beginning to end. We have wondered, for ourselves, whether we should not have been content to fancy him a better Catholic and more intellectually at rest in his priestly office,—so that his passion for the strange and lovely girl who is so suddenly thrust before him should, by itself, be left to account for his terrible trouble; but it is evident, on the other hand, that his confiding her his doubts and his inward rebellion forms the common ground on which they come closely together, and the picture of his state of mind has too much truthful color not to justify itself. He is a representation of extreme moral simplicity, and his figure might have been simpler if he had been a consenting priest, rather than a protesting one. But, though he might have been in a way more picturesque, he would not have been more interesting; and the charm of the portrait is in its suffering us to feel with him, and its offering nothing that we find mentally disagreeable,—as we should have found the suggestion of prayers stupidly mumbled and of the *odeur de sacristie*. The key to Don Ippolito's mental strainings and yearnings is in his fancy for mechanics, which is a singularly happy stroke in the picture. It indicates the intolerable *discomfort* of his position, as distinguished from the deeper unrest of passionate skepticism, and by giving a sort of homely practical basis to his possible emancipation, makes him relapse into bondage only more tragical. It is a hard case, and Mr. Howells has written nothing better—nothing which more distinctly marks his faculty as a story-teller—than the pages in which he traces it to its climax. The poor caged youth, straining to the end of his chain, pacing round his narrow circle, gazing at the unattainable outer world, bruising himself in the effort to reach it and falling back to hide himself and die unpitied,—is a figure which haunts the imagination and claims a permanent place in one's melancholy memories.

The character of Florida Vervain contributes greatly to the dusky, angular relief of Don Ippolito. This young lady is a singularly original conception, and we remember no heroine in fiction in whom it is proposed to interest us on just such terms. "Her husband laughed," we are told at the close of the book, "to find her protecting and serving [her children] with the same tigerish tenderness, the same haughty humility, as that with which she used to care for poor Mrs. Vervain; and he perceived that this was merely the direction away from herself of that intense arrogance of nature which, but for her power and need of loving, would have made her intolerable. What she chiefly exacted from them, in return for her fierce devotedness, was the truth in everything; she was content they should be rather less fond of her than of their father, whom, indeed, they found much more amusing." A heroine who ripens into this sort of wife and mother is rather an exception among the tender sisterhood. Mr. Howells has attempted to enlist our imagination on behalf of a young girl who is positively unsympathetic, and who has an appearance of chilling rigidity and even of almost sinister reserve. He has brilliantly succeeded, and his heroine just escapes being disagreeable, to be fascinating. She is a poet's invention, and yet she is extremely real,—as real, in her way, as that Kitty Ellison whom she so little resembles. In these two figures Mr. Howells has bravely notched the opposite ends of his measure, and there is pleasure in reflecting on the succession of charming girls arrayed, potentially, along the intermediate line. He has outlined his field; we hope he will fill it up. His women are always most sensibly women; their motions, their accents, their ideas, savor essentially of the sex; he is one of the few writers who hold a key to feminine logic and detect a method in feminine madness. It deepens, of course, immeasurably, the tragedy of Don Ippolito's sentimental folly, that Florida Vervain should be the high-and-mighty young lady she is, and gives an additional edge to the peculiar cruelty of his situation,—the fact that, being what he is, he is of necessity, as a lover, repulsive. But Florida is a complex personage, and the tale depends in a measure in her having been able to listen to him in a pitying, maternal fashion, out of the abundance of her characteristic strength. There is no doubt that, from the moment she learns he has dreamed she might love him, he becomes hopelessly disagreeable to her; but the author has ventured on delicate ground in attempting to measure the degree in which passionate pity might qualify her repulsion. It is ground which, to our sense, he treads very firmly; but the episode of Miss Vervain's seizing the young priest's head and caressing it will probably provoke as much discussion as to its verisimilitude as young Arbuton's famous repudiation of the object of his refined affections. For our part, we think Miss Vervain's embrace was more natural than otherwise—for Miss Vervain; and, natural or not, it is admirably poetic. The poetry of the tale is limited to the priest and his pupil. Mrs. Vervain is a humorous creation, and in intention a very happy one. The kindly, garrulous, military widow, with her lively hospitality to the things that don't happen, and her serene unconsciousness of the things that do, is a sort of image of the way human levity hovers about the edge of all painful occurrences. Her scatter-brained geniality deepens the picture of her daughter's brooding preoccupations, and there is much sustained humor in making her know so much less of the story in which she plays a part than we do. Her loquacity, however, at times, strikes us as of a trifle too shrill a pitch, and her manner may be charged with lacking the repose, if not of the Veres of Vere, at least of the Veres of Providence. But there is a really ludicrous image suggested by the juxtaposition of her near-sightedness and her cheerful ignorance of Don Ippolito's situation, in which, at the same time, she takes so friendly an interest. She *overlooks* the tragedy going on under her nose, just as she overlooks the footstool on which she stumbles when she comes into a room. The touch proves that with a genuine artist, like Mr. Howells, there is an unfailing cohesion of all ingredients. Ferris, the consul, whose ultimately successful passion for Miss Vervain balances the sad heart-history of the priest, will probably find—has, we believe, already found—less favor than his companions, and will be reputed to have come too easily by his good fortune. He is an attempt at a portrait of a rough, frank, and rather sardonic humorist, touched with the *sans gêne* of the artist and even of the Bohemian. He is meant to be a good fellow in intention and a likable one in person; but we think the author has rather over-emphasized his irony and his acerbity. He holds his own firmly enough, however, as a make-weight in the action, and it is not till Don Ippolito passes out of the tale and the scale descends with a jerk into his quarter that most readers—feminine readers at least—shake their heads unmistakably. Mr. Howells's conclusion—his last twenty pages—will, we imagine, make him a good many dissenters,—among those, at least whose enjoyment has been an enjoyment of his art. The story passes into another tone, and the new tone seems to *jurer*, as the French say, with the old. It passes out of Venice and the exquisite Venetian suggestiveness, over to Providence, to New York, to the Fifth Avenue Hotel, and the Academy of Design. We ourselves regret the transition, though the motive of our regret is difficult to define. It is a transition from the ideal to the real, to the vulgar, from soft to hard, from charming color to something which is not color. Providence and the Fifth Avenue Hotel certainly have their rights; but we doubt whether their rights, in an essentially romantic theme, reside in a commixture with the suggestions offered us in such a picture as this:—

> The portal was a tall arch of Venetian Gothic, tipped with a carven flame; steps of white Istrian stone descended to the level of the lowest ebb, irregularly embossed with barnacles and dabbling long fringes of soft green sea-mosses in the rising and falling tide. Swarms of water-bugs and beetles played over the edges of the steps, and crabs scuttled sidewise into deeper water at the approach of a gondola. A length of stone-capped brick wall, to which patches of stucco still clung, stretched from the gate on either hand, under cover of an ivy that flung its mesh of shining green from within, where there lurked a lovely garden, stately, spacious for Venice, and full of a delicious half-sad surprise for whoso opened upon it. In the midst it had a broken fountain, with a marble naiad standing on a shell, and looking saucier than the sculptor meant, from having lost the point of her

nose; nymphs and fauns and shepherds and shepherdesses, her kins-
folk, coquetted in and out among the greenery in flirtation not to be
embarrassed by the fracture of an arm or the casting of a leg or so;
one lady had no head, but she was the boldest of all. In this garden
there were some mulberry and pomegranate trees, several of which
hung about the fountain with seats in their shade, and, for the rest,
there seemed to be mostly roses and oleanders, with other shrubs of
the kind that made the greatest show of blossom and cost the least for
tendance.

It was in this garden that Don Ippolito told his love. We are
aware that to consider Providence and New York not worthy to be
mentioned in the same breath with it is a strictly conservative view
of the case, and the author of "Their Wedding Journey" and "A Chance
Acquaintance" has already proved himself, where American local color
is concerned, a thoroughgoing radical. We may ground our objection
to the dubious element, in this instance, on saying that the story is
Don Ippolito's, and that in virtue of that fact it should not have
floated beyond the horizon of the lagoons. It is the poor priest's property, as it were; we grudge even the reversion of it to Mr. Ferris. We
confess even to a regret at seeing it survive Don Ippolito at all, and
should have advocated a trustful surrender of Florida Verbain's subsequent fortunes to the imagination of the reader. But we have no
desire to expatiate restrictively on a work in which, at the worst, the
imagination finds such abundant pasture. "A Foregone Conclusion" will
take its place as a singularly perfect production. That the author was
an artist his other books had proved, but his art ripens and sweetens
in the sun of success. His manner has now refined itself till it gives
one a sense of pure *quality* which it really taxes the ingenuity to express. There is not a word in the present volume as to which he has not
known consummately well what he was about; there is an exquisite
intellectual comfort in feeling one's self in such hands. Mr. Howells
has ranked himself with the few writers on whom one counts with
luxurious certainly, and this little masterpiece confirms our security.

[Review of
The Lady of the Aroostook]

Mayo W. Hazeltine*

When it was remarked of an accomplished Bostonian that he gave you the impression of a sick Englishman, the key-note was struck of a movement which has already borne wholesome fruit in literature, and is not unlikely to exert a bracing influence on the national character. The criticism, by the way, was by no means leveled at the local affectations of a particular community: it was an argument *a fortiori*; it recognized in the society of a given city more successful adepts in imitative efforts practiced elsewhere with considerable assiduity; and the rejoinder was obvious that it is better, as regards robustness, genuineness, and elevation of type to resemble an invalid Englishman than, let us say, a moribund Gaul or a consumptive Italian. Of late, Mr. Howells and Mr. James have undertaken to interpret the profound concern and secret uneasiness of American society touching the judgment of foreign observers; to portray its studious approximation toward the English diction and point of view, and to indicate the shortcomings in the most painstaking reproduction. So far as their transcripts of life stopped short with the exposure of deficiencies and the dissipation of illusions, they were fraught with the delightful pungency but also with the sterility of satire. They pointed out in an effective and captivating way the more or less diverting failures to solve a certain problem, but they did not squarely pose the fundamental query, whether the problem, after all, is worth solution. It is because Mr. Howells has gone much further in his latest work—because he has not only disclosed the inevitable miscarriage of the Anglicizing aim, but has laid bare the mental obliquity of such a purpose, as well as the species of moral torpidity entailed by it—that we are led to pronounce "The Lady of the Aroostook" the most virile, healthful and estimable achievement in recent American fiction.

It is the scope and lesson of Mr. Howells's new novel to which we would especially direct attention. It would be superfluous to dwell on the artistic gifts which have been attested and developed by successive experiments, on the power of sharp characterization and the constructive skill too seldom found united in English novels, or on the Protean forms of a humor that knows no sting, but is now condensed into a grateful, subacid irony, now sublimated to a mild aroma. All these are the recognized professional qualifications, so to

*Reprinted from "Current Literature," *North American Review*, 128 (June 1879), 691–94.

speak, of the advocate who has consented to hold a brief in the cause of American ideals, manners, and diction, *versus* English formulas and standards. But we ought to glance at the artist's thorough mastery of the subject-matter—at his exhaustive and wellnigh irreproachable exhibition of the models whose authority he disputes. If any American can reproduce the English speech in precise conformity to the idiom sanctioned by the best London society, it would seem to be Mr. Howells. This he had already demonstrated, and he offers cumulative proof in the book before us. As regards the main texture of the story, where the author speaks in his own person or through the mouths of those whom he means to be authentic exponents of right colloquial use, we can note but three insignificant marks of inadvertence. Once, we light on the word "stylishness," employed as an equivalent to the last century term "modishness," for which we believe a paraphrase is now employed in Belgravia. So, too, the verb "to keep," which, if we are not mistaken, is always transitive or reflexive, is used in accordance with a New England idiom in such a phrase as "I can not keep from doing it." To these trivial oversights may be added the occasional employment of "won't" for the third person singular of the future indicative in the negative conjugation. Against these microscopic slips may be set the most complete and curious catalogue of American solecisms and archaisms that has ever in our recollection been collected in a work of fiction. The pretexts and devices, by means of which the writer contrives to float these curiosities of our Yankee tongue on the swift movement of his story, are most dexterous and satisfactory. With these revelations are adroitly interwoven suggestions of all those English words and turns of phrase most calculated to startle and depress the modest American whose energies are given to the secret and patient melioration of his native speech. To this end the author introduces two distinct types of the semi-Anglicized Bostonian. On the one hand we have the young man who, as yet unenlightened by foreign travel, essays to make good his loss by minute research, painstaking synthesis, and cautious divination—who ransacks English novels, notebook and pencil in hand, and drinks with hungry ear the colloquial droppings of British tourists. Ascending one step in the scale of oral accomplishment, we have the traveled Bostonian who has managed not only to remodel in a large measure his vocabulary, but has even superadded some tricks of intonation—exercising, moreover, these acquisitions with a facility which might seem second nature but for a strong infusion of self-complacency. When, beside these types of successive degrees in approximation is placed the genuine thing itself—namely, a well-born Englishman, possessed too of a mania for exploring the mysteries of the American language from the point of view of the philologist—we can not but acknowledge the perfection of Mr. Howells's machinery for evolving the points of likeness and difference in the British original and its Boston counterpart.

After this demonstration of his perfect right to pronounce judgment in the premises, Mr. Howells silently inculcates through the action of this story and by the eloquence of example his conviction that the imitative attitude is essentially abortive and inane. To this end he is careful not to choose for his heroine a daintily-nurtured and closely-environed girl like Miss Bessie Alden, or even an affluent but ill-schooled and frivolous young person whose transgressions after all might be confined to occasional walks with masculine companions in the public thoroughfares of European cities. He has boldly grappled with the most awkward and unpromising materials; he has selected a young woman whose social status may be precisely though crudely defined by the epithet "a Yankee schoolmarm," and he has placed her, not in a foreign town with her kinfolk within call, but on shipboard—not only unchaperoned, but utterly unprotected, without a relative on board or another person of her own sex in the ship's company. Among her fellow passengers are two more or less Europeanized Bostonians, and a third quite obnoxious individual, properly described in the British dialect as an acutely accented specimen of the genus "Cad." Such are the elements of the situation presented in the cabin of the Aroostook; and it must be admitted that the objectionable features of our indigenous social code are here exhibited in an intensely aggravated form. In a word, this is an extreme case; and, if Mr. Howells has succeeded in subverting the prejudice provoked in some of her fellow passengers by the unconventional isolation and colloquial deficiencies of Miss Lydia Blood, he will have gone far to stem the Anglicizing mania. He will have done much to rehabilitate the robust, unsuspicious simplicity of our native manners, and to promote that decisive act of social autonomy suggested by the late Mr. Motley, namely the affirmation of a distinct American language, and the adoption of independent canons of speech.

William Dean Howells

Thomas Sargent Perry*

It is now a little more than twenty years since Mr. Howells made his first visit to Boston, bringing in his carpet-bag a number of poéms, which were soon printed in "The Atlantic Monthly." He had already

*Reprinted from *Century Magazine*, 23 (March 1882), 680–85.

sent to the East some of his verses, which had appeared in the same magazine. Many of these, by their form, and still more by their deep, cheerless gloom, showed that their author had a great admiration for Heine, the wonderful master of epigrammatic sadness. With years and actual experience the sadness—which was of the willful sort that belongs to youth—wore away, but Mr. Howells's hand retained the neatness of touch which is apparent in even the slightest of these verses. At about the same time he published a few longer poems, in a narrative form, and it is curious to see in these some of the qualities that are familiar to us in his later novels. It was a novelist, for instance, who heard and told the "Pilot's Story" about the man

> Weakly good-natured and kind, and weakly good-natured and vicious,
> Slender of body and mind, fit neither for loving nor hating,

who gambled away the quadroon girl, his mistress. In every one of his stories, too, we come across bits of humorous or pathetic insight which might have stood by themselves as the subjects of little poems; and in all his subsequent work we find the poetic flavor which was here asserting itself. It was some time, however, before Mr. Howells tried the more serious business of writing novels. This delay is only natural; views about life are common property, but knowledge of what life really is is a rarer thing and more difficult of attainment.

These poems had been written by Mr. Howells in the scant leisure moments of a busy youth. He was born in Ohio, in the year 1837; his father was editor and publisher of a country newspaper, and it was at a very early age that the subject of this article began to set type and learn the printer's trade. Throughout his boyhood, and in fact until 1859, he worked in his father's printing-office, although for two or three years before that date he had exercised his pen as a legislative reporter, and then as "news editor" of "The Ohio State Journal" at Columbus. What intervals his work granted him were taken for reading and, in time, for writing, and the early fruits of his pen appeared in a volume called "Poems of Two Friends," which was published at Columbus, in December, 1859. The other writer, who indeed was the author of the greater number of the poems, was Mr. J. J. Piatt, who has since written many pleasing verses. These two young poets had worked together in a printing-office, where they spent the years which so many young men waste in college. In the summer of 1861[1] Mr. Howells wrote a life of Lincoln, a book which had a large sale in the West, and in the autumn of that year he was appointed consul at Venice.

This appointment was one of the sort which, doubtless, the stern civil-service reformer will have to condemn, in public, at least; but in private he will only congratulate himself upon it, as an Englishman might have done for the unsound system which found a place in Parliament for men like Pitt and Burke. Moreover, if the duties of a consul in Venice were slight—and the *Alabama* was at work beginning the warfare against American commerce which has since been carried on by legislators,—there was the more leisure for the study of this fascinating city. Indeed, the change from an Ohio city to Venice was the most complete that could be imagined. Even Hâvre or Bordeaux, with strictly commercial flavor, would have seemed like a glimpse of paradise to a young, untraveled, poetic consul, but to go to Italy, and of all Italian ports, to Venice! It must have seemed as if life had nothing more to grant to the imaginative young official.

It is with this new life that Mr. Howells's literary activity really begins, and the two volumes, "Venetian Life" and "Italian Journeys," bear witness to the impulse he received from this transplanting. These books are made up of essays and letters which were saved from the swift oblivion of bound magazines and newspapers. They are delightful reading, and they bear the promise of the future novelist in them. When he traveled to Italian towns he was studying human nature, and, fortunately, there have been preserved in these two books a vast number of little studies, minute observations, such as in abundance go to make the outfit of a writer of fiction. . . . take this account of the "patriarch," the government guide who accompanied Mr. Howells to Capri, and induced him to see the "tarantella" danced for two francs, "whereas down at your inn, if you hire the dancers through your landlord, it will cost you five or six francs. But," Mr. Howells goes on,

> The poor patriarch was also a rascal in his small way, and he presently turned to me with a countenance full of cowardly trouble and base remorse: "I pray you, little sir, not to tell the landlord below there that you have seen the tarantella danced here; for he has daughters and friends to dance it for strangers, and gets a deal of money by it. So, if he asks you to see it, do me the pleasure to say, lest he should take on (*pigliarsi*) with me about it: Thanks, but we saw the tarantella at Pompeii." It was the last place in Italy where we were likely to have seen the tarantella; but these simple people are improvident in lying, as in everything else.

Imagine a touch like that in Addison's "Remarks on Italy"!

These two volumes were not all that Mr. Howells brought back with him to America, when he returned home in the autumn of 1865. They show, however, how rich was the experience he had acquired, and with what a keen eye he had observed this foreign life. If he who knows two languages is twice a man, how much more can this be said of one who knows two peoples!

After doing a little journalistic work on "The Nation" in New York, Mr. Howells was invited by the late Mr. J. T. Fields to take the place of assistant editor of "The Atlantic Monthly," and in 1871 he assumed the full charge of that magazine, a position which he held until the spring of 1881. Much of his time and attention went into the composition of book-notices, a sort of writing which the public often neglects, and which is apparently without influence on writers; but he wrote a number of essays, which he collected into a volume called "Suburban Sketches," published in 1870, and "The Wedding Journey,"[2] which appeared serially in the year 1871, showed that he was gradually feeling his way to becoming a novelist. There was all the setting of a novel without a conventional plot; there were plenty of incidents, but they existed solely for their own sake; it was a prolonged sketch, full of all those qualities which readers have learned to associate with Mr. Howells's books.

The first of these to strike the reader's attention is the delightful humor, which is not the derisive horse-play of some of those writers who in foreign parts have acquired a reputation for American humor. Although that term is applied without much discrimination to very diverse ways of arousing laughter, varying from wit to buffoonery, we find in him, rather, a subtle, evasive humor, without geographical limitations, because it is so rare that no country can lay claim to its exclusive possession. Here is one bit, a trifle, to be sure, but a characteristic trifle; while going up the Hudson River there had been a slight accident, and the passengers had gathered on the deck to recount all the horrors which they had ever seen, or just escaped seeing:

"Well," said one of the group, a man in a hard hat, "I never lie down on a steam-boat or a railroad train. I want to be ready for whatever happens."

The others looked at this speaker with interest, as one who had invented a safe method of travel.

"I happened to be up to-night, but I almost always undress and go to bed, just as if I were in my own house," said the gentleman of the silk cap. "I don't say your way isn't the best, but that's my way."

The champions of the rival systems debated their merits with suavity and mutual respect, but they met with scornful silence a compromising spirit who held that it was better to throw off your coat and boots, but keep your pantaloons on.

Mr. Howells's humor is more noticeable when he is writing about women and their ways. Thus, when the couple whose journey is the subject of the book got to the furthermost of the little islands in the channel at Niagara, the heroine,

—without the slightest warning, sank down at the root of a tree, and said, with serious composure, that she could never go back on those bridges; they were not safe. He stared at her cowering form in blank amaze, and put his hands in his pockets. Then it occurred to his dull masculine sense that it must be a joke; and he said, "Well, I'll have you taken off in a boat!"

"O, *do*, Basil, *do*, have me taken off in a boat," implored Mabel, "you see yourself the bridges are not safe. *Do* get a boat."

He goes on with his ill-timed pleasantry, and she bursts into tears. He tries sarcasm, then kindness, proposing to carry her.

"No, that will bring double the weight on the bridge at once."
"Couldn't you shut your eyes, and let me lead you?"
"Why, it isn't the *sight* of the rapids," she said, looking up fiercely. "*The bridges are not safe.* I'm not a *child*, Basil. Oh, *what* shall we do?"

Then when he tells her some one is coming,—"Those people we saw in the parlor last night,"—she walks calmly back without a word. He asks her why she had so suddenly acted reasonably.

"Why, dearest! Don't you understand? That Mrs. Richard—whoever she is—is so much like me."

Or take that other instance, when "she rose with a smile from the ruins of her life, amidst which she had heart-brokenly sat down with all her things on."

If it is fair to make another quotation from this book, which, however, is wholly made up of these accessories, there is this:

They were about to enter the village, and he could not make any open acknowledgment of her tenderness; but her silken mantel slipped from her shoulder, and he embracingly replaced it, flattering himself that he had delicately seized this chance of an unavowed caress, and not knowing (O such is the blindness of our sex!) that the opportunity had been yet more subtly afforded him, with the art which women never disuse in this world, and which, I hope, they will not forget in the next.

Laughter at the alleged inconsequence of women is nothing new in literature, but it has not always been accompanied with the kindliness and reverence which Mr. Howells never fails to show. Occasionally, we come across a novelist who detects or fancies a resemblance between a woman and the domestic cat. With this slender stock in trade, he turns off numerous stories swarming with catlike women, who purr, glide over carpets, and, at times, scratch. This amount of lore is commonly taken for profound knowledge of the female heart, and the wrath of women over the analogy is taken for the shame of detection. Women have no cause to be indignant with Mr. Howells's kind comprehension of them; what he feels for them is not the exultation of a man who has found them out, or the pity of a superior being for attractive inferiors, but the sympathy of a man who understands them, and what we are all hungry for is not so much that we may be loved, as that we may be understood. Possibly, at times, we are overhasty in assuming that if we were understood we should be loved. There can be no dark doubt of this kind, however, in the case of Mr. Howells's girlish heroines. Take them in succession, and see their naturalness and consequent charm. The heroine of "A Chance Acquaintance" is not the same person as Lydia, the heroine of "The Lady of the *Aroostook*," or that of "Dr. Breen's Practice." Yet they are alike in their fearlessness before others and timidity before themselves, in their gracious innocence and generosity. No one has drawn such uncontaminated souls more delicately than Mr. Howells, because no one has drawn them more exactly. In the great whirl of life they would have but little show by the side of intenser people, more practiced plotters, and the victims of fiercer emotions; their kingdom, so to speak, is just out of the busy world, in some quiet corner, whence fancy and poetry are not banished.

Fond as Mr. Howells is of these independent girls with their romance awaiting them, he has also written about another sort of heroine, the full-blown coquette, the mature flirt, and he has made a most thorough study of her antics. The coquettes whom we meet in novels have commonly but one trick, although, to be sure, this is generally irresistible, or said to be irresistible; he has shown us accomplished experts in the gay science, who are not simply arch, or mischievous, or appealing, but much more, for at times they are frank. The art with which he draws his coquettes is most admirable, because here, as everywhere, Mr. Howells describes what he sees, and his eyes are exceedingly sharp. They see not only the grim, decrepit New England village in the brief season when "boarders" assemble, but also the perturbing flirt, the unworthy cause of tragedies, who is not condemned or apologized for, but is simply put before us.

There can be but little doubt that, whenever we are fortunate enough to have a novelist writing for us, we are only too apt to insist that he is not an artist, writing for his own delectation as well as ours, but that he is a political economist, or a patriot, or certainly a moralist, in disguise. To be sure, we are led into this error by the fact that every story, exactly in proportion to its truth to life, carries with it some lesson, just as all experience does; but that, I take it, is as secondary, in all real novels, as instruction in perspective is foreign to a painter's intentions. Yet we go on imagining that a novelist has anything in his mind except a story which exists for its own sake, and we torment one another with wondering what moral we were meant to draw, when the real question before us is: What is the fable? Do the little fishes talk like whales, or like little fishes? We may be sure of one thing: if the novelist will take care of his story, the moral will take care of itself.

Mr. Howells's novels have not wholly escaped discussion of this sort. Of late years, the American girl has become an object of great public interest, and the opinion seems to be held in some quarters that Mr. Howells has been retained, like a scientific expert, to support the views of one side of a controversy concerning the American young person, whereas it would be fairer to suppose that he chooses a certain sort of girl for his heroine, writes about her, and reads with wonder all the lessons that his critics find in the pages of his story.

And what charming girls they are! There is Florida Vervain in "A Foregone Conclusion," which is, perhaps, the most poetic of Mr. Howells's novels; we have here a distinctively American girl, with her keen moral sense, receiving a declaration of love from an Italian priest. That is the climax of the story, and the reader will recall how beautifully the whole tale is told, and how the girl's pity for the poor man is described. No other feeling would have served the author's purpose. Indignation would have been unnatural; any answer on her part to his affection would have repelled the reader, and her very pity makes his position the more hopeless. It is only the more cruel in its effect on the priest that the heroine, in absolute unconsciousness of what her words conveyed, had given the priest the very encouragement of which he stood most in need, that he should look upon himself as a man. . . .

When he ventures to take her really at her word, and discloses his long pent-up love, he sees the whole truth. Her cry, "You? A priest!" shows him the hopelessness of his passion; and her pity only seals his doom. Nothing could more completely sum up the book than the passage in which the heroine, as she bids farewell to the priest, throws her arms about his neck and kisses him, sealing, as it were, the impossibility of his love for her. With this, the story might well have ended; that the heroine should return to this country and marry an unromantic Yankee was, perhaps, inevitable, but was it not a sacrifice to conventionality?

In "The Lady of the *Aroostook*" we have the young girl, wholly without experience, triple-armed in her innocence, who is thrust fresh from South Bradfield, Mass., into semidisreputable foreign society in Venice, after crossing the ocean with no other woman on the ship, and two young men—for the little sot need not be counted—for her fellow-passengers. Certainly it would be hard to find a more dramatic contrast, and Mr. Howells is very fond of this plot—of placing an unconventional figure before all the complications of modern society, and letting the new-comer settle everything by her native judgment.

In so many formless English novels we see the frank acceptance of conventional rewards, the bride and the moneybags awaiting the young man who has artificially prolonged a tepid courtship, that the reader grows weary of the implied compliment to wealth and position. There is a truly national spirit in the way Mr. Howells shows the other side—the emptiness of convention and the dignity of native worth. Struggle as we may against it, it is one of the main conditions of American, if not of modern, society, that inborn merit has a chance to assert itself. The quality by which distinction is adjudged is, to be sure, too often unrelenting social ambition in combination with a long purse, but the destructon of old lines is going on, and even if movements of this kind could be stopped, society could not revert to its original condition of rigid divisions. As it is, however, these movements are irresistible—they move in any direction, save backward, and the democratic hero has done much in literature since Rousseau gave him citizenship in his "Nouvelle Héloïse."

After all, what can realism produce but the downfall of conventionality? Just as the scientific spirit digs the ground from beneath superstition, so does its fellow-worker, realism, tend to prick the bubble of abstract types. Realism is the tool of the democratic spirit, the modern spirit by means of which the truth is elicited, and Mr. Howells's realism is untiring. It is, too, unceasingly good-natured. Whether he is describing the Italian officers, or the wife in "Their Wedding Journey," with her firm devotion to Boston, or country people in "Dr. Breen's Practice," we feel that Mr. Howells is scrutinizing the person he is writing about with undisturbed calmness, and that no name and no person can impose upon him by its conventional value. His countrypeople are simple, shrewd, unimpassioned rustics; they are neither pastoral shepherds nor boors—they are human beings. In his "Wedding Journey" Mr. Howells introduces a conversation which he overheard in a steam-boat, between a young man who traveled "in pursuit of trade for the dry-goods house he represented," and two girls, "conjecturally sisters going home from some visit, and not skilled in the world, but of certain repute in their country neighborhood for beauty and wit." I will not quote the details of their romping flirtation, but these words of Mr. Howells deserve attention: "Ah! poor real life, which I love, can I make others share the delight I find in thy foolish and insipid face!"

This is his attitude throughout, and it is the one most fitting the writer who stands as interpreter between the world and his readers, who knows that it is his duty to tell us what he sees, not to pervert the truth according to his whims or prejudices. It would have been easy enough to sneer at these hoydenish girls and their bold admirer, but there is no ill-nature in the few lines devoted to them, and certainly no tendency to exaggerate their importance. This, it seems to me, is a saner way of looking at the world than that which we sometimes notice in "Punch," when "'Arry" comes under public censure. So long as realism gives us what is seen by intelligent eyes, without telling us what the emotions are with which we should dilate, it will have at least the charm of novelty. Although the tendency of modern literature is toward truthfulness, only a few writers dare to be honest, or, even if they dare, know how to be so. We can all sit down and write a very passable essay on the merits of cheerfulness, of punctuality, of patriotism, but how many people have the gift of seeing what goes on about them, and of stating it concisely, impressively, and yet dispassionately? They are few, indeed, and most of them, if they were to write a novel, would be likely to manufacture a story after the accustomed model, which would at least be safe.

After all, the world is very unfair to novelists; we all know that life is made up of disappointments, that the fervor of youth gives way to a chilly content with compromise, that no one carries his ideals far, but exchanges them for maxims of worldly prudence. We know all this, I say, and we tell novelists, above all things, to paint life as they see it; yet the moment one does so and gives us anything but the customary ending,—such as we see on the stage at about twenty-five minutes past ten o'clock, when the actors form in a semi-circle, and the green curtain begins to show signs of animation,—we are enraged, and we denounce the novelist as a foe to his kind. We ask, too, for faithful studies of men, yet it is seldom that a novelist gives us these; for one season the heroes are all consumptive, in the next they are all muscular. We are great sticklers, too, for the social position of the people we may meet in our reading; we do not care to make strange acquaintances.

For all these prejudices Mr. Howells has no patience, and in his pages one finds a tolerably full collection of the amusing figures who go to make up the American public. We pass them in the street without knowing them, and when we get home we groan over the monotony of American civilization; but they have not escaped the eyes of this busy student of his kind. The vulgarest of them he has put before us in their relations to some romantic incident; they are not merely collected and, as it were, pinned on the wall—they are brought into subservience to some romantic story. Of course, the mere accumulation of incidents does not make a novel, any more than the accidental juxtaposition of colors makes a picture: the informing spirit must control the selection and arrangement which go to every work of art. For my own part, I fail to feel the same interest in "Dr. Breen's Practice" that I feel in "A Foregone Conclusion" or "A Chance Acquaintance," or, indeed, in most of the others. But Mr. Howells is himself responsible for making his readers hard to please.

May I say the same thing about his plays, or, as they might be more properly called, his dramatic scenes? A novelist may well be anxious to set his characters on the stage, to see them walking before him, endowed with flesh and blood for at least a few hours' life, for the play promises to be more vivid than the printed page; yet often it is not. The lighter the play, the greater is the demand upon the skill of the actors, and there are but few of them who are capable of giving in the theater those delicate shades and implications which form the setting in which Mr. Howells always lays his scene. Occasionally we see a delicate French piece, such as one of Alfred de Musset's *proverbes*, in an English rendering; but all the graceful ease and finish of the original are evaporated in the removal from Paris, as if they were delicate wines incapable of transport. Mr. Howells's plays suffer from this very lightness, and we miss what are so noticeable in his novels—his own comments and ingenious side-remarks, which have no weight as stage directions, especially when translated into the ordinary gestures and motions of the stage. What endears his books to us as much as anything is what we see of the author in them; he lets us see through his eyes. Thus, in "The Lady of the *Aroostook*," Lydia is on the deck of the ship, talking with Staniford. He says:

> "I wish I could be with you when you first see Venice!"
> "Yes?" said Lydia.
> Even the interrogative comment, with the rising inflection, could not chill his enthusiasm.
> "It is really the greatest sight in the world."
> Lydia had apparently no comment to make on this fact. She waited tranquilly awhile before she said:
> "My father used to talk about Italy to me when I was little. He wanted to go. My mother said afterward—after she had come home with me to South Bradfield—that she always believed he would have lived if he had gone there. He had consumption."
> "Oh!" said Staniford, softly. Then he added, with the tact of his sex: "Miss Blood, you mustn't take cold, sitting here with me. This wind is chilly. Shall I go below and get you some more wraps?"

Or take this from the same book. Staniford says:

> "But we shall not see the right sort of Sabbath till Mr. Dunham gets his Catholic Church fully going."
> They all started, and looked at Dunham, as good Protestants must when some one whom they would never have suspected of Catholicism turns out to be a Catholic. Dunham cast a reproachful glance at his friend, but said simply:
> "I am a Catholic—that is true; but I do not admit the pretensions of the Bishop of Rome."

It is in just such scenes as these that Mr. Howells's peculiar power of seeing and putting before us little shades is most clearly marked, and we may be sure that we find these subtle distinctions more clearly presented in the story, with the aid of his lines or half-lines of characterization, than they are likely to be on the stage, where we are accustomed to broader effects and cruder methods. The delicate half-tints in which he works are too nearly indistinguishable in the dazzling, garish blaze of the theater. Such, at least, is one spectator's experience.

The traditions, too, of the stage are obstinate and would be slow in making themselves over, whereas Mr. Howells has made over the American novel, taught it gracefulness and compactness, and, with one predecessor and one or two contemporaries, given it a place in literature along with the best of modern work. That he has delighted us all, we all know. He has shown us how genuine, how full of romance, is the life about us which seems sordid and has a fine reputation for sordidness; and he has proved that realism does not mean groping in the mire. The main distinction, however, does not lie in the subject, but in the character of the man who writes about it. That is what gives the aroma of sincerity, sympathy, respect for what is honorable, or the contrary impression, to literary work. It is the tone of the author's mind that makes the mark upon that of the reader, and who that knows Mr. Howells's work does not feel that he learns new sympathies and gentler judgment from his generosity and careful study? The reader is not moved by eloquence to unknown feelings, which fade away when the book is closed, and give place to a critical reaction; no, he see things in a new light: Mr. Howells touches his shoulder, and points out the beauty hidden in simple actions, the pathos lurking beneath seemingly indifferent words,—in short, the humanity of life.

Above all, he does this with reverence, with the sort of regard which science has for small things as well as great. That small things are unimportant is a matter of convention, and, as we have seen, Mr. Howells does not care for conventions. What he cares for is to see and describe things as they are, and he does this with such sympathetic comprehension that our admiration for his books is enriched by a feeling of affection for the writer.

Notes

1. Publication date for *Lives and Speeches of Abraham Lincoln and Hannibal Hamlin* was 25 June 1860, or earlier.
2. The heroine of *Their Wedding Journey* was Isabel March.

1883-1886

American Literature in England

[Margaret Oliphant Oliphant]*

American enterprise has lately made a new departure in England. We all respect that energetic quality. We know what it has done in the past, we are aware that everything is expected from it in the future. In literature, perhaps, there are reasons, proper to the literary bosom, and in which the public on either side of the Atlantic has shown no very encouraging interest, which make us contemplate with a certain spitefulness the benevolence of the reception which has been awarded to our transatlantic brethren in this respect. It is futile, and it is perhaps not enlightened: but there are circumstances in which the principles of free trade, however entirely acquiesced in as a system, can be accepted only with a pang. When our own wares are heavily taxed by our neighbours—or à plus forte raison, when they are taken from us by our neighbours without any price paid at all—it would require a temper more than human to concur without the faintest grudge in the brilliant reception, the abundant recompense, the generous enthusiasm with which the productions of our fellow-tradesmen among those neighbours are received here. We are willing to allow that the sentiment is shabby, but it is human. There stands at the present moment before us a set of charming little books, most creditable in appearance to everybody concerned in their reproduction, with the words "Author's Edition" respectfully printed upon the title-page. Far be it from us to grudge that it should be so. We hope Mr. Howells finds the arrangement in every respect satisfactory; but when we remember not only the absolute want of any equivalent whatever, but even the slobbery broadsheet, like a double number of the 'Family Herald,' which is the shape in which English fiction is now presented to the American reader, it cannot be that we should view the contrast with the unalloyed satisfaction which we should desire to feel. When the reciprocity is all on one side, accord-

*Reprinted from *Blackwood's Edinburgh Magazine*, 133 (January 1883), 136–61.

ing to a vulgar but expressive description, a sigh cannot but heave the bosom of the unrecompensed. Delighted that you should have your due (we say), gentlemen all! but we should like on our own part to have some too. The wish may be selfish, but it is natural. And though it is Christian to do to others what you would that they should do to you, yet it is only human to wish, if no more, that they might be moved to reciprocate the treatment. It is even quite allowable, we hope, that a desire to move them to emulation of your Christian conduct should tell for something in your action. And when this return is refused to us, a certain regret may be permitted—not indeed because we have behaved honourably to them, but because they have not behaved quite so honourably to us.

We think this mild statement of the case may be ventured upon without offence even to the susceptible American, whose consciousness of what he himself calls spread-eagleism does not prevent him from being quite as determined as ever that criticism of the peculiar institutions which still remain to him is, as Dogberry says, tolerable, and not to be endured. . . .

It was exceedingly clever, what may perhaps be called smart, just at the moment when English authors were placed by a new efflorescence of piracy in a worse position than ever on the other side of the Atlantic, that the American periodical should have invaded our shores. But so it was. It has made, we believe, a successful invasion, and not without deserving its success. For the American magazines which England has accepted with cordiality are excellent in illustration; and if their literary qualities are not the highest, they have at least a certain novelty and freshness of flavour. There are, however, certain results of their introduction which are more important than the possibly ephemeral success which a public, more free from prejudices in favour of its own than ever public was before, has awarded to them: and these are, first, the revelation of some American authors little or not at all known in England; and second, a full perception, hitherto possible only to a few, of the claims of America in literature. These claims we have hitherto been very charitable to, as the early clutches of a great literature about to come into being, though as yet somewhat stunted and not of lavish growth, at the laurels of fame. But few perhaps were aware how little consideration was thought to be necessary, or how entirely sure our transatlantic relations were of having attained a standing-ground of certainty, much above that vague platform of hope. The readers of the 'Century,' which is the most ambitious, and we think the best, of our competitors, will have begun to realise by this time that there are a great many distinguished authors writing English whose names and works are entirely unknown to them. It may be that this discovery will have taught them to regret that literary piracy is coldly looked upon in England, and that consequently they are not in a position to judge for themselves what are the qualifications of these writers; or it may have moved them to a philosophical amusement at the limited nature of human reputation,—but in any case they will have received the information with a certain surprise. . . . Mr James in the 'Century' is illustrated only by a portrait, and—saving for a little autobiographical anecdote, in which Mr Howells, the writer of the article, comes himself to the front and informs us that it was his own discrimination which found out the qualities of the new writer—is legitimately enough treated in the way of criticism rather than gossip. "It still seems to me that the situation" (of the early tale submitted to him as assistant to Mr Fields, the publisher), "was strongly and finely felt," Mr Howells says, as if subsequent events had thrown some doubt upon this; and he adds with candour which seems uncalled for, considering how certainly the public has ratified his judgment, "One is much securer of one's judgment at twenty-nine than, say, at forty-five; but if this was a mistake of mine, I am not yet old enough to regret it." This is a fine specimen of the kind of delicate wit which it requires, it is said, a surgical operation to get into a Scotch intelligence. We are disposed, in the matter-of-fact method peculiar to our nation, to ask why should Mr Howells suppose that a time may come when he shall be old enough to regret it? Does he expect Mr James to "go off" like a professional beauty? or is this only American for the sentiment which, in England, would be expressed thus: "I am very proud of myself for having made such an excellent hit"?

We may add, before we go on, Mr Howells's opinion on a similar subject of literary art to that treated by Mr Warner. He does not tell us that he cannot understand English, nor we American; but he says that our old canons are worn out at least in fiction, of which craft he assures us Mr James is at present the head.

> The art of fiction has in fact become a finer art in our day than it was with Dickens and Thackeray. We could not suffer the confidential attitude of the latter now, nor the mannerism of the former, any more than we could endure the prolixity of Richardson or the coarseness of Fielding. These great men are of the past, they and their methods and interests; even Trollope and Reade are not of the present.

There is one great advantage which the artist who looks fondly back upon the past has over the worshipper of the present—his position is one of humility at least, and gracious decorum. He does not challenge a comparison between the old glories of his fathers and his own brannew and dazzling achievement. When a writer of fiction commits himself so terribly as to allege that the art of which he is a professor is finer than the art of Thackerary, the punishment which he prepares for himself is so prodigious that it becomes ridiculous. But no one we believe will be cruel enough to make the suggested comparison, and measure Mr Howells against Thackeray. He is so far safe in the inferiority of his stature. A little while ago it was Scott whom all our young cockerels had outgrown. For that matter, Shakespeare has been outgrown a number of times in the chronicles of the ages, both upon the stage and in the closet, but somehow has come back again, and still holds his own— though Pope and Voltaire were very sure that the dramatic art had improved immeasurably in the interval between his barbarous age and theirs. So we don't doubt that, even in America, the old gods will outlive the temporary dazzling of Mr Henry James's fine style, and delicate power of analysis, and even the setting down given to them by the critics. Mr Howells proceeds to add that the fine, nay finer, finest art of fiction in America is largely influenced by French fiction, especially by Daudet. Now M. Daudet is so largely influenced by Dickens, that we might, without extravagance, call him the literary son and heir of that great novelist; so it is evident that all this brave talk about that mannerism which cannot now be suffered, means only that the American likes a literary influence better when he gets it diluted by way of France, and through a strange land, than when it comes to him direct from his ancestral shores.

These two magnificent professions of faith, or of revolt, are both contained in the November number of the 'Century.' We shall in consequence look to that magazine for the fiction of the future—with hope, for Mr Howells says it is a finer art than any we have as yet known; yet with some alarm, for Mr Warner advertises us that we shall be utterly unable to understand it. This is sad, but it is an excitement to look forward to; and though it may be somewhat humiliating, it will be a fine lesson to see the critics of England gathered round the American periodical, endeavouring devoutly to spell out, through the intricacies of the American language, the last and greatest development of the novel—not as it was in the vulgar days of story-telling, but perfected with all the recent improvements, and adapted to the latest necessities of the time. . . .

American Novels

[Louis John Jennings]*

We regret to observe that some American writers still have much fault to find with us in England, especially with the language which is commonly in use here, and which to their gentle sense appears no better than a vulgar dialect. But there is one offence which they cannot fairly lay to our charge, no matter how much ingenuity they may apply to the task of lengthening the old indictment against us. It is impossible for them to allege that they have been denied the respectful attention to which they were justly entitled. It is, indeed, almost sufficient to make the success of a novel, to announce that it comes from the pen of an American. English readers appear, for a time at least, to have grown weary of most of their own novelists, who are perhaps not altogether guiltless of the sin of provoking weariness, by their persistency in reproducing the same set of puppets, and forcing upon our notice, year after year, the rusty springs and machinery which move them. Some of these writers had nothing to start with but the thinnest possible material, and the exigences of their trade have compelled them to go on painfully and laboriously beating it out, until it is difficult to say which has grown most weary of watching the process—the author or the reader. Even Sir Walter Scott could not multiply works of fiction continually without betraying manifest signs of exhaustion, and it is not surprising that writers, who never possessed a tenth part of his wealth of imagination or his fertility of invention, should fail where he did not succeed. Some had one good novel in them, and no more; some, perhaps, had half-a-dozen. But they have given us scores—each one, as a rule, more commonplace than its predecessor. The English public are slow to turn their backs upon an old favourite, but there is a limit to their great patience, and these too prolific writers have done their best to reach it.

It is partly owing to these circumstances that the American novelist has, of late years, received so effusive a welcome. Publishers have accepted blindfold anything he has chosen to offer them. The reason is, that he has either provided us with total change of scenery and of characters, or we take up his books in the expectation that he will do so. . . . With the exception of Mr. Bret Harte, whose admirable sketches of wild life in the West are thoroughly and distinctively American, owing very little to European 'culture' or influences, the writers whose works are so much in vogue in England either neglect their own country altogether, or introduce us to types of Europeanized Americans with which we are already too familiar, and which add nothing to our knowledge of Amer-

*Reprinted from Quarterly Review, 155 (January 1883), 201–229.

ican character. One little book of Hawthorne's—the 'Scarlet Letter'—is worth all the laboured and tedious writings of the novelists who boast of having founded a new school of fiction, based upon the principle that the best novelist is he who has no story to tell. A more convenient theory could scarcely be provided for those who have turned to novel-writing as a pleasant means of acquiring profit and reputation, without any natural gifts for the work, and without even a true insight into its nature. For writers who are unable either to invent a plot, or to infuse a spark of the fire of imagination into their 'analytical' studies, it is extremely satisfactory to have it laid down as a law, that a story is quite superfluous to a novel, and that wooden dummies are much more interesting than men and women. . . .

Any one who will go back to the works of the originators of American fiction will remark at once, how thoroughly imbued were their minds with the traditions and national feeling of their own country. . . .

It is true that these writers could not boast that they had made fiction a 'finer art' than it ever was before, and they did not enjoy the opportunity of publishing elaborate praises of each other's performances in the pages of illustrated magazines. The most successful of all 'fine arts' in the present day—the art of puffery—was then comparatively unknown. . . .

The fact is that, in our eager search for the American novel, we are in danger of overlooking the very writers who have the best claim to our attention. Instead of perpetually asking for something new, we shall do well to go back to the old, which for most of us will be new. How many English readers, for instance, have even heard of John P. Kennedy, the author of 'Swallow Barn,' a novel which contains vividly-drawn scenes of Virginian life, in the days when Virginia was still the proudest of the American States? We do not say that it is an exciting novel; but are the novels which we are now asked to read so thrilling in their interest, that poor Kennedy can no longer presume to hold up his head? Was ever any reader kept out of bed by his desire to finish the 'Portrait of a Lady' or 'A Modern Instance'?

That there are American girls like Mr. James's Daisy Miller, we are not prepared to deny; but if we were to exhibit her as a fair representative of young women in the United States, or of any large section of them, every American would think that he had a fair right to complain. Mr. Henry James has done scant justice to his country-women; perhaps he has studied them less than he has studied the women of Europe. In the truly 'first-class notice' (with a pretty portrait attached) which Mr. Howells has liberally devoted to Mr. James—Mr. Howells having received a similar notice, also with a pretty portrait, a few months previously—we are told that Mr. James's 'race is Irish on his father's side, and Scotch on his mother's;' that much of his early life was spent in Europe; that he was at Harvard a few years, and then 'took up his residence in England and Italy which, with infrequent visits home, has continued ever since.' It would therefore appear that the studies of Americans which Mr. James presents to us are made chiefly from a distance, and there are not a few Americans, proud of their own descent from the old stock, who would be inclined to receive with much coldness the credentials of his 'race.' New England blood was in Hawthorne's veins, but Mr. James comes almost as a stranger to make his 'analyses' of Americans, many of whom, in New York, New England, Virginia, or the Carolinas would have no difficulty in showing a family descent in their own country of two hundred and fifty years. This may have something to do with the singularity of the 'types' which supply Mr. James with his American portraits.... Since ["The American"] ... he appears to have been guided by the principle which is expressed in Mr. Howells's panegyric: 'Will the reader be content to accept a novel which is an anayltic study rather than a story?' The answer to this question, from nine readers out of ten, will be emphatically No: on that point neither Mr. Howells nor Mr. James need be in doubt for a single moment. When once the general reader is made to understand that he is not to go to these gentlemen for entertainment, even of the tamest kind, but only for philosophic instruction and dawdling sentimentality, their occupation will be gone. The one thing which the public exact of the dramatist or the novelist is, that they shall be amused. If the amusement is provided, they may perhaps be willing to take a little 'instruction' with it; but when it is all pill and no sugar, the dose will be rejected. Mr. Howells seems to be buoyed up with the hope of finding a much more accommodating frame of mind prevailing, at least in England. It is an act of kindness to warn him beforehand that he is providing for himself an ample fund of future disappointment....

Now no one is disposed to deny either to Mr. James or to Mr. Howells any reasonable degree of credit which they may choose to demand for this kind of work; the reception of their novels in this country is sufficient proof of that. But what we are not prepared to concede is the extraordinary claim which has recently been put forward by one of them, and not disavowed by the other, to be accounted superior to Dickens and Thackeray. 'The art of fiction,' Mr. Howells gravely tells us, 'has in fact become a finer art in our day than it was with Dickens and Thackeray. We could not suffer the confidential attitude of the latter now, nor the mannerism of the former.... These great men are of the past—they and their methods and interests. The 'school which is so largely of the future as well the present, finds its chief exemplar in Mr. James.' Mr. Howells has every reason to be satisfied, and perhaps astonished, at the progress which his 'school' is making in England, but surely it must grieve him to find that in his own country it has few adherents. . . .

Whatever may be the differences of opinion as to the value of the new 'school,' it must be acknowledged on all sides that a novelist enjoys an immense advantage in being a contributor to an illustrated magazine, which is ready not only to publish his works, but to issue elaborate articles on their merits—accompanied, as we have said, by that most affecting of souvenirs, a 'portrait of the author,' duly softened and idealized. The art of puffery gets 'finer' every day, whatever we may think about the art of novel-writing. Literary men are only just beginning to learn how to use it with effect. They have looked on for years at its successful application to various branches of commerce, and at length it has dawned upon their minds, that it may just as well be made serviceable to them as to the vendor of a new universal pain-killer or of a 'liver-pad.' In England we are still a little behind-hand in this field; the latest improvements have been brought out in America for special use in England. . . .

Numbers of American writers have given us stories, not deficient in general interest, and yet which are purely American, containing much that is most instructive and suggestive concerning their own country and its inhabitants. They must be amazed—such of them as are still living—when they find that while half England is running eagerly after the great American Novel, their own work has been left out of sight, and that English critics in important journals are declaring that now, for the first time, a school of 'imaginative composition' is making itself visible across the Atlantic.

. . . . We are, so we are informed, looking on at the 'modest and unpretending' beginnings of American fiction. Modest and unpretending are happy phrases to apply to the claims which have been put forward by writers who insist upon our acknowledging that they have compelled Thackeray and Dickens to 'take back seats.' and are masters of a style 'better than that of any other novelist.' Can we wonder that the very members of this 'school' should be tempted to tell us plainly that English criticism 'is only the result of ignorance—simply of inability to understand? This may appear a very ungrateful return for all the flattery which in this country has been lavished on the Howells and James school; but we cannot say that it is undeserved. Undoubtedly a good deal of 'ignorance' has been shown, and the present obsequious attitude of English critics in the presence of anything which is called 'American' reveals a clear 'inability to understand' true American literature. So far, then, the assertion is well founded. And as for its incivility, we have provoked that also. The respect of the Americans is never to be won by indiscriminate adulation. Before very long, the good sense of the public will correct the follies of the critics. They must already begin to have their doubts whether the water-gruel diet on which they have been placed can really be the strong American meat of which they have heard so much. Eventually the truth will become clear to them. They will see that imaginative literature in America had passed through a long and respectable life before the Boston Mutual Admiration Society was even heard of; and they will come to the conclusion that, if the American novel has reached its highest perfection in the works proceeding from this band of brothers, then that they have had quite enough of it, and they will turn with joy from the prophets of realism to the oldfashioned novelists who had no 'style' worth mentioning—to Georges Sand and Balzac, to Walter Scott and Jane Austen, and even in the last resort to Thackeray and Dickens.

Recent American Fiction

Horace E. Scudder*

While a novelist is living and at work, his growth in power is more interesting to critics than the expression of that power in any one piece of work. The Rise of Silas Lapham would probably affect a reader who should make Mr. Howells's acquaintance through it, in a different manner from what it does one who has followed Mr. Howells, as so many have, step by step, ever since he put forth his tentative sketches in fiction. We do not think that Mr. Howells has kept back the exercise of certain functions until he should have perfected his faculty of art by means of lighter essays, but that, in the process of his art, he has partly discovered, at any rate has convinced himself of the higher value to be found in a creation which discloses morals as well as manners. An art which busies itself with the trivial or the spectacular may be ever so charming and attractive, but it falls short of the art which builds upon foundations of a more enduring sort. A pasteboard triumphal-arch that serves the end of a merry masque is scarcely more ephemeral than the masque itself in literature.

The novel before us offers a capital example of the difference between the permanent and the transient in art. Had Mr. Howells amused himself and us with a light study of the rise of Silas Lapham in Boston society, what a clever book he might have made of it! We should have chuckled to ourselves over the dismay of the hero at the failure of the etiquette man to solve his problems, and have enjoyed a series of

°Reprinted from *Atlantic Monthly*, 56 (October 1885), 554–56.

such interior views as we get in the glimpse of Irene "trailing up and down before the long mirror in *her* new dress [Mr. Howells never seems quite sure that we shall put the emphasis where it belongs without his gentle assistance], followed by the seamstress on her knees; the woman had her mouth full of pins, and from time to time she made Irene stop till she could put one of the pins into her train;" we should have followed the fluctuations of pride and affection and fastidiousness in the Corey family, and have sent a final shuddering thought down the vista of endless dinner parties which should await the union of the two houses. All this and much more offered materials for the handling of which we could have trusted Mr. Howells's sense of humor without fear that he would disappoint us.

But all this is in the story; only it occupies the subordinate, not the primary place, and by and by the reader, who has followed the story with delight in the playful art, discovers that Mr. Howells never intended to waste his art on so shallow a scheme, that he was using all this realism of Boston society as a relief to the heavier mass contained in the war which was waged within the conscience of the hero. When in the final sentence he reads: "I don't know as I should always say it paid; but if I done it, and the thing was to do over again, right in the same way, I guess I should have to do it," he recognizes, in this verdict of the faithfully illiterate Colonel, the triumphant because unconscious attainment of a victory which justifies the title of the story. No mere vulgar rise in society through the marriage of a daughter to a son of a social prince, or the possession of a house on the water side of Beacon Street, would serve as a real conclusion to the history of a character like that of Silas Lapham; as if to flout such an idea, the marriage when it comes is stripped of all possible social consequences, and the house is burned to the ground. In place of so trivial an end there is a fine subjection of the mean and ignoble, and as in Balzac's César Birotteau, a man of accidental vulgarity discloses his essential nobility; with this added virtue in the case of Mr. Howells's hero, that we see the achievement of moral solvency unglorified by any material prosperity, and the whole history of the rise unadorned by any decoration of sentiment.

We have intimated that this bottoming of art on ethical foundations is a late development in Mr. Howells's work. In truth, this is but the second important example. An Undiscovered Country hinted at the possibility of there being other things than were dreamt of in the philosophy of light-minded young women, but it has always seemed to us that the book suffered from its use of an essentially ignoble parody of human far-sightedness. The real break which Mr. Howells made in his continuity of fiction was in A Modern Instance. That book suffered from too violent an effort at change of base. With all our respect for the underlying thought, a respect which we tried to make clear when we reviewed the book, we think that the author's habit of fine discrimination misled him into giving too much value in his art to the moral intention and too little to the overt act. The casual reader of A Modern Instance failed to be sufficiently impressed by the enormity of Bartley Hubbard's guilt. Mr. Howells was carrying over into the region of ethical art the same delicate methods which he had used so effectively in social art. But in affairs which touch the surface of life, such as etiquette, dress, the conventions of society in general, the difference between tweedledum and tweedledee is enormous, while the moment one pushes off into the deeper currents of impassioned human life, mere casuistry ceases to interest one who is struggling with vital problems. A close observer might accept at its real valuation Mr. Howells's reading of those penetrating words of the interpreter of the moral law which made sin to consist in the unacted thoughts of the heart, and found a man who was angry with his brother without a cause to be no better than a murderer; but the rough and ready critic would be impatient at an art which seemed to make no distinction between the little and the great in misdemeanor. Nor do we think such a critic unreasonable. If we are to have a portraiture of moral baseness, we have a right to ask for some shadows so deep as to leave no doubt of their meaning, instead of a multitude of little spots of darkness, any one of which may be indicative of turpitude, but all of which taken together do not accumulate into anything more than a character which repels one by its generally ignoble quality.

Was Mr. Howells faintly asserting his continued belief in the artistic justification of Bartley Hubbard, when he introduced him anew in this last story? If he was, we are much obliged to him for not pressing his acquaintance farther upon us. Still, we are so far obliged to him that we must thank him for supplying by means of the juxtaposition a possible comparison between Hubbard and Lapham. They are both self-made men, but Hubbard is essentially vulgar, while Lapham is only accidentally so; the former thrusts his vulgarity through the thin covering of education and aptitude for the world, the latter thrusts his essential manliness through the equally thin covering of an uneducated manner and a hopeless condition of social outlawry.

Nevertheless, though there can be no mistaking Mr. Howells's intention in this novel, and though he uses his material with a firmer hand, we confess, now that we are out of the immediate circle of its charm, that The Rise of Silas Lapham suffers from the same defect as A Modern Instance. The defect is not so obvious, but arises from the same super-refinement of art. In brief, Silas Lapham, a man of coarse grain and excessive egotism, is, in the crucial scenes, treated as a man of subtlety of thought and feeling. We do not say that the turnings and windings of his conscience, and his sudden encounters with that delicious Mephistopheles, Milton K. Rogers, are not possible and even reasonable; but we complain that the author of his being, instead of preserving him as a rustic piece of Vermont limestone with the soil clinging to it, has insisted upon our seeing into the possiblities of a fine marble statue which reside in the bulk. Moreover, when one comes to think of it, how little the rise of this hero is really connected with the circumstances which make up the main incidents of the story. The relations with Rogers, out of which the moral struggle springs, are scarcely complicated at all by personal relations with the Corey family arising from the love of young Corey for Penelope Lapham. The Colonel goes through the valley of tribulation almost independently of the fact that he and his are sojourning meanwhile in another half grotesque vale of tears.

This same over-refinement of motive, as supposed in natures which are not presumably subtle, impresses us in the whole history of Penelope's love affair. We feel, rather than are able to say why we feel it, that there is something abnormal in the desolation which falls upon the entire Lapham family in consequence of Irene's blindness and Penelope's over-acuteness. We frankly confess that when reading the scenes, it seemed all right, and we gave ourselves up to the luxury of woe without a doubt as to its reality. But when *thinking* about them (forgive the italics), it seems an exaggeration, a pressing of the relations between these interesting people beyond the bounds of a charitable nature.

But when all is said, we come back with satisfaction to the recollection that Mr. Howells has distinctly set before himself in this book a problem worth solving, and if his statement and solution are presented with an art which has heretofore been so cunning as quite to reconcile one to the fragility of the object under the artist's hand, and this art still seems sometimes to imply the former baselessness, we can at least thank our stars that when we criticise such a book as The Rise of Silas Lapham, we are dealing with a real piece of literature, which surely will not lose its charm when the distinctions of Nankeen Square and Beacon Street have become merely antiquarian nonsense.

Novel Writing as a Science

"R.P."*

Mr. Howells, in *The Rise of Silas Lapham*, takes several occasions to give vent to his theory of novel-writing. He does well. What he and his kind are really driving at when they write novels is something that

*Reprinted from the *Catholic World*, 42 (October 1885 to March 1886), 274–80.

many people have been puzzling to find out. It is a good thing that at last he should formulate his purposes in more or less plain black and white. In the following conversation about novels Mr. Howells gives us many hints of his belief:

> "It's astonishing," said Charles Bellingham, "how we do like the books that go for our heart-strings. And I really suppose that you can't put a more popular thing than self-sacrifice into a novel. We do like to see people suffering sublimely."
> "There was talk, some years ago," said James Bellingham, "about novels just going out."
> "They're just coming in!" cried Miss Kingsbury.
> "Yes," said Mr. Sewell, the minister, "and I don't think there ever was a time when they formed the whole intellectual experience of more people. They do greater mischief than ever."
> "Don't be envious, parson," said the host.
> "No," answered Sewell, "I should be glad of their help. But these novels with old-fashioned heroes and heroines in them—excuse me, Miss Kingsbury—are ruinous! ... The novelists might be the greatest possible help to us if they painted life as it is, and human feelings in their true proportion and relation; but for the most part they have been, and are, altogether noxious."
> This seemed sense to Lapham; but Bromfield Corey asked: "But what if life as it is isn't amusing? Aren't we to be amused?"
> "Not to our hurt," sturdily answered the minister.

We cannot help fancying—the similiarity of the names Sewell and Howells seems to favor the notion—that in the character of this minister Mr. Howells himself aspires to enact the part of Greek chorus to his story. At any rate, it is plain from the above passage that Mr. Howells regards the profession of the novelist as quite missionary; and his minister confirms this conclusion by several other dogmatisms. In fact, he uses a crisis of the story to point the moral of his theory, and one of the most vivid impressions taken from *The Rise of Silas Lapham* is that of the Rev. Mr. Sewell, with the air of a Boston Chadband, delivering a severe homily to a pair of old people on the part played by the novels of the old fashion in creating the love-tangle between their children that they have come to consult him about.

It is really very commendable of Mr. Howells to take this high and severe view of his mission in life. And there are many reasons why it is important that we should watch with interest how he proceeds when he sets out to teach the world the way novels ought to be written. There is no use denying it, light literature forms an enormous share—perhaps, with the newspapers, the entire amount—of the reading done by a large mass of our people; and it is useless to pretend that such constant dropping does not wear an impress on the minds and consciences on which it falls. The fact may be deplored, but it is a fact nevertheless and should be recognized. And since it is ever the aim of the church to seize the weapons of the enemy and turn them against himself, there is no reason why light literature should form an exception. The novelist who can handle his art so as at the same time to delight and to better his readers performs a mighty and a good work. Mr. Howells' minister is almost right in placing his influence as next to that of the clergyman.

Mr. Howells has never hesitated to roundly express his contempt for the methods of all the novelists that preceded him. It is not very long ago since he wrote that he and Mr. Henry James, Jr., were the only novelists who understood their business; all others, even Thackeray and Dickens, were only tinkers at the art as compared with these accomplished craftsmen. He goes still further now, and declares in effect that what the others wrote were not novels at all. "Novels are only just coming in," says one of his characters, meaning the novels of Mr. Howells and Mr. James.

This is a great deal to undertake; but Mr. Howells means what he says. His method of writing novels is certainly revolutionary, and we have seen that he writes them with the hope of serving a praiseworthy end. Let us take a glance at Mr. Howells's method, and see whether it is calculated to serve the end he has in view.

The revolution attempted by Mr. Howells is as simple as it is great. He regards novel-writing as science and not as art.

This is, perhaps, a natural outcome of what Mr. Spencer would call heredity and environment. The Puritan mind is scientific, analytical. It is too severe and cold and suspicious to fuse into the constructive enthusiasm of art. And the last thing it would dream of would be to pursue art for art's sake, or even science for the sake of science alone. It must have an object in view, some useful end to serve. Thus it is curious to note how the Puritan mind in Mr. Howells, finding itself, by a freak of circumstance, working at an art, takes it strongly in its hands and transforms it into a science, and a science intended to have a useful application.

Two men study some object in nature, say a plant. One of them will drink in with his eye all its visible beauty, its form, its color, the stirring of the wind and the delicate play of light and shade among its leaves. He seizes a brush and with a few bold strokes reproduces all these traits upon a canvas. That is Art. The other observer plucks up the plant by the roots and brings it home to his herbarium. There he makes minute and careful diagrams of it, probably with the aid of a camera. He measures it and weighs it. He cuts it up into sections and makes drawings of the sections. He analyzes the clay at its roots, he counts its juices and tests for acids in them. That is Science; and therein lies the difference between the novel-writing of, say, Nathaniel Haw-thorne and novel-writing as Mr. Howells pursues it.

In this way Mr. Howells has produced the most scientifically real-istic novel that has yet been written. M. Zola's books are as the awkward gropings of an amateur compared with this finished treatise. The field that Mr. Howells takes for his investigation is, he tells us, "the common-place." By studying "the common feelings of common people" he believes he "solves the riddle of the painful earth."

Silas Lapham is a type of the self-made American. He has grown rich through the instrumentality of a mineral paint of which he is the proprietor. He lives in Boston and entertains social ambitions for his wife and two daughters. Bromfield Corey is a Boston aristocrat with a wife, two daughters, and a son. The Laphams and the Coreys are thrown together in consequence of a contemplated misalliance between young Corey and one of the Lapham daughters; and in the contrasts and developments that appear among all these "types" is supposed to consist the main interest of the story. There are no incidents that are not sternly commonplace, but everything connected with these incidents and their psychological effect on the actors is analyzed and detailed with microscopic accuracy.

The realism of Mr. Howells has been compared to photography, it is so exact and so minute. We do not think this is a fair criticism. Exacti-tude and minuteness are not to be quarrelled with on the score of art. They are admissible, and have been admitted, into the finest art. No photograph can be more exact and minute than the little canvases of Meissonier, and the undue rendering of detail does not offend critics in the works of pre-Raphaelite artists. If Mr. Howells adhered to the principles of art, placing the details in their proper perspective, and so forth, we think he should be welcome to as many of them as he pleased. Tourguénieff, in some of his scenes, manages not to omit a single de-tail, but he manages it with such artistic feeling and skill that the effect is ilke that of a picture by Meissonier.

Photography is too near akin to art—even though it be a relation-ship by the left hand—to be used as a comparison for any work of Mr. Howells'. Photography, as generally understood and practised, aims first of all at the picturesque. Art is the sun that warms its horizon; to be as close an imitation of art as possible is its highest aspiration. Now, Mr. Howells, though a mechanic—an anatomist, shall we say?—of exquisite skill, despises art. Therefore his work should be compared rather to a series of scientific diagrams than to photographs. It is not Mr. Howells' details that offend the artistic eye; it is the plans, the sections, the front elevations, the isometric projections he gives of his subjects.

He studies men and women as a naturalist does insects. We read his book on the manners, habits, sensations, nerves of a certain set of people as we might a treatise on the coleoptera. And he investigates and expounds his theme with the same soullessness and absence of all emotion. Even Mr. Henry James, beside this chilly *savant*, appears quite a child of sentiment. He is capable of receiving "impressions"—which, in Mr. Howells' eyes, would be a most unscientific weakness—and he manages to retain some smack of art about the work he does.

Is this kind of novel-writing an elevating pursuit? and is the reading of it beneficial? To these two queries the answer must be emphatically, No.

Novels like *Silas Lapham* mark a descent, a degradation. Of course art is debased when it has fallen so low into realism. Art is ever pointing upward, and the influence of true art upon man is to make him look upward, too, to that vast where his Ideal sits.

—pinnacled in the lofty ether dim

where all is beautiful, but where all is immeasurable by him until he beholds it with his glorified intelligence. Science points downward, and when science is unguided by religion it leads its followers lower and lower into the mud beneath their feet. And even as we see some scientists making a distinct "progress" downward from the study of the higher to that of the lower forms of animal life, so in the novel-writing of Mr. Howells we can already mark this scientific decadence. He began with people who were not quite commonplace, whose motives and acts and ideas were a little bit above the common. He now declares that nothing is worthy to be studied but the common feelings of common people; and having begun *Silas Lapham* with people who were inoffensively commonplace, he was unable to finish the book without falling a stage lower. Towards the end he introduces a young woman who speaks thus of her husband: "If I could get rid of Hen I could manage well enough with mother. Mr. Wemmel would marry me if I could get the divorce. He said so over and over again." He introduces a scene in which this young woman, her tipsy sailor-husband, her drunken mother, and Silas Lapham as the family benefactor figure—a scene that, for hopeless depravity both in the author and subject, out-Zolas Zola. The old woman, who has a bottle in her hand, complains of her son-in-law not giving the daughter an opportunity to obtain a divorce. "'Why don't you go off on some them long v'y'ges?' s'd I. It's pretty hard when Mr. Wemmel stands ready to marry Z'rilla and provide a comfortable home for us both—I han't got a great many years more to live, and I *should* like to get more satisfaction out of 'em and not be beholden and dependent all my days—to have Hen, here, blockin' the way. I tell him there'd be more money for him in the end; but he can't seem to make up his mind to it.'" Again says this old harridan: "Say, Colonel, what should you

advise Z'rilla do about Mr. Wemmel? I tell her there an't any use goin'
to the trouble to git a divorce without she's sure about him. Don't you
think we'd ought to git him to sign a paper, or something, that he'll
marry her if she gits it? I don't like to have things goin' at loose ends
the way they are. It an't sense. It an't right.'" Before Mr. Howells reaches
the end of the book he makes even the worthy Mrs. Lapham suspect
her husband of infidelity and make a scene, accusing him, in the hearing
of her children. It has seldom been our duty to read a book whose moral
tone was so unpleasantly, so hopelessly bad; it is a book without heart
or soul, neither illumined by religion nor warmed by human sympathy.
This is all the more astonishing that Mr. Howells seems convinced that
he is fulfilling a high moral purpose in writing it. It might be explicable
on the theory that it was the legitimate outcome of the doctrine of total
depravity; but it is more probably the logic of the downward progress
of godless science. We shall not be surprised if the next book of Mr.
Howells deal with characters and feelings that shall be so far below the
commonplace from which he has already fallen that even M. de Gon-
court will not enjoy reading about them. It is the progress from man to
the apes, from the apes to the worms, from the worms to bacteria, from
bacteria to—mud. It is the descent to dirt.

But the consolation in regarding Mr. Howells' work is that it is
bound to sicken of its own poison. It cannot do any appreciable damage
to the novel-reading public, for the very good reason that the novel-reading public, when the present access of curiosity has subsided, are not
likely to read it. The force of the novel consists in its popularity, and
the popularity of the novel depends on certain well-defined elements,
all of which Mr. Howells discards from his work. Dramatic action, surprising plot, thrilling and unusual incidents, interesting and uncommon-
place characters, breadth of scene—all of these, among many other things,
people look for in their novels, for they look to their novels to take
them out of themselves, out of their everyday lives, and to lead them
into other worlds for the time being. In these and similar things lies
the novel's mighty and subtle spell; and the only way the reformer can
succeed in this field is by snatching this spell from the hands of the
evil-worker and using it himself as a beneficent power. Mr. Howells
seems to have as great a horror of such sorcery as his Puritan forbears
had of the arts of the witches of Salem. Therefore he can never hope
to reach the class he expects to benefit by his new style of literature.
People read novels to be amused, and he hotly repudiates the intention
of amusing them. People read novels because they are "light literature."
Mr. Howells offers them heavy literature. Instead of reforming the novel
he has transformed it, so that what he produces is not a novel at all.
Consequently the people who want novels will not want Mr. Howells';
and this is surely a relief to know. Mr. Howells will be read only by a

species of scientific and hard-minded people, which we are led to understand flourishes best in Boston; and this species is past harming. But such a class of readers would be just as well, if not better, satisfied if Mr. Howells called his work by its right name—a treatise—and not by its pseudonym; and it would simplify matters if the scientific school generally were to label their books "Treatise on Commonplace People," "Treatise on Drabs," "Treatise on Drunkards," and so on, as they went through the catalogue.

A Typical Novel

Hamilton Wright Mabie*

In "The Rise of Silas Lapham" Mr. Howells has given us his best and his most characteristic work; none of his earlier stories discloses so clearly the quality and resources of his gift or his conception of the novelist's art. As an expression of personal power and as a type of the dominant school of contemporary fiction in this country and in France, whence the special impulse of recent realism has come, this latest work of a very accomplished and conscientious writer deserves the most careful and dispassionate study. If Mr. Howells's work possessed no higher claim upon attention, its evident fidelity to a constantly advancing ideal of workmanship would command genuine respect and admiration; whatever else one misses in it, there is no lack of the earnestness which concentrates a man's full power on the thing in hand, nor of the sensitive literary conscience which permits no relaxation of strength on subordinate parts, but extracts in every detail the skill and care which are lavished on the most critical unfoldings of plot or disclosures of character. Mr. Howells evidently leaves nothing to the chance suggestion of an inspired moment, and takes nothing for granted; he verifies every insight by observation, fortifies every general statement by careful study of facts, and puts his whole force into every detail of his work. In spite of its evident danger in any save the strongest hands, there is a tonic quality in this exacting conscientiousness which writers of a different school often lack, and the absence of which is betrayed by hasty, unbalanced, and incomplete workmanship. It is this quality which discovers itself more and more distinctly in Mr. Howells's novels in a constant development of native gifts, a stronger grasp of facts, and a more comprehensive dealing with the problems of character and social life to which he has given atten-

*Reprinted from the *Andover Review*, 4 (November 1885), 417–29.

tion. In fact, this popular novelist is giving thoughtful readers of his books a kind of inspiration in the quiet but resolute progress of his gift and his art; a progress stimulated, no doubt, by success, but made possible and constant by fidelity to a high and distinterested ideal.

Nor has Mr. Howells spent his whole force on mere workmanship; he has made a no less strenuous endeavor to enlarge his knowledge of life, his grasp of its complicated problems, his insight into the forces and impulses which are the sources of action and character. If he has failed to touch the deepest issues, and to lay bare the more obscure and subtle movements of passion and purpose, it has been through no intellectual willfulness or lassitude; he has patiently and unweariedly followed such clews as he has been able to discover, and he has resolutely held himself open to the claims of new themes and the revelations of fresh contacts with life. The limitations of his work are also the limitations of his insight and his imagination, and this fact, fully understood in all its bearings, makes any effort to point out those limitations ungracious in appearance and distasteful in performance; if personal feeling were to control in such matters, one would content himself with an expression of hearty admiration for work so full of character, and of sincere gratitude for a delicate intellectual pleasure so varied and so sustained. The evidence of a deepened movement of thought is obvious to the most hasty backward glance from "The Rise of Silas Lapham" and "A Modern Instance" to "Their Wedding Journey" and "A Chance Acquaintance." In the early stories there is the lightness of touch, the diffused and delicate humor, which have never yet failed Mr. Howells; but there is little depth of sentiment, and almost no attempt to strike below the surface. These slight but very delightful tales discover the easy and graceful play of a force which deals with trifles as seriously as if it were handling the deepest and most significant problems of life. Seriousness is, indeed, the habitual mood of this novelist, and in his early stories it was the one prophetic element which they contained. There is a progressive evolution of power through "The Lady of the Aroostook," "The Undiscovered Country," "Dr. Breen's Practice," and "A Modern Instance"; each story in turn shows the novelist more intent upon his work, more resolute to hold his gift to its largest uses, more determined to see widely and deeply. His purpose grows steadily more serious, and his work gains correspondingly in substance and solidity. The problems of character which he sets before himself for solution become more complex and difficult, and, while there is nowhere a really decisive closing with life in a determined struggle to wring from it its secret, there is an evident purpose to grapple with realities and to keep in sympathy and touch with vital experiences.

In "The Rise of Silas Lapham" Mr. Howells has made a study of social conditions and contrasts everywhere present in society in this country; not, perhaps, so sharply defined elsewhere as in Boston, but to be discovered with more or less definiteness of outline in all our older communities. His quick instinct has fastened upon a stage of social evolution with which every body is familiar and in which everybody is interested. The aspect of social life presented in this story is well-nigh universal; it is real, it is vital, and it is not without deep significance; in dealing with it Mr. Howells has approached actual life more nearly, touched it more deeply, and expressed it more strongly than in any of his previous stories. The skill of his earliest work loses nothing in his latest; it is less evident because it is more unconscious and, therefore, more genuine and effective. There is the same humor, restrained and held in check by the major interests of the story, but touching here and there an idiosyncrasy, an inconsistency, a weakness, with all the old pungency and charm; a humor which is, in fact, the most real and the most distinctive of all Mr. Howells's gifts. There is, also, stronger grasp of situations, bolder portraiture of character, more rapid and dramatic movement of narrative. Still more important is the fact that in this novel life is presented with more of dramatic dignity and completeness than in any of Mr. Howells's other stories; there is a truer and nobler movement of human nature in it; and the characters are far less superficial, inconsequential, and unimportant than their predecessors; if not the highest types, they have a certain force and dignity which makes us respect them, and make it worth while to write about them. Add to these characteristics of "The Rise of Silas Lapham" the statement that Mr. Howells has never shown more complete mastery of his art in dealing with his materials; that his style has never had more simplicity and directness, more solidity and substance, and it will be conceded that the sum total of excellence which even a reader who dissents from its underlying conception and method discovers in this story is by no means inconsiderable; is, indeed, such as to entitle it to very high praise, and to give added permanence and expansion to a literary reputation which, from the standpoint of popularity at least, stood in small need of these things.

And yet, when all this has been said, and said heartily, it must be added that "The Rise of Silas Lapham" is an unsatisfactory story; defective in power, in reality, and in the vitalizing atmosphere of imagination. No one is absorbed by it, nor moved by it; one takes it up with pleasure, reads it with interest, and lays it down without regret. It throws no spell over us; creates no illusion for us, leaves us indifferent spectators of an entertaining drama of social life. The novelist wrote it in a cool, deliberate mood, and it leaves the reader cold when he has finished it. The appearance and action of life are in it, but not the warmth; the frame, the organism, are admirable, but the divine inbreathing which would have given the body a soul has been withheld. Everything that art could do has been done, but the vital spark has not been transmitted. Mr. Howells never identifies himself with his characters; never becomes one with them in the vital fellowship and communion of the imagination; he constructs them with infinite patience and skill, but he never, for a moment, loses consciousness of his own individuality. He is cool and collected in all the emotional crises of his stories; indeed, it is often at such moments that one feels the presence of a diffused satire, as if the weakness of the men and women whom he is describing excited a little scorn in the critical mind of the novelist. The severest penalty of the persistent analytic mood is borne by the writer in the slight paralysis of feeling which comes upon him at the very moment when the pulse should beat a little faster of its own motion; in the subtle skepticism which pervades his work, unconsciously to himself, and like a slight frost takes the gloom off all fine emotions and actions. There are passages in Mr. Howells's stories in reading which one cannot repress a feeling of honest indignation at which is nothing more nor less than a refined parody of genuine feeling, sometimes of the most pathetic experience. Is Mr. Howells ashamed of life in its outcries of pain and regret? Does he shrink from these unpremeditated and unconventional revelations of character as vulgar, provincial, inartistic; or does he fail to comprehend them? Certainly the cool, skillful hand which lifts the curtain upon Silas Lapham's weakness and sorrows does not tremble for an instant with any contagious emotion; and whenever the reader begins to warm a little, a slight turn of satire, a cool phrase or two of analysis, a faint suggestion that the writer doubts whether it is worth while, clears the air again. Perhaps nothing more decisive on this point could be said of Mr. Howells's stories than that one can read them aloud without faltering at the most pathetic passages; the latent distrust of all strong feeling in them makes one a little shy of his own emotion.

This failure to close with the facts of life, to press one's heart against them as well as to pursue and penetrate them with one's thought; this lack of unforced and triumphant faith in the worth, the dignity, and the significance for art of human experience in its whole range; this failure of the imagination to bridge the chasm between the real and the fictitious reproduction of it, are simply fatal to all great and abiding work. Without faith, which is the very ground upon which the true artist stands; without love, which is both inspiration and revelation to him, a true art is impossible. Without faith there would never have come out of the world of the imagination such figures as Jeanie Deans, Colonel Newcome, Eugénie Grandet,

Père Goriot, and Hester Prynne; without love—large, warm, generous sympathy with all that life is and means—the secret of these noble creations would never have been disclosed. Mr. Howells and Daudet practice alike the art of a refined realism, but what a distance separates the Nabob from Silas Lapham! Daudet is false to his theory and true to his art; life touches him deeply, fills him with reverence, and he can no more rid himself of the imagination than he can part the light from the flower upon which it falls. The Nabob might have suggested a similar treatment of Silas Lapham. How tenderly, how reverently, with what a sense of pathos, through what a mist of tears, Daudet uncovers to us the weakness and sorrows of Jansoulet! The Nabob is always touched by a soft light from the novelist's heart; poor Silas Lapham shivers in a perpetual east wind. Imagine the "Vicar of Wakefield" treated in the same spirit, and the fatal defect of Mr. Howells's attitude towards life is apparent at a glance.

The disposition to treat life lightly and skeptically, to doubt its capacity for real and lasting achievement, to stand apart from it and study it coolly and in detail with dispassionate and scientific impartiality, is at bottom decisive evidence of lack of power; that is, of the dramatic power which alone is able to reproduce life in noble dramatic forms. A refined realism strives to make up in patience what it lacks in genius; to make observation do the work of insight; to make analysis take the place of synthesis of character, and "a more analytic consideration of the appearance of things"—to quote Mr. James—the place of a resolute and masterly grasp of characters and situations. The method of the realism illustrated in "The Rise of Silas Lapham" is external, and, so far as any strong grasp of life is concerned, necessarily superficial. It is an endeavor to enter into the recesses of character, and learn its secret, not by insight, the method of the imagination, but by observation, the method of science; and it is an endeavor to reproduce that character under the forms of art, not by identification with it, and the genuine and almost unconscious evolution which follows, but by skillful adjustment of traits, emotions, passions, and activities which are the result of studies more or less conscientiously carried on. The patience and work involved in the making of some novels constructed on this method are beyond praise; but they must not make us blind to the fact that no method can take the place of original power, and that genius in some form—faith, sympathy, insight, imagination—is absolutely essential in all true art. The hesitation, the repression of emotion, the absence of color, are significant, not of a noble restraint of power, a wise husbanding of resources for the critical moment and situation, but of a lack of the spontaneity and overflow of a great force. Ruskin finely says that when we stand before a true work of art we feel ourselves in the presence, not of a great effort, but of a great force. In most of the novels of realism it is the effort which impresses us, and not the power. In Turgénieff and Björnson, masters of the art of realism, and yet always superior to it, the repression and restraint are charged with power; one feels behind them an intensity of thought and feeling that is at times absolutely painful. No such sensation overtakes one in reading "The Rise of Silas Lapham" or "The Bostonians"; there is no throb of life here; the pulse of feeling, if it beats at all, is imperceptible; and of the free and joyous play of that supreme force which we call genius there is absolutely not one gleam. If either novelist possessed it, no method, however rigidly practiced, could wholly confine it; it would flame like lightning, as in Björnson, or suffuse and penetrate all things with latent heat, as in Turgénieff, or touch all life with a soft, poetic radiance, as in Daudet.

Mr. Howells has said, in substance, that realism is the only literary movement of the day which has any vitality in it, and certainly no one represents this tendency on its finer side more perfectly than himself. Its virtues and its defects are very clearly brought out in his work: its clearness of sight, its fixed adherence to fact, its reliance upon honest work; and, on the other hand, its hardness, its lack of vitality, its paralysis of the finer feelings and higher aspirations, its fundamental defect on the side of the imagination. Realism is crowding the world of fiction with commonplace people; people whom one would positively avoid coming in contact with in real life; people without native sweetness or strength, without acquired culture or accomplishment, without the touch of the ideal which makes the commonplace significant and worthy of study. To the large, typical characters of the older novels has succeeded a generation of feeble, irresolute, unimportant men and women whose careers are of no moment to themselves, and wholly destitute of interest to us. The analysis of motives that were never worth an hour's serious study, the grave portraiture of frivolous, superficial, and often vulgar conceptions of life, the careful scrutiny of characters without force, beauty, aspiration, or any of the elements which touch and teach men, has become wearisome, and will sooner or later set in motion a powerful reaction. One cannot but regret such a comparative waste of delicate, and often genuine, art; it is as if Michael Angelo had given us the meaningless faces of the Roman fops of his time instead of the heads of Moses and Hercules.

It is certainly a mental or a moral disease which makes such trivial themes attractive to men of real talent. The "storm and stress" period returns at intervals, and, in spite of its extravagances of feeling, is respectable because of the real force and promise that are in it; one has a certain amount of patience with Werther, and with the hero of Schiller's "Robbers." But our modern misanthrope gropes feebly about for some clew to the mystery of his existence, and, not finding it ready to hand, snuffs out the flame of life in obedience, not to an honest conviction of the hopelessness of things, but because something goes wrong at the moment. Here is the modern hero skillfully displayed on a small canvas:—

> Vane walked up to Central Park, and returned to dress for dinner. Where was he to dine? The Club was the best place to meet people. His lodgings were dark, and he had some difficulty in finding a match; then he dropped one of his shirt-studs on the floor, and had to grope for it. Another one broke, and he threw open the drawer of his shaving-stand, impatiently, to find one to replace it. Lying in the drawer was an old revolver he had brought from Minnesota two years before. He took it out, placed the muzzle at his chest, and drew the trigger. As he fell to the floor, he turned over upon his side, holding up his hands before his eyes.

If such diseased and irresolute youths as Vane were the refuge of weak but ambitious writers groping for subjects with which to illustrate their own feebleness, there would be no significance in the fact; there is deep significance, however, in the fact that the man who wrote this story has genuine strength and skill. That such a character as Vane should attract such a writer, that Mr. James's stories should uniformly convey the impression, not of the tragic pathos of life, but of its general futility, that Mr. Howells should, for the most part, concern himself with men and women of very slender endowments and very superficial conceptions of life, are phenomena which lead us very directly to a conclusion somewhat similar to that reached by Mr. Stedman, after a survey of the present condition of poetry in this country, in his article on the "Twilight of the Poets" in a recent issue of the "Century Magazine." The work of the younger generation of American poets, in the judgment of this acute and accomplished critic, is full of the resources of a delicate art, and not without qualities of individual insight and imagination; but, as a whole, it lacks vigor, variety, grasp, and power. It is an interlude between the poetic activities of a generation now fast becoming silent and a generation not yet come to the moment of expression. Fiction has, however, a better outlook than poetry; there are already in the field novelists to whom life and art speak as of old with one voice, and who are illustrating under new forms those imperishable truths of character and destiny, the presence of which lifts the most obscure life into the realm of art, and the absence of which leaves life without a meaning, and devoid of all interest. It is very significant that realism either fails to grasp life firmly and present it powerfully, or else seizes upon its ignoble aspects; its vigor is mainly on the side of moral pathology. The great name of Balzac is a word of power among the realists; and yet it is not easy to find in this master of fiction on a great scale either the principles or the method of the writers who profess to stand in direct line of succession from him. His realism was of that genuine order which underlies the noblest art of every age; it studies with most patient eye, and reproduces with most patient hand, the facts of life, in order that it may the more powerfully and the more faithfully discover the general law, the universal fact, which are the sole concern of art, behind them. The "more analytic consideration of the appearance of things" which one finds in Balzac is accompanied by a more powerful irradiation of the imagination. It is easy to understand Zola when he says "l'imagination de Balzac m'irrite;" it is just this imagination, this penetration of the real with the ideal, which makes the *Comédie Humaine* such a revelation of the age, such a marvelous reproduction of the complex life of the most complex epoch of history. The Naturalism of Zola, which is not psychological but physiological, which reduces life to its lowest factors, has little in common with the art of Balzac, which found all methods and facts inadequate for the complete illustration of the sublime, all-embracing fact of life. Naturalism is worthy of study, not only because of the great place it fills in contemporary literature, but because it is the logical result of realism, and, by exaggeration, makes the defects and limitations of realism more apparent.

The issue between the theoretical realism of the day and the older and eternal realism of fidelity to nature as the basis of all art is the more momentous because it is concealed in many cases by so much nice skill, and so much subtlety and refinement of talent. The divergence between the two is in the nature of a great gulf fixed in the very constitution of things; it goes to the very bottom of our conceptions of life and art. To see nature with clear eyes, and to reproduce nature with deep and genuine fidelity, is the common aim of the old and the new realism; the radical character of the difference between them is made clear by the fact that the realists of the new school deny the existence in nature of the things which the older realists have held to be deepest and truest. The new realism is not dissent from a particular method; it is a fundamental skepticism of the essential reality of the old ends and subjects of art. It strikes at the very root of the universal art growth of the world; adherence to its fundamental precepts would have made Greek art an impossibility; would have cut the ground from under Aeschylus, Sophocles, and Euripides; would have prevented the new growth of art and literature in the Renaissance; would have paralyzed the old English drama, the classical French drama, and the late but splendid flowering of the German genius from Lessing to Heine. If the truth lies with modern realism, we must discard all those masters by whom the generations have lived and died, and seek out other teachers and shrines. Realism writes failure and barrenness across the culture of the world as the hand once wrote a similar judgment on the walls of an Assyrian palace. Fortunately, the parallel fails at the vital point; it requires a stronger faith than realism is able to furnish to identify the inspiration of the modern and the ancient interpreter, to discover in Zola the successor of Daniel.

The older art of the world is based on the conception that life is at bottom a revelation; that human growth under all conditions has a spiritual law back of it; that human relations of all kinds have spiritual types behind them; and that the discovery of these universal facts, and the clear, noble embodiment of them in various forms, is the office of genius and the end of art. The unique quality of the Greek race lay in its power to make these universal, permanent elements of life controlling. This is the secret of its marvelous and imperishable influence upon the minds of men. This was the work for which it was so lavishly endowed with genius. The art instinct among the Greeks was so universal and so controlling that all individual thought, feeling, and living seemed to be a kind of transparent medium for the revelation of elements and qualities which are common to the race. What was personal, isolated, unrelated to universal life has largely disappeared, and there remains a revelation, not of Greek character, but of human life of unequaled range and perfection. Every great Greek character is a type as truly as every Greek statue; and it is the typical quality which lifts the whole race into the realm of art. But modern realism knows nothing of any revelation in human life; of any spiritual facts of which its facts are significant; of any spiritual laws to which they conform in the unbroken order of the Universe. It does more than ignore these things; it denies them. Under the conditions which it imposes art can see nothing but the isolated physical fact before it; there are no mysterious forces in the soil under it; there is no infinite blue heaven over it. It forms no part of a universal order; it discovers no common law; it can never be a type of a great class. It is, in a word, practical atheism applied to art. It not only empties the world of the Ideal, but, as Zola frankly says, it denies "the good God;" it dismisses the old heaven of aspiration and possible fulfillment as an idle dream; it destroys the significance of life and the interpretive quality of art.

Such was not the conception of the great Balzac. With characteristic acuteness and clearness he puts the whole issue in a paragraph: "A writer who placed before his mind the duty of exact reproduction might become a painter of human types more or less faithful, successful, courageous, and patient; he might be the annalist of the dramas of private life, the archaeologist of the social fabric, the sponsor of trades and professions, the registrar of good and evil. And yet to merit the applause at which all artists should aim, ought he not also to study the reasons—or the reason—of the conditions of social life; ought he not to seize the hidden meaning of this vast accretion of beings, of passions, of events? Finally, having sought—I will not say found— this reason, this social mainspring, is he not bound to study natural law, and *discover why and when Society approached or swerved away from the eternal principles of truth and beauty?*" And he adds, to the same end, "History does not, like the novel, hold up the law of a higher ideal. History is, or should be, the world as it has been; the novel—to use a saying of Madame Necker, one of the remarkable minds of the last century—*should paint a possible better world.*" Readers of Balzac do not need to be told that his work, defective as it is on the side of moral insight, is still a commanding interpretation of life because it penetrates through individual fact to the universal fact, and through particular instances to the common law. It is only when one sees clearly this denial of the spiritual side of life, and sees it in all its results, that one understands why Naturalism inevitably portrays the repellant, and a refined realism the superficial, aspects of life. In this pregnant fact lies the secret of its rigidity, its coldness, its inevitable barrenness. A natural method, a true and vital conception, are always capable of further expansion. Is there anything beyond Zola? He has pressed his theory so far that even his hottest adherents see no step left for another to take. The energetic Naturalist—a man of great force and splendid working power—has left his followers not a single fig leaf to be plucked off the shameless nudity of the "bête humaine"—the human animal—in the delineation of which he rivals the skill of Barye. It is equally difficult to imagine any further progress along the lines of a refined realism; it has brought us face to face with the hard, isolated facts of life, and, having discarded the only faculty that can penetrate those facts to their depths and set them in the large order of the higher reason, there remains nothing more to be done by it. Materialism in art reaches its limits so soon that it never really gets into the field at all.

This denial of the imagination, this effort to discard it entirely and banish it into the region of moribund superstitions, is at bottom a confession of weakness. It is the refuge of writers who have inherited the skill, but not the impulse, of the great literary creators, and who are driven, unconsciously no doubt, to adopt a theory of art which makes the most of their strength and demands the least of their weakness. It is a new illustration of the old tendency to elevate individual limitations into universal laws, and to make the art bend to the man rather than the man to the art. We need not concern ourselves about the imagination, as if any man, or body of men, could discard it, or, for any long time, even obscure it; the imagination may safely be left to care for itself; what we need to concern ourselves about is the fact that we are on the wrong road, and that men of genius, unconsciously mistaking the way along which the sign-boards have all been carefully misplaced, may lose time and heart in the struggle to free themselves from misleading aims. We are in great danger of coming to accept as work of the first order that which has no claim to any such distinction, and adopt as the standards of the noblest literary art the very delightful but very inadequate creations of some of our contemporary writers. It is always wisest to face the truth; if the poets of the time lack the qualities which go to the making of great singers, let us acknowledge the fact and make the best of it; if our realistic novelists are more skillful than powerful, more adroit and entertaining than original and inspiring, let us admit this fact also. But, in the name and for the sake of art, let us decline to accept these charming story-tellers as the peers of the great masters, and, above all, let us refuse to impose their individual limitations upon the great novelists of the future. "The Rise of Silas Lapham" and the novels of its class are additions to the literature of fiction for which we are grateful; but it is a great injustice to them and to their writers to insist upon placing them side by side with the great novels of the past.

What is needed now, in fiction as in poetry, is a revitalization of the imagination and a return to implicit and triumphant faith in it. The results of the scientific movement are misread by men of literary genius no less than by religious people; in the end, they will be found to serve the noblest uses of art no less than of religion. Their first effect is, indeed, to paralyze all superficial faiths and inspirations, by disturbing the order of facts upon which these rested, or from which they were derived; but, in the end, it will be found that the new order of the universe has under it a harmony of sublime conceptions such as no art has ever yet so much as dreamed of, no religion ever yet grasped with clearness and certainty. Science not only leaves the imagination untouched, but adds indefinitely to the material with which it works. The more intelligent study of facts which it has made possible and inevitable purifies and enlarges in a corresponding degree the conceptions which underlie them, and will add in the end immeasurably to the scope and majesty of life. The hour is fast approaching for a new movement of the imagination; a new world awaits interpretation and reproduction in art at its hands. The first effects of the scientific tendency, evident in the uncertain note of contemporary poetry and the defective insight of realistic fiction, must not be mistaken for the final effects; it is this mistake which gives our poetry its elegiac note and our fiction its general confession of the futility of all things. Great works of art never come from lands afflicted with this kind of paralysis. The real outcome of the scientific spirit is something very different from the interpretation of realism; for its interpreters and prophets the time is fast approaching, and no blindness and faintheartedness of this generation will delay their coming when the hour is ripe. They, too, will be realists as all the great artists have been; realists like Dante and Shakespeare; like Balzac and Thackeray; like the wise Goethe, who held resolutely to the fact because of the law behind it, who saw that the Real and the Ideal are one in the divine order of the universe, and whose clear glance into the appearance of things made him the more loyal to the Whole, the Good, and the True.

The Home of Fiction

Anonymous*

"I must say that the capital is a pleasant place and the society democratic enough to suit the taste of the most ultra republican," said William Dean Howells, the novelist, to a *Mail and Express* writer yesterday at the Murray Hill Hotel. Mr. Howells has been spending a brief social period at Washington and several receptions were given specially to him and his wife. He leaned back in a deep-seated arm chair and the light from a window gave a clear view of his features. In stature he is low, with great broad shoulders and full chest. His face is large, regular in its oval outlines, and devoid of whiskers save a heavy iron gray moustache, that is kept closely cropped. His blue eyes sparkle beneath a high, classical forehead, and his light-colored hair is neatly combed and parted. In conversation he speaks without studied effort in a well-modulated voice, and wins his hearers, by the charm of his manner.

"You don't mean that Washington society is too democratic, do you, Mr. Howells?"

"Oh, no," he answered in substance. "I was charmed by the freedom and the genial way social receptions were conducted. Any one almost can go and leave a card. I saw no snobbery of any kind, nothing but pure, good American customs, the outcome of a republican form of government and the liberty all people enjoy under it. I consider Washing-

*Reprinted from *Mail and Express*, (London) 10 April 1886, p. 6.

ton, socially speaking, the typical city of the Union. There all sections of the country are represented, and they usually bring with them the peculiarities of their surroundings."

"Do you intend to write a novel of Washington life?"

"No; my stay of a few days there gave me no chance to make any observations for a novel. Necessarily, what I saw was in a hurried and superficial way. I cannot write about countries and social conditions of any section unless I have visited and studied them. That would be going into the romantic school of fiction. At present I belong to the realistic. No, my visit to the capital was to rest from work a few days and enjoy recreation. I also visited Virginia."

"Are you engaged on a novel now?"

"Yes, I have a novel under way. Whether I am writing or not, I am busy working out the story and the characters."

"Do you work thirteen hours a day, as Balzac was reported to have done?"

"No, I do about three hours mental labor each day—actual writing. I begin writing at 9 o'clock in the morning and quit at noon. But after that I go about thinking it all over, and when I cross the street I keep one eye on my character and the other on the cabs. I once thought novel writing would come easy, that I could sit down and a beautiful book would just flow spontaneously from my pen. That was a foolish thought and an egregious error. Of course, I was a young man then and indulged in dreams and idle fancies. The first novel I wrote I worked. Ah! I flattered myself that I would not have to labor at fiction any more after the first—that was the arduous task, and all else would come naturally. I know now that novel-writing is always labor—hard, unremitting work. It seems that each book I write I work as hard, if not harder than on my first. Success, I think, depends on labor! Young writers beginning doubtless live on the flattering idea that at a certain time it will be simply play to put together a novel. They soon discard that notion. Then, too, many imagine that a close reading of books will fit them for fiction-writing. That is a mistake.

OFFERED A CITY EDITORSHIP.

"When I was a young man I was offered the position of city editor on a Cincinnati paper. I have regretted to this day that I did not accept it. It would have given me a great schooling in studying human nature. Besides, I should have been taught many things in a general and practical way that books never can teach. Instead, I went to my books. When I was 24 years old President Lincoln appointed me Consul at Venice. I remained there for a number of years. That is why I lay many of my scenes in Italy. I have seen and studied the country."

"Some critics allege that you are on the wrong tack—that you have scarcely any plot and break all the rules of novel-writing."

"I have no special answer to make to such criticisms. I write a novel to suit myself, and do not proceed by rule and model. My plan is to work out everything in a natural way. I try not to draw improbable characters. A novel-writer should have no model, but strive for probability and reality. The old romantic school is fast dying out, and with it the complicated and often impossible plots. The grange, the moat, the ancient castle, are relegated to legendary writers, and have no part and place in our advanced and matter-of-fact days. The great romancers are dead, and only a few are left in England to produce that unreal style of fiction."

"Is England behind other countries in novel-writing?"

"Yes, for there the romantic school still flourishes to some extent. Of course, there are some exceptionally great and realistic writers in England. At the head of the list I place Thomas Hardy, whose novels I read with absorbing interest. I have not read so many of Mr. William Black's novels, but I know their charm. I don't know why; but England is far behind the countries on the Continent. Russia has the greatest novel-writers. They stand ahead of all others in the world. Why? They are natural. You read Tolstoi or Tourguenieff, especially the former, and you become at once enchained by his realism. Tolstoi's story, Anna Kassenius,[1] is not only great but carries with it the conviction that it is true and really happened. These writers have no models, no rules to go by; they seem to proceed by the rule of their feeling and judgment and what they see and know. In France the old sensational school has long given way to the natural. When Victor Hugo died the deathknoll of the romantic school was sounded. Emile Zola, Daudet and others are rapidly bringing credit to France by their natural methods. In Italy and Spain the class of fiction writers are ahead of England in method. They have caught the spirit of truth, and write what was, and is and may be, and not what was not, and is not and never can be."

THE FUTURE OF AMERICA.

"How is America as a home for the realistic school?"

"The United States is, perhaps, destined to outstrip the other countries in realistic novel-writing. True, we haven't the old history, the castles and knights, all prolific themes for the imaginative writer, and we don't want them; but we have more novel phases of life and character to study and depict than any other country on the face of the globe. Our institutions, too, are different, and everything is favorable to the production of a class of original fiction-writers. We have some already that are eminent in their line. Geo. W. Cable, Miss Murfree, G. P. Lathrop and others. Of course, we have some who still are guided by the old methods. Those who succeed, in my opinion, will have to study out character—and every section of this country has a local peculiarity that fiction can portray. Now I have nothing to do with day before yesterday; I deal with the present and fear to trespass on the morrow. I came from Ohio. I have not written anything about the people and their characteristics, yet I have a lively recollection of everything connected with my early life there. Don't ask me about the natural school in America; it really exists and is the predominating fiction."

"Some criticisms have been passed on your last novel, Indian Summer, that your style is somewhat changed."

"Yes, and what makes it more amusing is that Indian Summer is not my last novel. I wrote it before I did The Rise and Fall of Silas Lapham.[2] It was not published owing to certain editorial exigencies. I laid the scene in Florence instead of here, but the characters were Americans. I made the grouping at Florence because it is a fact that so many Americans of all sorts meet there, and there was nothing unusual about it. I could have placed the whole action in America for that matter. It is unnecessary for writers to go out of America to get character and material for a novel. The material is at our very feet, and requires natural gift and practice to put into reality and artistic shape. The more practice a writer has the better."

"What do you think of our modern school of drama?"

"It is analogous to fiction, and I think the tendency is to discard the lurid melodrama and deal in the natural. My idea is that the old plot invented by the early dramatists will yield to character-sketches. There will be a plot still, but not so complicated and all absorbing, whirling the characters, like so many automatons, through to a great climax. It will be the reverse; the characters will be the central figures and a thin plot will simply be to permit them to develop. This will afford great scope for really good actors to come to the front. I think that Harrigan is moving in the right direction. His creations are natural and can be seen any day in certain parts of the city. I went to see his play of Dan's Tribulations. It pleased me immensely. He has caught the true spirit of the future dramatist and he is an admirable actor. I was so impressed with his work that I mentioned him to an English critic of ability and advised him by all means to go and see the play. He did so and was impressed similarly to myself. Before I leave the city I intend to go and see Harrigan in his new play, The Leather Patch. Why have I never written plays? Well, I have. Mr. Barrett put one of my plays on, The Counterfeit Presentment.[3] I prefer writing novels, because I can appeal directly to the public with my work. In writing a play it must be adapted to the manager's wishes, so that the play virtually is an instrument in the hands of the manager. I cannot criticise the manager, because he knows what the public desires and what will be a success. All of them are anxious to get good plays. I think they read nearly all plays they receive in hopes of finding one that will make a success when put on with all the costly accessories of stage setting and scenery. Do I think the war will furnish good material for the dramatics? Yes, most assuredly, but not more so than real things that occur daily.

TO WRITE SHORT STORIES.

"Is it true that you intend to write some short stories?"

"Yes, I have an idea of trying my hand in that line. It is an exceptional case, I know, where the writer of a novel writes short stories. The line seems to be drawn, but yet as a rule all novelists have written short stories. Many short story writers, though, have never written novels. Some suppose that a novelist has no art in that direction. The greater can include the less, and hence many short story writers never become novelists. It is a fine field for young writers and gives them practice. There is nothing like practice. Then, too, there is always a demand for short stories of a high order, and the Americans have done almost their best work at that sort."

"How do you begin to write a novel; does a certain method prevail all the time?"

"I have no special method. I get an idea and begin to evolve it. Characters, scenes and plots come to me while I am trying to work the idea to a tangible and natural conclusion. That idea pervades the whole work. I work like a pilot on a Mississippi river steamboat, with certain landmarks to shape my course by; I keep a phrase, an attitude, a situation in mind, from the beginning, and steer by those successive points to the end."

"Do you ever strive to make a certain effect?"

"No, I never attempt to write artificially. Whenever I have written anything of the kind my feelings repudiate it and I say, 'Now, I am lying,' and immediately tear up the copy. Such writing might deceive young writers and readers, but those who are older would know that it was not natural and understand my attempt for effect at once. As to humor, that is something that should come easily and naturally too. It cannot be forced. My only advice to young writers is to write as they feel, in the simplest style, and make no attempts to strive for grand effects. Take no special model: work out everything according to their own conception, and put nothing in the book that could not be in real life."

"Do you go over your work, or send it to the printer without revising?"

"I often revise my manuscript, sometimes changing it almost entirely. Then I frequently make many changes when I receive the proof sheets. Publishers are very kind these days, and consent to any amount of changing. The more work given to a novel makes it all the more perfect. It is labor, always labor, novel-writing."

Notes

  1. Apparently the interviewer did not know *Anna Karenina*.
  2. *The Rise of Silas Lapham*.
  3. *A Counterfeit Presentment*.

William Dean Howells

Henry James*

As the existence of a man of letters (so far as the public is concerned with it) may be said to begin with his first appearance in literature, that of Mr. Howells, who was born at Martinsville, Ohio, in 1837, and spent his entire youth in his native State, dates properly from the publication of his delightful volume on *Venetian Life*—than which he has produced nothing since of a literary quality more pure—which he put forth in 1865, after his return from the consular post in the city of St. Mark which he had filled for four years. He had, indeed, before going to live in Venice, and during the autumn of 1860, published, in conjunction with his friend Mr. Piatt, a so-called "campaign" biography of Abraham Lincoln; but as this composition, which I have never seen,[1] emanated probably more from a good Republican than from a suitor of the Muse, I mention it simply for the sake of exactitude, adding, however, that I have never heard of the Muse having taken it ill. When a man is a born artist, everything that happens to him confirms his perverse tendency; and it may be considered that the happiest thing that could have been invented on Mr. Howells's behalf was his residence in Venice at the most sensitive and responsive period of life; for Venice, bewritten and bepainted as she has ever been, does nothing to you unless to persuade you that you also can paint, that you also can write. Her only fault is that she sometimes too flatteringly—for she is shameless in the exercise of such arts—addresses the remark to those who cannot. Mr. Howells could, fortunately, for his writing was painting as well in those days. The papers on Venice prove it, equally with the artistic whimsical chapters of the Italian Journeys, made up in 1867 from his

*Reprinted from *Harper's Weekly*, 30 (19 June 1886), 394–95.

notes and memories (the latter as tender as most glances shot eastward in working hours across the Atlantic) of the holidays and excursions which carried him occasionally away from his consulate.

The mingled freshness and irony of these things gave them an originality which has not been superseded, to my knowledge, by any impressions of European life from an American stand-point. At Venice Mr. Howells married a lady of artistic accomplishment and association, passed through the sharp alternations of anxiety and hope to which those who spent the long years of the civil war in foreign lands were inevitably condemned, and of which the effect was not rendered less wearing by the perusal of the London *Times* and the conversation of the British tourist. The irritation so far as it proceeded from the latter source, may even yet be perceived in Mr. Howells's pages. He wrote poetry at Venice, as he had done of old in Ohio, and his poems were subsequently collected into two thin volumes, the fruit, evidently, of a rigorous selection. They have left more traces in the mind of many persons who read and enjoyed them than they appear to have done in the author's own. It is not nowadays as a cultivator of rhythmic periods that Mr. Howells most willingly presents himself. Everything in the evolution, as we must all learn to call it to-day, of a talent of this order is interesting, but one of the things that are most so is the separation that has taken place, in Mr. Howells's case, between its early and its later manner. There is nothing in *Silas Lapham*, or in *Doctor Breen's Practice*, or in *A Modern Instance*, or in *The Undiscovered Country*, to suggest that its author had at one time either wooed the lyric Muse or surrendered himself to those Italian initiations without which we of other countries remain always, after all, more or less barbarians. It is often a good, as it is sometimes an evil, that one cannot disestablish one's past, and Mr. Howells cannot help having rhymed and romanced in deluded hours, nor would he, no doubt, if he could. The repudiation of the weakness which leads to such aberrations is more apparent than real, and the spirit which made him care a little for the poor factitious Old World and the superstition of "form" is only latent in pages which express a marked preference for the novelties of civilization and a perceptible mistrust of the purist. I hasten to add that Mr. Howells has had moments of reappreciation of Italy in later years, and has even taken the trouble to write a book (the magnificent volume on *Tuscan Cities*) to show it. Moreover, the exquisite tale *A Foregone Conclusion*, and many touches in the recent novel of *Indian Summer* (both this and the *Cities* the fruit of a second visit to Italy), sound the note of a charming inconsistency.

On his return from Venice he settled in the vicinity of Boston, and began to edit the *Atlantic Monthly*, accommodating himself to this grave complication with infinite tact and industry. He conferred further distinction upon the magazine; he wrote the fine series of "Suburban

Sketches," one of the least known of his productions, but one of the most perfect, and on Sunday afternoons he took a suburban walk—perfect also, no doubt, in its way. I know not exactly how long this phase of his career lasted, but I imagine that if he were asked, he would reply: "Oh, a hundred years." He was meant for better things than this—things better, I mean, than superintending the private life of even the most eminent periodical—but I am not sure that I would speak of this experience as a series of wasted years. They were years rather of economized talent, of observation and accumulation. They laid the foundation of what is most remarkable, or most, at least, the peculiar sign, in his effort as a novelist—his unerring sentiment of the American character. Mr. Howells knows more about it than any one and it was during this period of what we may suppose to have been rather perfunctory administration that he must have gathered many of his impressions of it. An editor is in the nature of the case much exposed, so exposed as not to be protected even by the seclusion (the security to a superficial eye so complete) of a Boston suburb. His manner of contact with the world is almost violent, and whatever bruises he may confer, those he receives are the most telling, inasmuch as the former are distributed among many, and the latter all to be endured by one. Mr. Howells's accessibilities and sufferings were destined to fructify. Other persons have considered and discoursed upon American life, but no one, surely, has *felt* it so completely as he. I will not say that Mr. Howells feels it all equally, for are we not perpetually conscious how vast and deep it is?—but he is an authority upon many of those parts of it which are most representative.

He was still under the shadow of his editorship when, in the intervals of his letter-writing and reviewing, he made his first cautious attempts in the walk of fiction. I say cautious, for in looking back nothing is more clear than that he had determined to advance only step by step. In his first story, *Their Wedding Journey*, there are only two persons, and in his next, *A Chance Acquaintance*, which contains one of his very happiest studies of a girl's character, the number is not lavishly increased.

In *A Foregone Conclusion*, where the girl again is admirable, as well as the young Italian priest, also a kind of maidenly figure, the actors are but four. Today Mr. Howells doesn't count, and confers life with a generous and unerring hand. If the profusion of forms in which it presents itself to him is remarkable, this is perhaps partly because he had the good fortune of not approaching the novel until he had lived considerably, until his inclination for it had ripened. His attitude was as little as possible that of the gifted young person who, at twenty, puts forth a work of imagination of which the merit is mainly in its establishing the presumption that the next one will be better. It is my im-

pression that long after he was twenty he still cultivated the belief
that the faculty of the novelist was not in him, and was even capable
of producing certain unfinished chapters (in the candor of his good
faith he would sometimes communicate them to a listener) in triumphant
support of this contention. He believed, in particular, that he could not
make people talk, and such have been the revenges of time that a cynical critic might almost say of him to-day that he cannot make them
keep silent. It was life itself that finally dissipated his doubts, life that
reasoned with him and persuaded him. The feeling of life is strong in
all his tales, and any one of them has this rare (always rarer) and indispensable sign of a happy origin, that it is an impression at first hand. Mr.
Howells is literary, on certain sides exquisitely so, though with a singular
and not unamiable perversity he sometimes endeavors not to be; but
his vision of the human scene is never a literary reminiscence, a reflection of books and pictures, of tradition and fashion and hearsay. I know
of no English novelist of our hour whose work is so exclusively a matter
of painting what he sees and who is so sure of what he sees. People are
always wanting a writer of Mr. Howells's temperament to see certain
things that he doesn't (that he doesn't sometimes even want to), but
I must content myself with congratulating the author of *A Modern Instance* and *Silas Lapham* on the admirable quality of his vision. The
American life which he for the most part depicts is certainly neither
very rich nor very fair, but it is tremendously positive, and as his manner of presenting it is as little as possible conventional, the reader can
have no doubt about it. This is an immense luxury; the ingenuous character of the witness (I can give it no higher praise) deepens the value
of the report.

Mr. Howells has gone from one success to another, has taken possession of the field, and has become copious without detriment to his
freshness. I need not enumerate his works in their order, for, both in
America and in England (where it is a marked feature of the growing
curiosity felt about American life that they are constantly referred to for
information and verification), they have long been in everybody's hands.
Quietly and steadily they have become better and better; one may like
some of them more than others, but it is noticeable that from effort to
effort the author has constantly enlarged his scope. His work is of a
kind of which it is good that there should be much today—work of observation, of patient and definite notation. Neither in theory nor in practice is Mr. Howells a romancer; but the romancers can spare him; there
will always be plenty of people to do their work. He has definite and
downright convictions on the subject of the work that calls out to be
done in opposition to theirs, and this fact is a source of much of the
interest that he excites.

It is a singular circumstance that to know what one wishes to do should be, in the field of art, a rare distinction; but it is incontestable that, as one looks about in our English and American fiction, one does not perceive any very striking examples of a vivifying faith. There is no discussion of the great question of how best to write, no exchange of ideas, no vivacity nor variety of experiment. A vivifying faith Mr. Howells may distinctly be said to possess, and he conceals it so little as to afford every facility to those people who are anxious to prove that it is the wrong one. He is animated by a love of the common, the immediate, the familiar and vulgar elements of life, and holds that in proportion as we move into the rare and strange we become vague and arbitrary; that truth of representation, in a word, can be achieved only so long as it is in our power to test and measure it. He thinks scarcely anything too paltry to be interesting, that the small and the vulgar have been terribly neglected, and would rather see an exact account of a sentiment or a character he stumbles against every day than a brilliant evocation of a passion or a type he has never seen and does not even particularly believe in. He adores the real, the natural, the colloquial, the moderate, the optimistic, the domestic, and the democratic; looking askance at exceptions and perversities and superiorities, at surprising and incongruous phenomena in general. One must have seen a great deal before one concludes; the world is very large, and life is a mixture of many things; she by no means eschews the strange, and often risks combinations and effects that make one rub one's eyes. Nevertheless, Mr. Howells's standpoint is an excellent one for seeing a large part of the truth, and even if it were less advantageous, there would be a great deal to admire in the firmness with which he has planted himself. He hates a "story," and (this private feat is not impossible) has probably made up his mind very definitely as to what the pestilent thing consists of. In this respect he is more logical than M. Émile Zola, who partakes of the same aversion, but has greater lapses as well as greater audacities. Mr. Howells hates an artificial fable and a *dénouement* that is pressed into the service; he likes things to occur as they occur in life, where the manner of a great many of them is not to occur at all. He has observed that heroic emotion and brilliant opportunity are not particularly interwoven with our days, and indeed, in the way of omission, he *has* often practised in his pages a very considerable boldness. It has not, however, made what we find there any less interesting and less human.

The picture of American life on Mr. Howells's canvas is not of a dazzling brightness and many readers have probably wondered why it is that (among a sensitive people) he has so successfully escaped the imputation of a want of patriotism. The manners he describes—the desolation of the whole social prospect in *A Modern Instance* is perhaps the strongest expression of those influences—are eminently of a nature to dis-

courage the intending visitor, and yet the westward pilgrim continues
to arrive, in spite of the Bartley Hubbards and the Laphams, and the
terrible practices at the country hotel in *Doctor Breen*, and at the Boston
boarding-house in *A Woman's Reason*. This tolerance of depressing revelations is explained partly, no doubt, by the fact that Mr. Howells's
truthfulness imposes itself—the representation is so vivid that the reader
accepts it as he accepts, in his own affairs, the mystery of fate—and
partly by a very different consideration, which is simply that if many
of his characters are disagreeable, almost all of them are extraordinarily
good, and with a goodness which is a ground for national complacency.
If American life is on the whole, as I make no doubt whatever, more
innocent than that of any other country, nowhere is the fact more
patent than in Mr. Howells's novels, which exhibit so constant a study
of the actual and so small a perception of evil. His women, in particular,
are of the best—except, indeed, in the sense of being the best to live
with. Purity of life, fineness of conscience, benevolence of motive, decency of speech, good-nature, kindness, charity, tolerance (though, indeed, there is little but each other's manners for the people to tolerate),
govern all the scene; the only immoralities are aberrations of thought,
like that of Silas Lapham, or excesses of beer, like that of Bartley Hubbard. In the gallery of Mr. Howells's portraits there are none more living
than the admirable, humorous images of those two ineffectual sinners.
Lapham, in particular, is magnificent, understood down to the ground,
inside and out—a creation which does Mr. Howells the highest honor.
I do not say that the figure of his wife is as good as his own, only because I wish to say that it is as good as that of the minister's wife in
the history of *Lemuel Barker*, which is unfolding itself from month to
month at the moment I write. These two ladies are exhaustive renderings
of the type of virtue that worries. But everything in *Silas Lapham* is
superior—nothing more so than the whole picture of casual female youth
and contemporaneous "engaging" one's self, in the daughters of the
proprietor of the mineral paint.

   This production had struck me as the author's high-water mark, until
I opened the monthly sheets of *Lemuel Barker*, in which the art of im-
parting a palpitating interest to common things and unheroic lives is
pursued (or is destined, apparently, to be pursued) to an even higher
point. The four (or is it eight?) repeated "good-mornings" between
the liberated Lemuel and the shopgirl who has crudely been the cause
of his being locked up by the police all night are a poem, an idyl, a trait
of genius, and a compendium of American good-nature. The whole episode is inimitable, and I know fellow-novelists of Mr. Howells's who
would have given their eyes to produce that interchange of salutations,
which only an American reader, I think, can understand. Indeed, the

only limitation, in general, to his extreme truthfulness is, I will not say his constant sense of the comedy of life, for that is irresistible, but the verbal drollery of many of his people. It is extreme and perpetual, but I fear the reader will find it a venial sin. Theodore Colville, in *Indian Summer*, is so irrepressibly and happily facetious as to make one wonder whether the author is not prompting him a little, and whether he could be quite so amusing without help from outside. This criticism, however, is the only one I find it urgent to make, and Mr. Howells doubtless will not suffer from my saying that, being a humorist himself, he is strong in the representation of humorists. There are other reflections that I might indulge in if I had more space. I should like, for instance, to allude in passing, for purposes of respectful remonstrance, to a phrase that he suffered the other day to fall from his pen (in a periodical, but not in a novel), to the effect that the style of a work of fiction is a thing that matters less and less all the while. Why less and less? It seems to me as great a mistake to say so as it would be to say that it matters more and more. It is difficult to see how it can matter either less or more. The style of a novel is a part of the execution of a work of art; the execution of a work of art is a part of its very essence, and that, it seems to me, must have mattered in all ages in exactly the same degree, and be destined always to do so. I can conceive of no state of civilization in which it shall not be deemed important, though of course there are states in which executants are clumsy. I should also venture to express a certain regret that Mr. Howells (whose style, in practice, after all, as I have intimated, treats itself to felicities which his theory perhaps would condemn) should appear increasingly to hold composition too cheap—by which I mean, should neglect the effect that comes from alternation, distribution, relief. He has an increasing tendency to tell his story altogether in conversations, so that a critical reader sometimes wishes, not that the dialogue might be suppressed (it is too good for that), but that it might be distributed, interspaced with narrative and pictorial matter. The author forgets sometimes to paint, to evoke the conditions and appearances, to build in the subject. He is doubtless afraid of doing these things in excess, having seen in other hands what disastrous effects that error may have; but all the same I cannot help thinking that the divinest thing in a valid novel is the compendious, descriptive, pictorial touch, *à la Daudet*.

It would be absurd to speak of Mr. Howells to-day in the encouraging tone that one would apply to a young writer who had given fine pledges, and one feels half guilty of that mistake if one makes a cheerful remark about his future. And yet we cannot pretend not to take a still more lively interest in his future than we have done in his past. It is hard to see how it can help being more and more fruitful, for his face is turned in the right direction, and his work is fed from sources which play us no tricks.

Notes

1. It was, of course, *Poems of Two Friends* which Howells published in collaboration with Piatt, not the campaign biography. Like T. S. Perry, James had an inexact notion of their friend's Ohio career. *Poems of Two Friends* actually appeared in December 1859 and the Lincoln volume in June 1860.

1887-1891

Statesman and Novelist:
A Talk Between Senator Ingalls
and Mr. Howells

Harriet E. Monroe*

On the evening of March 12, 1886, I spent a few hours at the Washington home of Senator and Mrs. Ingalls, whither I had accompanied Mr. and Mrs. Howells, and there heard about the following conversation.

The sketch is, of course, stripped of the picturesque language of the speakers; but the spirit and sentiment are retained.

In person Mr. Howells is about five feet four inches in height, quite stout, with short neck, large head carried a little in front,—probably a result of continual leaning forward to write,—pleasant blue eye, iron-gray hair and moustache, colorless Napoleonic face.

Senator Ingalls, tall, straight, slender, with large head, piercing black eye, gray hair and moustache, looks the scholar and distinguished man even in a crowd of distinguished people.

Two persons could scarcely be more antipodal: Ingalls argumentative, pungent, picturesque; Howells gentle, graphic, and absorbent.

After the preliminaries, Mr. Howells said, "Mr. Ingalls, what do you think of Cleveland?"

"In many respects I have not made up my mind. I will give you my data, and you can come to your own conclusions. It was something to see a man who had been in Washington but once before, enter the Senate-chamber with perfect self-possession in company with Mr. Arthur, that polished, self-poised gentleman. The leading men of the nation were present; the galleries were full of distinguished people. More anxious to see him even than the others were the leaders of his own party from the South, to whom he was personally unknown. Amid such surroundings he coolly took his seat beside Mr. Arthur, with every eye, every opera-

*Reprinted from *Lippincott's Magazine*, 39 (January 1887), 128–32.

glass, centred on him. He looked neither embarrassed nor nervous in the least. He never moved during that half-hour of preliminary exercises,—not his hand, not his foot; he did not wink oftener than usual: he might have been bronze, for any effect the inspection seemed to produce. He then moved out to the front, where he took the oath of office and delivered the first inaugural I ever heard pronounced without manuscript. He stood there and delivered that harangue of dogmatic platitudes without any attempt at oratory."

"Did he not have notes?" asked Mr. Howells.

"He held a card between the second and third fingers of the left hand, which he kept mostly behind him. Occasionally he would bring that card in front of him; it probably contained only a few catchwords. The fact that in the few months of intense excitement between the time of his election and inauguration he should have gotten that speech into his mind so as to give it calmly before that vast multitude, whom no man could number, was to me inexplicable."

"Was his immobility training or temperament?" asked Mrs. Howells.

"Temperament, I should say," continued the Senator. "Then he has what his friends call firmness, what his enemies denominate obstinacy. He is perfectly self-reliant. I have quietly asked nearly every Democratic Senator, 'With whom does Mr. Cleveland advise? Who is his best friend?' Not one of them knows; and it is now acknowledged by them that he has no intimate friend, no adviser, no counsellor: no one but Grover Cleveland is responsible for his acts. Now draw your own conclusions."

"Do you think he has kept faith with the Mugwumps?"

"Yes, if he has kept faith with any party. The Democrats certainly think he has failed them."

Mrs. Howells then said, "That Mugwumpian movement was very singular, was it not? It was considered a gentlemanly movement. The aesthetic men lost their heads, and staked everything on this man without a history except as mayor of Buffalo and a one-term governor of New York."

"Yes," said the Senator, "a man who left a lucrative professional practice at thirty-five to become sheriff of his county, and hung two prisoners with his own hand to save the fee he would have been compelled to pay a deputy: it seems rather ghastly, does it not?"

Mrs. Howells said, "May he not have thought it more noble, as he had accepted the office, to personally fulfil all its duties?"

"You are very kind, Mrs. Howells, to take such a charitable view of the case," said Mr. Ingalls. "If you want charity you must go to women."

"Y—e—s," said Mr. Howells, with a little shrug,—"charity to the—actions—of—men."

"Those Mugwumps," continued Mr. Ingalls, "thought to purify the country by precipitating into the Presidential chair the representative of its worst element. Is there not some Mugwumpian influence generated from Harvard University?"

"Mr. Ingalls," said Mr. Howells, "you may be said to represent both the East and the West. You are originally from New England, aren't you?"

"Yes; I was born and brought up in Essex County, Massachusetts, educated at Williams College, went to Kansas in 1858, where I have been ever since. Yes, I think I am both Eastern and Western."

"That West is a marvellous country, and I hope I shall yet see it."

"Yes," said the Senator, "Kansas is more truly the New England of books and ideas than what is now left in New England. The enterprising young New England graduate has gone West, carrying with him the church, the school, the Puritan ideas, the *moral earnestness* attributed to New England in books. The foreign element has captured New England farming-land. My father's farm has long been occupied by an English peasant. We have the real New England in the West."

"You will hear," said Mrs. Ingalls, "more profanity in an hour around a New England railway-station than you would hear in Kansas in a month. Western people also observe the Sabbath."

"We are not Sabbatarians," said Mr. Howells.

"Mr. Howells, you should come to Washington and write the great American novel," said Mr. Ingalls. "We have had 'Democracy' and 'Through One Administration,' but they have not hit it."

Mr. Howells replied, "I am too old now" (he does not look over forty). "I could not stand the going into society to catch the spirit of things. There will come a young man who will yet write it. Every good English novel has some politics in it; but *there* it is the fashion. Ladies, and even children, talk public affairs in London."

"So they do in Washington; and in a residence of two years here you would get the spirit of things. Have you ever thought how well Washington is situated for a capital? It has no manufacturing or commercial interests. Had the complications of '76 occurred in New York instead of Washington, there would have been revolution. The fathers were wise to make this strictly a political capital. Mr. Howells, do you think 'Uncle Tom's Cabin' a great novel?"

"Yes; I have read it of late years, and I consider it one of the great novels."

Mr. Howells, in some connection, remarked,—

"When I first went to Boston the literary men were very kind to me. Longfellow gave a dinner every Wednesday evening, where I met Agassiz, Holmes, Lowell, Tom Appleton, Emerson, and many others. No one who rang the door-bell was admitted. To knock was the sign of membership. Longfellow was translating Dante. Before dinner he would read his translations, while we kept the Italian in hand and commented upon and criticised his work."

"Is it a literal translation?"

"Yes; it is an exact reproduction of the Italian poem."

"Was Longfellow a good talker?" said the Senator.

"Yes: he did not talk as much as Lowell, Holmes, or others, but he gave the *flavor* to the evening. He had a personal loveliness and sweetness quite indescribable. When the evening was gone, you would find what Longfellow said or did pre-eminent in memory."

Mr. Ingalls said, "Of course Longfellow is not to be ranked with Shakespeare and the greatest poets; but he has lines of descriptive poetry unsurpassed. That description of a New England snow-storm is perfect of its kind. It begins,—

> Out of the bosom of the air,
> Out of the cloud-folds of its garments shaken, etc.

Did Longfellow keep his powers to the last?"

"Yes," said Mr. Howells: "he suffered much from neuralgia of the head, and complained of feeling confused, but he did not show it: he suffered much from insomnia, that disease of the aged. Emerson, you know, totally lost his memory. I saw him looking at Longfellow in his coffin with a dazed, confused look, and I said to myself, 'He does not know his old friend.' When the funeral was over, he said to Mrs. Agassiz, 'The gentleman whose funeral we have attended was a sweet and beautiful soul; but I cannot recall his name.' Emerson remembered the use of things, but not their names. He would speak of 'that we use to keep the rain off' for the word umbrella. His daughter went everywhere with him, to be memory for him."

Mr. Ingalls said, "I remember Emerson came to Williams College in 1854 to address the societies. I was sent to his room to tell him the particulars as to hour and place. He was yet writing his address. As he finished page after page he flung them to the floor, and they were scattered all over the room. We took a walk before sunrise, and as we saw the sun come up over the horizon he said, 'O Sunrise and Sunset, ye great magicians!' I never saw him again. Does Dr. Holmes retain all his powers?"

"Yes; when you meet him he may be dim a moment, then his mind instantly clears, and he is the same brilliant, wonderful talker. How many good things he has said and written! Lowell is probably the most charming living talker. When he talks, everybody else listens."

Some one said, "What of Whittier?"

Mr. Ingalls replied,—

"Longfellow and Whittier are so different as not to be comparable. Whittier always wrote to help some good cause: he writes for a purpose.

Longfellow wrote as the birds sing. Mr. Howells, is Whittier a good talker?"

"Whittier is double-distilled silence. He is from New England, and a Quaker; but what he *does* say is always worth hearing."

Some one asked Mr. Howells if he had read Tennyson's last. He replied, "Yes: it is hardly equal to his other work: he is growing Tennysonian,—has mannerism rather than matter."

Mr. Ingalls said, "With the first money I earned I bought Whittier's 'Voices of Freedom.' The school-mistress was sick, and I took charge of the school. I was only sixteen, and the students thought they wouldn't obey. I did not teach much. The week was chiefly spent in flagellations. Many stayed away, and I was fast scattering the school. Luckily, the teacher got well. The committee handed me five dollars. With that I bought a copy of Whittier, a portfolio which I have yet, and a copy of Byron."

Mrs. Howells here rose to go. The Senator said to Mr. Howells, "May I offer you a cigar?"

"No: I don't smoke."

"No vices?"

"Yes; but I conceal them."

Mr. Howells on Realism

Anonymous*

Never has Lake George been more beautiful or more popular than now. . . . The author of "Silas Lapham" likes Lake George. I called upon him yesterday, and found him with his family about him, seated upon the front piazza of his cottage in a soft felt hat, a white flannel shirt, and a large easy pair of corduroy trousers. He looked the picture of good health. Evidently he had not shunned the sunlight, for his face was darkly tanned. He answered the question as to how in the world he had ever ventured into New-York State for a summer vacation by saying that though warmly attached to Boston, he was not to the manor born, and found it less difficult to do strange and unusual things than if he were native Bostonese.

"We left early," he said, "spending June in Carbondale without having our summer plans definitely arranged, though feeling that our faces were rather surely turned in the direction of Lake George. What a

*Reprinted from the *New York Tribune*, 10 July 1887, p. 12.

lovely place it is! We are enjoying it immensely. Dr. Eggleston lives across the lake almost opposite this place. He and Miss Eggleston rowed over to see us the other day."

"Are you contemplating any new literary work, Mr. Howells?"

"Yes. I have just written the first pages of a new novel not yet announced. I began it, in fact, only the day before yesterday. It will be a purely American story, its chief events centred in a New England country town, though it will relate to both city and country life. I have not thought of a name for it yet, nor, though I have its plot pretty well sketched out in my mind, should I feel at liberty to detail it to you just now. The nature of my arrangements with the Harpers, who have contracted with me for all I write, is such that entire good faith requires me to leave with them the time and form of any extended announcement. We shall not leave Lake George before October, and by that time I hope to have the book in fairly good shape."

"How do you work here?"

"There is my little office," replied the novelist, pointing to a little one-storied wing of the house. "Will you look at it?"

It is a pretty room, with a hard-wood floor and plenty of shelving, plentifully stored with books. A picture of Lincoln, after that lately reproduced in *The Century*, and pictures of Tolstoi, Björnson, Hawthorne, and others were on the walls. A large flat desk and several easy chairs completed the room's furniture.

"I write here for about four hours every morning after breakfast," continued Mr. Howells. "Yes, I become vastly interested in my work. It quite possesses me. Of course, there are times when I feel myself unable to think and when it really palls on me, but that is every man's experience in every kind of effort. . . . The real sentiment of to-day requires that the novelist shall portray a section of real life, that has in it a useful and animating purpose. All the good work of our time is being done on this theory."

"In proof of this, just glance at the work which public sentiment has passed favorably upon in all intelligent countries. Russia has led in the new school, and holds the foremost place among the nations that have produced great modern novelists. England stands at the very bottom of the list. Hardy is a great, I may say, a very great novelist. His pictures of life are life itself. Mrs. Howells and I have heard under our windows in England the very thoughts, yes, the very accents, which he has attributed to his English peasantry. His truth and sincerity are admirable. And Black, too, so far as I have read him, is an able skilful writer. But the Russian novelists lead the world. Indeed, I affirm that Tolstoi occupies to all fiction the same relation that Shakespeare occupies to all drama. He has a very strong ethical side, and not only teaches it and portrays it, but lives it. He has given himself up to it. He believes that men should live precisely and literally as Christ lived, and abandoning literature, where he stood at the summit of fiction, he has adopted the daily life of a Russian peasant."

I remarked that that seemed like simplicity itself, and received this retort:

"Isn't that because our civilization is so sophisticated? We read, and say we believe that Christ is God, but sometimes our actions imply that we scarcely think He meant what He said about the conduct of life."

"Who do you think ranks next to Tolstoi as a writer of fiction?"

"Turgenieff."

"Do you mean to say that the greatest writers of fiction that the world has ever produced are both Russians?"

"Yes, I think I am prepared to say just that. The novels of these men are absolute truth. They are nature bared. They are greatest because their writers have the ability and the courage to paint humanity and its affairs just as they are. That I regard as the highest art. . . ."

The Russians, "and the realistic school they lead, . . . contend that the daily life of men and women with its thousand cares and hopes and ambitions and sorrows is of itself full of interest. If any one dared to show it as it really is, without the slightest gloss or draping, he would be giving out the most absorbing fiction."

"How do you answer the charge that real life is commonplace?"

"By asserting that the very things that are not commonplace are those commonly called commonplace. All the rest has long since become hackneyed. In the preposterous what is there to invent? Nothing, except what is so preposterous as to be ludicrous.

"I think my first ideas as to the rare beauty of natural simple fiction that dealt with the actual hopes and fears of men as they are universally shown, came from reading Björnson's exquisite stories. In Scandinavian literature realism has attained a rare degree of perfection. Most of the modern Italian and modern Spanish novels are of the new school, and it cannot be denied that the best works in all the Continental tongues show the growth of this tendency.

"Of course we all know the character of the modern French writers. Zola is a great writer. I may regret that he has concerned himself so much with the disagreeable and unhappy things of life, but I do not base my objection to him on that ground. Strange as it may seem, if I objected to him at all it would be that he was a romanticist. . . . A true arrangement of the literatures in which realism has obtained the supremacy over romance would place the Russian first; the French, by virtue of Zola's strength, second; the Spanish next; the Norwegian fourth; the Italian fifth, and the English last."

November's Come

Anonymous*

The London *Standard*, apropos of Mr. Childs' gift to Stratford-on-Avon, goes so far as to assert editorially that America has never produced a writer equal to Shakespeare.

Here is an opportunity for Count Tolstoi to say something pleasant about Mr. Howells.

SEVEN UP.

A game that will be played in Chicago next month.

Jacob Sharp may have been a foolish old man, but he never paid $385 for a private box for the opening performance of an aspiring young amateur.

Mr. Pulitzer is requested to paste this in his hat.

*Reprinted from *Life*, 10 (3 November 1887), p. 244.

[Howells and the Anarchists]

Anonymous*

Because Mr. W. D. Howells in his "realistic" fiction sometimes seems to waste good literature on petty subjects, it must not be supposed that he lacks manly fibre or humane impulses. His studies of Italian life show him a man in whom sympathy with the sufferers and

*Reprinted from the *Pilot* [New York], 12 November 1887, p. 4.

the fighters of wrong is instinctive and impellent. He has shown the courage of his humanity in a more daring manner recently by petitioning the Governor of Illinois on behalf of the condemned Anarchists—a thing which few of his milk-and-water critics would have the honorable impulse to think of or the independence to carry out. Mr. Howells deserves all honor for such an action.

Novels and Agnosticism

Julian Hawthorne*

. . . the ideal novel, conforming in every part to the behests of the imagination, should produce, by means of literary art, the illusion of a loftier reality. This excludes the photographic method of novel-writing. "That is a false effort in art," says Goethe, towards the close of his long and splendid career, "which, in giving reality to the appearance, goes so far as to leave in it nothing but the common, every-day actual. . . ." He who claims the name of artist must rise to that vision of a loftier reality—a more true because a more beautiful world—which only imagination can reveal. A truer world,—for the world of facts is not and cannot be true. . . . One fact, considered in itself, has no less importance than any other; a lump of charcoal is as valuable as a diamond. But that is the philosophy of brute beasts and Digger Indians. . . .

In proceeding from the general to the particular,—to the novel as it actually exists in England and America,—attention will be confined strictly to the contemporary outlook. The new generation of novelists (by which is intended not those merely living in this age, but those who actively belong to it) differ in at least one fundamental respect from the later representatives of the generation preceding them. Thackeray and Dickens did not deliberately concern themselves about a philosophy of life. . . .

But of late years a new order of things has been coming into vogue, and the new novelists have been among the first to reflect it; and of these the Americans have shown themselves among the most susceptible. Science, or the investigation of the phenomena of existence (in opposition to philosophy, the investigation of the phenomena of being), has proved nature to be so orderly and self-sufficient, and inquiry as to the origin of the primordial atom so unproductive and quixotic, as to make it convenient and indeed reasonable to accept nature as a self-

*Reprinted from *Confessions and Criticism* (Boston: Ticknor, 1887), pp. 35–70.

existing fact, and to let all the rest—if rest there be—go. From this point of view, God and a future life retire into the background; not as finally disproved,—because denial, like affirmation, must, in order to be final, be logically supported; and spirit is, if not illogical, at any rate outside the domain of logic,—but as being a hopelessly vague and untrustworthy hypothesis. The Bible is a human book; Christ was a gentleman, related to the Buddha and Plato families; Joseph was an ill-used man; death, so far as we have any reason to believe, is annihilation of personal existence; life is—the predicament of the body previous to death; morality is the enlightened selfishness of the greatest number; civilization is the compromises men make with one another in order to get the most they can out of the world; wisdom is acknowledgment of these propositions; folly is to hanker after what may lie beyond the sphere of sense. The supporter of these doctrines by no means permits himself to be regarded as a rampant and dogmatic atheist; he is simply the modest and humble doubter of what he cannot prove. He even recognizes the persistence of the religious instinct in man, and caters to it by a new religion suited to the times—the Religion of Humanity. Thus he is secure at all points: for if the religion of the Bible turn out to be true, his disappointment will be an agreeable one; and if it turns out false, he will not be disappointed at all. He is an agnostic—a person bound to be complacent whatever happens. He may indulge a gentle regret, a musing sadness, a smiling pensiveness; but he will never refuse a comfortable dinner, and always wear something soft next his skin, nor can he altogether avoid the consciousness of his intellectual superiority.

Agnosticism, which reaches forward into nihilism on one side, and extends back into liberal Christianity on the other, marks, at all events, a definite turning-point from what has been to what is to come. The human mind, in the course of its long journey, is passing through a dark place, and is, as it were, whistling to keep up its courage. It is a period of doubt: what it will result in remains to be seen; but analogy leads us to infer that this doubt, like all others, will be succeeded by a comparatively definite belief in something—no matter what. It is a transient state—the interval between one creed and another. The agnostic no longer holds to what is behind him, nor knows what lies before, so he contents himself with feeling the ground beneath his feet. That, at least, though the heavens fall, is likely to remain; meanwhile, let the heavens take care of themselves. It may be the part of valor to champion divine revelation, but the better part of valor is discretion, and if divine revelation prove true, discretion will be none the worse off. On the other hand, to champion a myth is to make one's self ridiculous, and of being ridiculous the agnostic has a consuming fear. From the superhuman disinterestedness of the theory of the Religion of Humanity, before which angels might quail, he flinches not, but when it comes to the risk of being laughed at by certain sagacious persons he confesses that bravery has its limits. He dares do all that may become an agnostic,—who dares do more is none.

But, however open to criticism this phase of thought may be, it is a genuine phase, and the proof is the alarm and the shifts that it has brought about in the opposite camp. "Established" religion finds the foundation of her establishment undermined. . . . the outlook may fairly be described as confused and the issue uncertain. And—to come without further preface to the subject of this paper—it is with this material that the modern novelist, so far as he is a modern and not a future novelist, or a novelist *temporis acti,* has to work. Unless a man have the gift to forecast the years, or, at least, to catch the first ray of the coming light, he can hardly do better than attend to what is under his nose. He may hesitate to identify himself with agnosticism, but he can scarcely avoid discussing it, either in itself or in its effects. He must entertain its problems; and the personages of history, if they do not directly advocate or oppose agnostic views, must show in their lives either confirmation or disproof of agnostic principles. It is impossible, save at the cost of affection or of ignorance, to escape from the spirit of the age. It is in the air we breathe, and, whether we are fully conscious thereof or not, our lives and thoughts must needs be tinctured by it. . . .

And, as a matter of fact, art already shows the effects of the agnostic influence. Artists have begun to doubt whether their old conceptions of beauty be not fanciful and silly. They betray a tendency to eschew the loftier flights of the imagination, and confine themselves to what they call facts. Critics deprecate idealism as something fit only for children, and extol the courage of seeing and representing things as they are. Sculpture is either a stern student of modern trousers and coat-tails or a vapid imitator of classic prototypes. Painters try all manner of experiments, and shrink from painting beneath the surface of their canvas. Much of recent effort in the different branches of art comes to us in the form of "studies," but the complete work still delays to be born. We would not so much mind having our old idols and criterions done away with were something new and better, or as good, substituted for them. But apparently nothing definite has yet been decided on. Doubt still reigns, and, once more, doubt is not creative. One of two things must presently happen. The time will come when we must stop saying that we do not know whether or not God, and all that God implies, exists, and affirm definitely and finally either that he does not exist or that he does. That settled, we shall soon see what will become of art. If there is a God, he will be understood and worshipped, not superstitiously and literally as heretofore, but in a new and enlightened spirit; and an art will arise commensurate with this new and loftier revelation. If there is no God, it is difficult to see how art can have the face to show herself any more. There is no place for her in the Religion of Humanity; to be true and living she can be nothing which it has thus far entered into the heart of man to call beautiful; and she could only serve to remind us of certain vague longings and aspirations now proved to be as false as they were vain. Art is not an orchid: it cannot grow in the air. Unless its root can be traced as deep down as Yggdrasil, it will wither and vanish, and be forgotten as it ought to be; and as for the cowslip by the river's brim, a yellow cowslip it shall be, and nothing more; and the light that never was on sea or land shall be permanently extinguished, in the interests of common sense and economy, and (what is least inviting of all to the unregenerate mind) we shall speedily get rid of the notion that we have lost anything worth preserving.

This, however, is only what may be, and our concern at present is with things as they are. It has been observed that American writers have shown themselves more susceptible of the new influences than most others, partly no doubt from a natural sensitiveness of organization, but in some measure also because there are with us no ruts and fetters of old tradition from which we must emancipate ourselves before adopting anything new. We have no past, in the European sense, and so are ready for whatever the present or the future may have to suggest. Nevertheless, the novelist who, in a larger degree than any other, seems to be the literary parent of our own best men of fiction, is himself not an American, nor even an Englishman, but a Russian—Turguénieff. His series of extraordinary novels, translated into English and French, is altogether the most important fact in the literature of fiction of the last twelve years. To read his books you would scarcely imagine that their author could have had any knowledge of the work of his predecessors in the same field. Originality is a term indiscriminately applied, and generally of trifling significance, but so far as any writer may be original, Turguénieff is so. He is no less original in the general scheme and treatment of his stories than in their details. Whatever he produces has the air of being the outcome of his personal experience and observation. He even describes his characters, their aspect, features, and ruling traits, in a novel and memorable manner. He seizes on them from a new point of vantage, and uses scarcely any of the hackneyed and conventional devices for bringing his portraits before our minds; yet no writer, not even Carlyle, has been more vivid, graphic, and illuminating than he. Here are eyes that owe nothing to other eyes, but examine and record for themselves. Having once taken up a character he never loses his grasp on it: on the contrary, he masters it more and more, and only lets go of it when the last recesses of its organism have been explored. In the quality and conduct of his plots he is equally unprecedented. His scenes are modern, and embody characteristic events and problems in the recent history of Russia. There is in their arrangement no attempt at symmetry, nor poetic justice. Temperament and circumstances are made to rule, and against their merciless fiat no appeal is allowed. Evil does evil to the end; weakness never gathers strength; even goodness never varies from its level: it suffers, but is not corrupted; it is the goodness of instinct, not of struggle and aspiration; it happens to belong to this or that person, just as his hair happens to be black or brown. Everything in the surroundings and the action is to the last degree matter-of-fact, commonplace, inevitable; there are no picturesque coincidences, no providential interferences, no desperate victories over fate; the tale, like the world of the materialist, moves onward from a predetermined beginning to a helpless and tragic close. And yet few books have been written of deeper and more permanent fascination than these. Their grim veracity; the creative sympathy and steady dispassionateness of their portrayal of mankind; their constancy of motive, and their sombre earnestness, have been surpassed by none. This earnestness is worth dwelling upon for a moment. It bears no likeness to the dogmatism of the bigot or the fanaticism of the enthusiast. It is the concentration of a broadly gifted masculine mind, devoting its unstinted energies to depicting certain aspects of society and civilization, which are powerfully representative of the tendencies of the day. "Here is the unvarnished fact—give heed to it!" is the unwritten motto. The author avoids betraying, either explicitly or implicitly, the tendency of his own sympathies; not because he fears to have them known, but because he holds it to be his office simply to portray, and to leave judgment thereupon where, in any case, it must ultimately rest—with the world of his readers. He tells us what is; it is for us to consider whether it also must be and shall be. Turguénieff is an artist by nature, yet his books are not intentionally works of art; they are fragments of history, differing from real life only in presenting such persons and events as are commandingly and exhaustively typical, and excluding all others. This faculty of selection is one of the highest artistic faculties, and it appears as much in the minor as in the major features of the narrative. It indicates that Turguénieff might, if he chose, produce a story as faultlessly symmetrical as was ever framed. Why, then, does he not so choose? The reason can only be that he deems the truth-seeming of his narrative would thereby be impaired. "He is only telling a story," the reader would say, "and he shapes the events and persons so as to fit the plot." But is this reason reasonable? To those who believe that God has no hand in the ordering of human affairs, it undoubtedly is reasonable. To those who believe the contrary, however, it appears as if the story of no human life or complex of lives could be otherwise than a rounded and perfect work of art—provided only that the spectator takes note, not merely of the superficial accidents and appearances, but also of the underlying divine purpose and significance. The absence of this recognition in Turguénieff's novels is the explanation of them: holding the creed their author does, he could not have written them otherwise; and, on the other hand, had his creed been different, he very likely would not have written novels at all. . . .

There is no commanding individual imagination in England—nor, to say the truth, does there seem to be any in America. But we have what they have not—a national imaginative tendency. There are no fetters upon our fancy; and, however deeply our real estate may be mortgaged, there is freedom for our ideas. England has not yet appreciated the true inwardness of a favorite phrase of ours,—a new deal. And yet she is tired to death of her own stale stories; and when, by chance, any one of her writers happens to chirp out a note a shade different from the prevailing key, the whole nation pounces down upon him, with a shriek of half-incredulous joy, and buys him up, at the rate of a million copies a year. Our own best writers are more read in England, or, at any rate, more talked about, than their native crop; not so much, perhaps, because they are different as because their difference is felt to be of a significant and typical kind. It has in it a gleam of the new day. They are realistic; but realism, so far as it involves a faithful study of nature, is useful. The illusion of a loftier reality, at which we should aim, must be evolved from adequate knowledge of reality itself. The spontaneous and assured faith, which is the mainspring of sane imagination, must be preceded by the doubt and rejection of what is lifeless and insincere. We desire no resurrection of the Ann Radclyffe type of romance: but the true alternative to this is not such a mixture of the police gazette and the medical reporter as Émile Zola offers us. . . .

We are thus brought face to face with the two men with whom every critic of American novelists has to reckon; who represent what is carefullest and newest in American fiction; and it remains to inquire how far their work has been moulded by the skeptical or radical spirit of which Turguénieff is the chief exemplar. . . .

. . . . It cannot be said of any one of Mr. James's stories, "This is his best," or "This is his worst," because no one of them is all one way. They have their phases of strength and veracity, and, also, phases that are neither veracious nor strong. The cause may either lie in a lack of experience in a certain direction on the writer's part; or else in his reluctance to write up to the experience he has. The experience in question is not of the ways of the world,—concerning which Mr. James has every sign of being politely familiar,—nor of men and women in their everyday aspect; still less of literary ways and means, for of these, in his own line, he is a master. The experience referred to is experience of passion. If Mr. James be not incapable of describing passion, at all events he has still to show that he is capable of it. . . .

The other one of the two writers whose names are so often mentioned together, seems to have taken up the subject of our domestic and social pathology; and the minute care and conscientious veracity which he has brought to bear upon his work has not been surpassed, even by Shakespeare. But, if I could venture a criticism upon his productions, it would be to the effect that there is not enough fiction in them. They are elaborate and amiable reports of what we see around us. They are not exactly imaginative,—in the sense in which I have attempted to define the word. There are two ways of warning a man against unwholesome life—one is, to show him a picture of disease; the other is, to show him a picture of health. The former is the negative, the latter the positive treatment. Both have their merits; but the latter is, perhaps, the better adapted to novels, the former to essays. A novelist should not only know what he has got; he should also know what he wants. His mind should have an active, or theorizing, as well as a passive, or contemplative, side. He should have energy to discount the people he personally knows; the power to perceive what phases of thought are to be represented, as well as to describe the persons who happen to be their least inadequate representatives; the sagacity to analyze the age or the moment, and to reveal its tendency and meaning. Mr. Howells has produced a great deal of finely wrought tapestry; but does not seem, as yet, to have found a hall fit to adorn it with.

And yet Mr. James and Mr. Howells have done more than all the rest of us to make our literature respectable during the last ten years. If texture be the object, they have brought texture to a fineness never surpassed anywhere. They have discovered charm and grace in much that was only blank before. They have detected and described points of human nature hitherto unnoticed, which, if not intrinsically important, will one day be made auxiliary to the production of pictures of broader as well as minuter veracity than have heretofore been produced. All that seems wanting thus far is a direction, an aim, a belief. Agnosticism has brought about a pause for a while, and no doubt a pause is preferable to some kinds of activity. It may enable us, when the time comes to set forward again, to do so with better equipment and more intelligent purpose. It will not do to be always at a prophetic heat of enthusiasm, sympathy, denunciation: the coolly critical mood is also useful to prune extravagance and promote a sense of responsibility. The novels of Mr. James and of Mr. Howells have taught us that men and women are creatures of infinitely complicated structure, and that even the least of these complications, if it is portrayed at all, is worth portraying truthfully. But we cannot forget, on the other hand, that honest emotion and hearty action are necessary to the wholesomeness of society, because in their absence society is afflicted with a lamentable sameness and triviality; the old primitive impulses remain, but the food on which they are compelled to feed is insipid and unsustaining; our eyes are turned inward instead of outward, and each one of us becomes himself the Rome towards which all his roads lead. Such books as these authors have written are not the Great American Novel, because they take life and humanity not in their loftier, but in their lesser manifestations. They are the side scenes and the background of a story that has yet to be written. That story will have the interest not only of the collision of private passions and efforts, but of the great ideas and principles which characterize and animate a nation. It will discriminate between what is accidental and what is permanent, between what is realistic and what is real, between what is sentimental and what is sentiment. It will show us not only what we are, but what we are to be; not only what to avoid, but what to do. It will rest neither in the tragic gloom of Turguénieff, nor in the critical composure of James, nor in the gentle deprecation of Howells, but will demonstrate that the weakness of man is the motive and condition of his strength. It will not shrink from romance, nor from ideality, nor from artistic completeness, because it will know at what depths and heights of life these elements are truly operative. It will be American, not because its scene is laid or its characters born in the United States, but because its burden will be reaction against old tyrannies and exposure of new hypocrisies; a refutation of respectable falsehoods, and a proclamation of unsophisticated truths. Indeed, let us take heed and diligently improve our native talent, lest a day come when the Great American Novel make its appearance, but written in a foreign language, and by some author who—however purely American at heart—never set foot on the shores of the Republic.

Mr. Howells at Nahant

"E.J.C."*

....Mr. Howells is so retiring in his disposition and so seldom seen in public that his figure is not as familiar as those of Dr. Holmes, John Boyle O'Reilly or, possibly, Mr. Aldrich, although the latter seldom ventures out of the seclusion of the Atlantic office into the public view. Here then is a pen portrait of the author of "A Foregone Conclusion," "The Lady of the Aroostook," "The Undiscovered Country," "The Rise of Silas Lapham," and nearly a score more of novels which half the world has read and the other half is now reading. Short of stature, round of build, a smoothly shaven round face, adorned with a moustache of iron gray, thin hair combed smoothly forward, gray eyes which see all that

*Reprinted from *Boston Daily Advertiser*, 20 September 1888, p. 5.

there is to see about them,—this is the man. His manner is quiet and genial, impressing one at once with his entire sincerity of motive and his thorough candor.

Seating his visitor the other day upon a comfortable sofa in his pleasant library, and himself taking a wide, leather-covered easy chair, he chatted pleasantly.

"Oh! yes I have finished 'Annie Kilburn,' I am glad to say, and now I am ready to begin on something new. I always plan to have a new work ready to begin upon about as soon as I have finished with one story. I shall begin to write in a few days. I think it would hardly be fair to my publishers to say what I shall treat next, for they prefer to make their own announcements. I am quite busy, nearly all the time, with my critical work for the Harper 'Study.' You see the quantity of books I have on hand," he said, smiling, indicating a pile of books, fresh from the publishers and still unopened. "I have a great many books sent me, far more than I can begin to notice. But I do not pretend, as you know, to review books, but only to use them as topics for literary chat and discussion."

"How did you enjoy your life in New York, last winter, Mr. Howells?" was asked.

"New York is to me a very interesting city. It gives one much the impression of London, that is, in the sense of being a great city. New York is far more cosmopolitan than London. London is homogenous. They are overwhelmingly English there. But in New York we find people of all nations in great numbers, and I suppose that it is this quality, also, that gives to the city much of its charm. I regard Boston as the most beautiful city in the world. I will not even except the beautiful cities of Europe. Her suburbs are unsurpassed for beauty and extent. Now New York has practically no suburbs, that is, none through which one can drive and enjoy himself. One cannot get out of New York without crossing a ferry. But of Boston one never tires."

"The view of the Charles River basin from the water-side of Beacon St. I know you admire," suggested the visitor. "I remember the view from your study windows on Beacon St. Silas Lapham, too, admired it, you know."

"Yes," said Mr. Howells, smiling at the allusion, "I never tired of that view. It was delightful, unsurpassed. I was very sorry to leave it."

"You have, doubtless, enjoyed your life here this summer?"

"Oh, very much. You see what a beautiful view we have, and what delightful air. We shall remain here, probably, until about the first of November and then return to New York for the winter. But we still regard the region of Boston as our summer home."

"You see here," he continued, as his mail was laid upon his desk; "how I manage my English copyrights."

Opening a small package, he displayed a pamphlet containing the fourth instalment of "Annie Kilburn."

It bore the imprint of a Scotch publisher.

"Each instalment of a story," said Mr. Howells, "is forwarded to the British publishers and put into type upon the other side. It is then published in pamphlet form simultaneously with its publication in Harper's Magazine in this country. To meet the requirements of law, at least 25 copies are printed, and a bona-fide sale of at least one copy is made. This secures the copyright."

"The story is not published as a serial in an English magazine, simultaneously with its appearance in Harper's?"

"No. The publishers of Harper's would scarcely agree to that. Harper's Magazine circulates 60,000 copies in Great Britain and that covers the ground pretty well. When the story is completed a duplicate set of plates is made by the English publishers and forwarded to me so that the book may be printed upon either side of the water as may be desired, and it is covered by copyright in both countries."

"The practice, then, of having the type for the book set upon the other side will account for the use throughout your novels of the 'u' in such words as 'honour' and 'labour?'"

"Yes, I follow the American spelling, in which I am a firm believer, in my manuscripts, but the English method is followed by the British compositors and proof-readers. I have been severely criticized for following the English mode of spelling these words, but I do not like it any better than do my critics."

"Which of your books has the best sale, Mr. Howells?"

"Of all my books, 'Venetian Life' has had by far the best sale. But of my novels, 'Silas Lapham' is most in demand. 'Their Wedding Journey' is also having an excellent sale, especially since the new edition with an additional chapter on 'Niagara Revisited' was issued. The three publishers of my books, Houghton, Mifflin & Co., Ticknor & Co. and Harper & Bros. have agreed upon a uniform binding of all my books, of which I am very glad. Hitherto there has been no uniformity, one publisher following one style and another another. Hereafter all my books will be issued in the plain red binding, which is seen in 'April Hopes,' and in the new edition of 'Their Wedding Journey.'"

Literary Notes

Laurence Hutton*

"Our Father which art in heaven, help us to remember those who have nothing to eat. Amen."

So spoke the crippled child of a confirmed drunkard in a New England town, and at a dinner-table so dreadfully old-fashioned that Mr. Howells's *Annie Kilburn* felt the persons who sat about it to be entirely out of the world she had grown to look upon as the only world worth knowing. There was a platter of stewed fowl and a plate of high-piled waffles, there were soda biscuit and canned cherries, there was a clean white cloth, and with all there was love! " 'Winthrop!' said Putney, and the father and mother bowed their heads. The boy dropped his over his folded hands, and piped up, clearly, 'Our Father which art in heaven, help us to remember those who have nothing to eat. Amen!' 'That's a grace that Win got up himself,' his father explained, 'and we think it suits the Almighty as well as anything.' " Whoever its author may be, it seems to contain the sum of the Golden Rule, and to those who only remember to thank the Lord that they themselves have meat to eat, it is here presented as a motto text for the new year.

On social as well as on moral grounds Annie Kilburn is well worth studying and well worth knowing; if not particularly interesting in herself, she is surrounded by men and women whom, in the jargon of society, "we are pleased to have met," notwithstanding the fact that we meet them and their kind every day. Mr. Chapley, the publisher, of New York, had a summer home at South Hatboro', and there is even one family from Chicago there, who are recognized "as quite nice, you know, because New England by birth!" Hatboro' is the typical New England town, with all its virtues and all its faults, including private theatricals, a soldiers' monument, Queen Anne houses, and railroad tracks crossing the principal streets; and it contains all of those delightful and varied phases of human nature to be found in the villages of the Eastern States and nowhere else. The bell of the orthodox church at Hatboro', which called the members of Mr. Peck's society together for the business meeting, in Chapter XXV. of "Annie Kilburn," sounded in the ears of a body of men and women absolutely true to the life; and if the proceedings had been reported by a stenographer, with a detective camera and a perfected phonograph as assistants, they could not be more clearly reproduced than in Mr. Howells's book, from the sputtering of the electric-lights over Mr. Gates's head to the sharp cutting eloquence of the

*Reprinted from *Harper's Monthly*, 78 (January 1889), 145–46.

irrepressible lawyer who loves his fellow-men and goes on periodical and dreadful "sprees."

Mr. Ralph Putney is the most admirable creation of Mr. Howells's since the days of Bartley Hubbard, but a more delightful and more satisfactory character in every way than the illustrious journalist of "A Modern Instance," because more lovable and more worthy of respect. His weakness is a great weakness, and there is nothing in all fiction more pathetic than the manner in which he discusses his failings with his wife and his friends; nor anything more realistic or more terrible than the scene at Mrs. Munger's "party," when the lemonade he tasted turned out to be rum-punch in disguise. The temptation to quote Ralph Putney— when he is himself—is very strong. His picture of the Boston millionaire who goes to Hatboro' long enough in the spring "to dodge his taxes," is only equalled by his account of the minister who behaved toward the poor in his parish in a way to make it simply uninhabitable to the standard Christian! Putney confesses that he is not a hypocrite, simply because hypocrisy will avail him nothing in a town where all the inhabitants have seen him in the gutter; and this, he declares, is the only advantage he has over his fellow-citizens; but the good that is in him is very good, as his own boy will tell you, notwithstanding the fact that in his drunken helplessness once he ruined his boy's physical life.

The hero whom Annie Kilburn worships, while she cannot love, however, is not the village lawyer, whose piety and irony are so curiously blended, but a member of that cloth which has furnished so many heroes lately to the more serious novel. He is a minister as consistently Calvinistic as John Ward, and as broadly humanitarian as Robert Elsmere; he has no wife to torture, although he does make life burdensome to his infant daughter; he gives his coat to those who take his cloak, and he meekly turns both cheeks to the smiter; he is only a self-educated man, who has not had time to attain to that state of high culture which leads his brother Elsmere to apply the scourge of introspection upon the bare skin of his own conscience, and he forgets himself entirely, and his own hunger, in his earnest endeavors to remember those who have nothing whatever to eat!

In this respect, if in no other, is he a better teacher than the now famous men who preach the gospel of Mrs. Deland or Mrs. Humphrey Ward.

The Moral Purpose
in Howells's Novels

Anna Laurens Dawes*

Mr. Howells's writings cannot be confined within any one depart-
ment of literature, since among the thirty or more titles given us by the
catalogues we find travel, biography, essays, poetry, drama, and criticism
mingled with a sort of psychological autobiography making up fully
half the list. Yet he is so prominently and preëminently a novelist that
any general view of his work may well confine itself for the most part to
the consideration of fiction. Indeed it would be superfluous to justify
such a course. The subject also of a greater variety of opinions—covering
the whole range of praise and blame—than perhaps any other of his
contemporaries, that last and worst of literary experiences has not fallen
to his lot: Mr. Howells has never been forgotten! From school-girls to
philosophers the whole gamut of criticism has been sounded over his
style, his theories of art and life, his place in literature. But amongst it
all his end in writing has been too little considered, and the fact that
his fiction has always and increasingly a purpose in view has been altogether ignored, or the absence of such an intention has been deplored
as an acknowledged lack. It is still pertinent, therefore, to declare this
fact, whether it be for good or ill in the eye of the critic. It is especially
timely just now when the appearance of "Annie Kilburn" is thought by
many to mark a new departure in this author's work, a sudden turning off
from his usual *rôle* of social observer. It is quite unnecessary to consider
at this time Mr. Howells's well-known theory of realism. That is altogether a question of *method,* and as such belongs to the technical critique
alone. If the finest judges are to be believed, this is not the test of the
success or failure of a novel. In his famous essay on the "Art of Fiction,"
Henry James says: "It is not till I have accepted your data that I can
measure you: I have the standard, I judge you by what you propose."
If, then, the *end proposed* is the real criterion of novel-writing, it may
be well to first consider that. And here we are met with as many theories
as there are writers. Mr. Charles Dudley Warner claims that its object
is to entertain, and an English bishop has just now ably borne him out.
Mr. James himself declares, in his essay on Daudet, that the main object
of the novel is "to represent life"; but few would claim that this would be
always entertaining. It is obvious at least that no proper judgment of
Howells's work can be made without considering, first of all, what he
proposes. The further question of how far he has accomplished his object

Andover Review, 11 (January 1889), 23–36.

may still be left to the critics and the public. Carelessly enough, both these judges have too often been able to see in Mr. Howells only a superficial observer of life, a photographer of society, a dissecter of butterflies, or one who draws loathsome pictures of people and places quite unknown to eyes polite. He is not even wicked,—that were eagerly forgiven,—but he deals with the common and the vulgar, and that finds no forgiveness in this world. Let us try him by Henry James's fine test, and see if this is all. Let us hear his own words as to what he proposes. In a review of a certain novel we find this passage: "It can hardly fail to stir the reader into the wish to be a little truer, and this, young ladies and gentlemen who intend writing novels for the consideration of our successors, is a finer thing for the novel to do than to be entertaining." And, again, in an evidently authorized sketch of himself, he says that he has "never written a book yet simply for the sake of writing something for somebody to read, but always with the purpose of giving his readers something to thing about that should be useful and profitable to them, and to the world as well. . . ." Here is a writer whose books will not do for the idle hour. . . . they must be read in a strenuous mood. This view of the possible place and power of Howells's fiction raises it to a very high rank, and puts the question of its value to a different test from that commonly adopted.

    . . . . It is true that he who harnesses his muse to a horse-car cannot expect the rush and glory of the race-course, nor, indeed, is there that excitement in the palace-car that hangs about the chariot. Nevertheless, it is in this inglorious shape that, in our time, chivalry seeks love, and heroism finds a real expression. Therefore, when Mr. Howells chooses the streets of Boston rather than the heart of Africa for the setting of his picture, it is but another evidence of the purpose underlying his work. It is to prove that chivalry still exists, that heroism has found new channels rather than disappeared, that he tells us the story of "The Lady of the Aroostook," that he shows us Silas Lapham fighting the fires of temptation. He does not give us a glorification of the commonplace, but a revelation of it. Living will look no differently to our breakfast-table view of it, but the meaning of life—ah, the meaning in it—which will appear to him who reads Howells aright! We shall discover, if we will, the hope, the deep inspiration, even the high self-sacrifice in those we have thought to call the vulgar; the need of thought and care, and a sometimes tedious self-sacrifice for our fellow-men round about us here in the very streets of the town; the duties we will not see, because, forsooth, our brothers and sisters are of the horse-car, not the chariot. It may be that the general reader, as well as the critic, has somewhat captiously misunderstood Mr. Howells. Because he makes a strong and constant claim for realism in fiction, we have forgotten that he is dealing with the *methods* of his art, and not of the art itself, with its expression, not its substance. And if it be objected that he chooses too small a canvas, the picture cannot be forbidden its place on the line on account of its size. He himself has somewhere called this view of things "not breadth sidewise, but breadth upward and downward." Because Mr. Howells believes in a certain method of expression and certain lines of work, we have quarreled with all his ideas, and insist that he has no ends. It is perhaps, a little crass, this judgment. For not only has the author a high purpose, but his very method is an effort to realize it. You have but to hear him on that subject to discover that to him it is a vocation. Speaking in general of the realistic writer, Mr. Howells says: "In life he finds nothing insignificant; all tells for destiny and character; nothing that God has made is contemptible. He cannot look upon human life and declare this thing or that thing unworthy of notice, anymore than the scientist can declare a fact beneath the dignity of his inquiry. He feels in every nerve the equality of things and the unity of man; his soul is exalted, not by vain shows and shadows and ideals, but by realities in which the truth lives." These are the things William D. Howells would show us,—this is the mood in which he sets them down.

Mr. Howells's books are said to be written in two different manners. If this be true, and doubtless it is, the second manner is but the flower and fruit of the first. The later novels are intended as factors in a result; but if this cannot quite be said of the earlier efforts, they are by no means without their ends, and these also break out everywhere into high thought and noble aim. Single sentences, pregnant paragraphs, turns of action, subtle analyses of motive, all go to show the moral outlook, that unmistakable atmosphere of the heights that marks off the citizen thereof, wherever you find him. To the man furnished with this insight, *progress* can be only in one direction. The vision of the relationship of things, of the moral issues of thought and deed, cannot result in indifference, for by their own laws these develop purpose. Thus it is by no violent change that Howells's novels become novels with a direct purpose, "tendency novels" in some sense of the term. Beginning with the scarcely realized point of view, of character first and foremost, he has gone on to the position where he would fain bring about that character, but the beautiful meadows in the highlands of the Rocky Mountains are only another stage of the same journey that began in the foot-hills. Through the long series of his books, Howells has never been without some desire to disclose a hidden beauty, to unstop deaf ears, or to open blind eyes, and through the whole, the Pharisee is shown his true relation to the publican, Nicodemus is made to see that, after all, Zaccheus is nobler than he. If the better class gets no new view of itself, it certainly gets an entirely new view of the middle class, and even of the common people. . . .

Another much discussed story is "The Minister's Charge," frequently known as "that horrid story of Lemuel Barker." We have here a country boy with some genius and more character, but with all the limitations of a very narrow experience upon him, who comes to town relying upon the friendship of those who have interested themselves in him at home. These fail him signally at every turn, and we are shown the dangers and the friendships that do beset him, and we are shown also to what and whither necessity will drive him, and the effect upon him. In due course of affairs he imagines himself in love with a girl of his own sort but not of his own calibre, and then as life and experience develop his possibilities, he finds what a galling chain such connection may become through the teaching of a real and worthy love, and fights the old battle between conflicting duties. "Men are more like than unlike one another," says Mr. Howells in the Study; "let us make them know one another better that they may be all humbled and strengthened with a sense of their fraternity." Incidentally we are given several side issues of no small value, such as night lodging-houses, police courts, and the like. But especially does Lemuel Barker's history teach the need of friendly sympathy to those ignorant of life, and our culpability if we are too self-indulgent to give it. It is largely an exposition of our sins of omission. Lemuel himself, with his character mixed of strength and weakness, appeals to us all. His ability and his energy, his dogged perseverance and his weak yielding to circumstances, his exasperating vanity and pride, his impulsive and vacillating affections, make a very real whole, but his character appears in his moral strength which not only never entirely deserts him, but constantly dominates his action. His refusal to lie down upon Mr. Sewell for help given grudgingly, his various efforts to honestly help himself, his treatment of his friend the tramp, and his very devotion to that wretch contrasted with the always failing friendship of his own more sophisticated friends,—these and many other things show the strength and force of this character, trans-figured in his final determination to take up his life with Statira in all its hideousness. Poor pathetic Statira, alternately winning and repelling the reader, much as she did Lemuel himself! Is not her simplicity and her trust, and her devotion, the womanliness of her? Is not the silliness and vulgarity of that saleslady the product of an environment we will not lift a finger to help her out of—she nor one of her sisters? But never was anything better shown than the mixed nature of Sewell,—all the brave words of inspiration and helpfulness he could and did speak to his people as their minister, all his weakness as a man when duty laid off the gown and came down out of the pulpit and confronted him in unaccustomed place and time. From the title onward the story is an arraignment—how severe need not be said—of a philanthropy and a Christianity that has no room for constant brotherly care, and an argu-ment for something better. Nothing could be finer than Mr. Sewell's principles, but they are not put in practice, and in their place is Miss Vane's spasmodic intermittent charity, and Corey's dilettante interest, and that other futile selfishness which mistakes æsthetics for ethics, and thinks to give a flower when bread is asked. How eagerly we hope that Sewell will rise to his best self in the repeated chances the author gives him! But always he fails of his possibilities, loses his chance, and the reason for the failure we are made to see is the unwillingness on his part—the unreadiness is a better word—to put himself into mental sympathy with the man who asks his help. From beginning to end there is no lack of willingness to help Lemuel if he will take the ordinary methods of help which lie ready to hand—money, patronage, charity. This is the subtle but striking lesson of this book. It is a great deal of trouble to patiently seek the special mental attitude of those we would help, to put ourselves beside them and look at life with their eyes, to take them by the hand and lift them up. This requires time, thought, persistent patience, and the gift of ourselves; here is the real force of that simple word brotherliness, a word of which we have quite lost the meaning in losing out of it the figure of speech that is in it. Sewell would not where he could—could not always from a long lack of habit that way—put himself beside Lemuel, but looking down upon him from intellectual heights and moral highlands, he got no common ground with that unclassified youth, and the opportunity for help was gone.

Of such sort as I have tried to show are the books we cannot read, because they contain such odious characters, and the surroundings are so uninteresting. I have not heard that the "Inferno" is especially pleasant reading, nor "Les Miserables," for instance, nor even those modern favorites, the Russian novels. There is a famous old picture which represents the Holy Mother interceding for the plague-stricken city of Tours. She and all her heavenly train are contemplating the desolated city. In one corner a plump little angel shows his fellow a noisome skull, and the fascinating cherub is holding his nose at the sight! Nevertheless, it is averred that Tours was cured of the plague. . . .

Take "April Hopes," for example, where we have not only the inter-play of character, but the withering, blasting effect of a poor character, even though it is not a bad one; and the story is threaded through and through with ethical suggestion, reflection, analysis. The general reception of this novel, however, is another good example of the difficulty first referred to under which Mr. Howells labors. Here the sapient reader chiefly concerns himself with the wisdom or folly of the relations between the hero and the heroine. That is the sum of any novel, doubtless, but in this case it is not the *substance* of it. The havoc which may be wrought in life—her own and others—by the arrant egotism and unreal religion of a self-centered girl is very plainly drawn, and yet the critics ask what there is in this young woman's story that it should be writ large for the world to read. But these same critics find in Rosamond Vincy a lesson of selfishness and vanity for all the world, while Alice Pasmer, forsooth, is only "a bit of realism." It is true that the author of "Middlemarch," possibly wiser than the author of "April Hopes," always suggested to us the evil or the good we should find in her characters, but Mr. Howells leaves us with the photograph before us to draw our own inference. Hereafter he would do well, it would appear, to write after his work "This fable teaches." Nor is the character of Alice the only lesson of this book. Quite as strongly exhibited is the other sort of selfishness practiced by the charming Dan Mavering,—and by so many of his brothers and sisters outside of fiction,— that refined and subtle form of selfishness which must be comfortable even at the cost of truth itself, and which is ready to face any perplexity for other people in the future, if so be the present as a joyous hour. It is not for nothing that Mr. Howells so holds the mirror up to life for his readers.

The complications of love form the basis of all romance, even the romance of realism, but a comparative study of Mr. Howells's novels shows a frequency of treatment of one phase of the subject which cannot be accidental. The much mooted question of the nature and permanency and value of the bond that binds husband and wife is his text so often that he might almost be called the apostle to the married. We have two books definitely and directly related to this question, "Modern Instance" and "April Hopes," while "Dr. Breen's Practice" is about as much given over to the married flirt as to the woman doctor, and scarcely one of the other novels but deals in some way with the question of the mutual influence for good or ill of husbands and wives, or with the difficult question of mistaken marriages. Constantly we are reminded of the need of the iron band of duty for that dark hour when the silken bond of love has yielded to the strain. By plot, by character-drawing, by incidents minor and major, and by that privilege of the chorus granted to the impersonality of the author, Mr. Howells preaches the lesson that marriage is a high and holy thing, a sacrament and not a contract, and he brings before our consciences again and again the remembrance that obligation, opportunity, and rights are not the watchwords of married life, but love, and duty, and service.

Incidental evidence of the general position taken is found outside of the fiction proper. The claim that Mr. Howells has always been interested in the moral aspect of life is more than substantiated by his poems, written, some of them, at the very beginning of his career, or by "The Three Villages," with its story of high faith and martyrdom, and by many little touches in his sketches or his miscellaneous work. Of the other claim, that his present point of view is altogether ethical, an unintentional corroboration is found in the wails of a recent critic over his "Italian Poets." It is complained that the poets selected for discussion are chosen on the ground of their devotion to principle, their fervid patriotism, their zeal for an idea, and that they are edited with enthusiasm! This enthusiasm for the seer rather than the singer seems to be the heaviest point in the indictment. Still stronger proof, however, is found in the Editor's Study, especially in the reviews. Books are good or bad to him, in the last result, not only according to whether they are true to life, but chiefly by their sympathy with the higher nature, by their appreciation of purpose, their nobility or weakness. Very trifling work finds high appreciation at his hands if it has this spirit and quality, and much more ambitious writing falls before him wanting it; as he says in his sympathetic and most commendatory review of Cabot's "Emerson," "The literary merit of the book, to our present thinking, is always the least merit of a good book." Whether its editor deals with literature or life, every number of the Study shows a depth and active expression of the moral element becoming in these last days what may perhaps be called an outspoken *religious* view of life. Another evidence of Mr. Howells's position is his petition for clemency to the Anarchists. The present writer has no sympathy whatever for this particular position, but there have been of late few pieces of moral courage greater than this action. We can ask no stronger evidence of the strength of a man's convictions than the price he is willing to pay for them. By no means without sense or observation, Mr. Howells knew as well beforehand as we do now the storm of derision and wrath which would fall upon him on account of this action. It is possible to stand against wrath for any length of time, but derision drives us indoors at once. He must certainly have counted the cost before taking that most unpopular and most derided step. But having adopted the theory that peace is not to be purchased by bloodshed, nor right to be supported by the gallows, he must needs say so, let the result be what it would. There is no particular reason why the public should insist on calling him a dynamiter, or in laughing at him on that account, but he certainly knew beforehand that this would happen. It may be doubted if any of us are eager to face such results of our convictions. We find it very convenient to keep silent. at least when no questions are asked, in this matter of our unpopular convictions.

Mr. Howells's skill in accomplishing the ends he proposes is a question for the critic. It is sometimes objected that whatever he may intend. his books leave no strong moral impression and do not become factors in the reader's life. If this be true, a reason for the failure might perhaps be found in the fact that they are projected on the negative lines. Mr. Howells does not so much aim at making us love virtue as to make us hate vice. He shows us, for the most part, the hatefulness of evil, the shame of carelessness and neglect, the folly of our foibles. This method is more effective, doubtless, but hardly as effectual. He aims at the consciences of men, not their hearts; but men are wont to be moved by their hearts, and the conscience was ever a fearsome master, and sadly disobeyed. Neither are we now concerned with the influence of Count Tolstoi over his *style*, whether for good or ill. But the public and the critics in confining themselves to these questions strangely fail to discover that the great impelling force in this man's work has become a moral force. The direct influence of Leon Tolstoi's life and teachings on William Dean Howells is greater by an immeasurable power than any literary influence the novelist may have had. Mr. Howells sometimes invites the public into his holy places of late, and we do not find an empty sanctuary or vacant altars. "It is always possible," he says, in a paragraph which hardly needs reading between the lines to seem a sort of Apologia, "it is always possible to be unaffected, just as it is to be morally honest, to put our object before ourselves, to think more of the truth we see than of our poor little way of telling it, and to prize the fact of things beyond the effect of things. What if, after all, Tolstoi's power came from his conscience, which made it as impossible to caricature and dandify any feature of life as to lie or cheat? What if he were so full of the truth and so desirous to express it for God's sake and man's sake that he would feel the slightest unfaithfulness to it a sin? This is not wholly incredible of such a man, though it is a hard saying for those who write merely from the artistic standpoint long vaunted as the highest."

The Editor's Easy Chair

George W. Curtis*

The literary judgments which are handed down in the neighboring tribunal, the Study, are so sound and thoughtful and humane, so obviously rendered solely in the interest of truth and candor, of good literature and morality, that, although like all judgments of that character, they sometimes arouse dissent, they never draw into question either the ability or the purpose of the bench. Even in the great case in which Thackeray and Dickens appeared as defendants, although upon certain important points judgment went against them, there is no doubt that the opinion of the court induced a very general reconsideration of the merits, and there was some revising of conclusions believed to be immutably settled. The Easy Chair, of counsel, asked

*Reprinted from *Harper's Monthly*, 80 (January 1890), 313–14.

respectfully, indeed, to have certain exceptions noted to the judicial description of the defendant Thackeray as "caricaturist," but with a becoming sense of the weight which must always attach to the decisions of the full bench of the Study upon all such points.

In re Walter Scott, there was some strenuous demur, but whether strictly upon the merits, or from pious or other deference to tradition, did not clearly appear. The general ground, however, seemed to be that where unquestionable genius had produced undeniable effects of the highest value to universal harmless recreation, it must be held to have satisfied the purposes of literary art, and the old case was cited of the birds pecking at the grapes, which was held to establish the fact that the fruit was well painted. The opinion in the famous case of the Jane Austen miniatures is, however, undisputed. That no more exquisite work of the kind has been accomplished, and that all its effects are legitimately produced, is not questioned even by the captious. It is harmoniously acknowledged that the power of machine is as finely demonstrated in paring an apple as in driving a pile.

The prodigious service of the high court of the Study lies in the fact that its judgments proceed upon clearly conceived fundamental principles. The function of criticism is something else than the expression of a feeling. It is the estimate of works of the imagination by the canons of literary art, which are not arbitrary and whimsical, and the very first and chief of which is holding the mirror up to nature. The genius may be gladly acknowledged and its power felt, but it must not be supposed that consequently its methods are the best, even for its own expression or object. This is a point made in the case of Laurence Sterne at the close of the last century—a case well worthy of study, as it is set forth in the volume of cases of the English Humorists (Thackeray, W. M.).

A novel or story is a work of art, and the primary condition of art is that it shall represent what is, not what is not. It is obvious that unless it conforms to this rule—if it represents what is not—it is at once beyond the pale of intelligent or intelligible judgment. This is but to say that the work must be real. In the celebrated case of William Wordsworth, who alleged a certain "light that never was on sea or land," it was not claimed that he had depicted it, or asserted that it could be depicted, except by means of a skillful use of the light which, it is common knowledge, lies visibly both upon land and sea. Thus realism is of the very substance of legitimate fiction, and Tom Thumb and the *Arabian Nights* cannot be pleaded in bar. Indeed, even the Arabian decisions hold that "in all true poetry there must be palmtrees and running water," and mirages are ruled out of court because they are not real, or admitted only because they represent familiar reality.

The object of the Easy Chair in alluding to the neighboring tribunal, however, is less to speak of the judgments rendered in the Study than to note one which has not been and will not be handed down, but which relates to a case even more important than the larger part of the current cases of which the Study disposes. The default arises from no carelessness or forgetfulness, but from reasons which will be readily comprehended. Upon the calendar of new cases of fiction that of *A Hazard of New Fortunes,* by Howells, W. D., appears at the head, but the decision of the Study, C. J., will be awaited in vain, and the Easy Chair, J., must therefore read the opinion.

The story is entirely a tale of to-day, and of to-day in New York. It is what has been long desired and often attempted, but never before achieved, a novel of New York life in the larger sense. In reading a book like Dickens's *Mutual Friend,* with its vivid pictures of certain aspects of London Life, or in recalling the many famous stories of which the interest and character and life are all of London, how often the American reader has wondered when will this spell be woven from observation of the life of New York! Is it an essentially unsuggestive city? Was Hawthorne's sigh in the last generation justified, that there is nothing picturesque, nothing to stimulate the creative imagination in America? Or is it rather all latent there, and awaiting only the sympathetic eye and mind and hand to reveal it, as the kindly heat discloses invisible writing?

This question is answered by Mr. Howells's latest story. It shows that New York supplies all the elements and conditions that creative fiction requires, and that their proper romantic effect demands the realism, as it is called, which characterizes his genius. Great and vulgar wealth, the contrasts of social condition, the "push" and advertising instinct, the tender cynicism of refined intelligence, the mingling of Southern, Western, and Eastern traditions and characters in the cosmopolitan Babel, all shot through with individual passion, aspiration, sympathy, affection, with dramatic incident, pathos, humor, and tragedy, the whole web held and woven by a firm, sympathetic, comprehensive master-hand, produce such a piece of realism as holds the mirror up to nature, and at once illustrates and vindicates every principle which the Study has maintained and applied in its judgments of contemporary story.

The taste which is "tired of humdrum commonplace people," which does not "find stupid folks entertaining because they are described in novels," which wishes "to be cheered and recreated by being lifted out of the familiar rut, and introduced to stirring and romantic incident, to the stormy play of passion and sweet emotion, afar from tea parties and Newport flirtations," will find in this tale its desire of passion, romance, and emotional interest gratified, but gratified in the familiar figures and characteristic incidents of New York life. It deals with the springs of that life which is but a part of universal human life. The tender-hearted reader who was weeping yesterday over Scott's *Pirate*, or any other novel that seems to stir the soft source of tears even more delightfully, will find not less pathos and romantic charm here, although there be Lindau for Norna of the Fitful Head, and the drama proceed in the houses and streets that the reader knows. It is a story of real life in the truest sense, a microcosm of America, a table which, like all works of the imagination, reveals another world beneath itself.

This is the general character of *A Hazard of New Fortunes*. The details of the story the reader would not thank us for disclosing. Its earnestness, force, and humanity are all characteristic of sincere art. It might be alleged that the tale lags a little in getting under way, but the shrewd humor of the dalliance is full compensation. Then how clean it is! how wholesome! how temperate! how true! Like Balzac, here is a student of life; but, unlike Balzac, here is a sweet and open and generous mind, and a picture firm with clear insight and glowing with human sympathy.

Mr. Howells's Latest Novels

Hamlin Garland*

There is no man in American literature to-day who so challenges discussion as the candid writer of the *Editor's Study*, which has come to be the expression of Americanism in art and literature. Mr. Howells has become an issue in the literary movement of the day, and his utterances from month to month have the effect of dividing the public into two opposing camps. It is no common man whose name can thus become the synonym for a great literary movement; and those who know him the most intimately feel the greatest admiration for him as he pursues his way calmly through the hail of ignoble personalities which opposing critics have ceaselessly rained upon him. He is writing upon conviction, and convictions are not changed by splenetic assaults, especially if these convictions are begotten and sustained by the spirit of a great social movement. The innovator in literature is a sort of Arnold Winkelried; and though he receives the lances of the confronting host, he feels that he has a dauntless band behind him, small though it may be.

*Reprinted from the *New England Magazine*, NS 2 (May 1890), 243–250.

Fifteen years ago Mr. Howells was one of the novelists most favorably received by the general careless American public. He wrote charming and graceful stories and essays, and no one thought of assaulting him. He did not stand for progress, did not enunciate definite opinions, and the conservative public considered him delightful for summer reading. He amused the public. Fifteen years is a short time, but it has brought to the author of *A Hazard of New Fortunes* more changes mentally than fall to the lot of most men during an entire lifetime. He has deepened and broadened, gathering sympathy and tenderness, and as a consequence his books have deepened in insight and broadened in humanity. The attention to style, the graceful turn of a phrase are there still, but they are only the scrolls on the column. The first need now is utterance; the form, although not less finished and faithful, has become secondary.

If we attempt to trace out this change in Mr. Howells, we find it beginning in *A Woman's Reason*, where he first grapples with the false and incomplete education of women. This book was in fact a satire, very tender and subtle, and those who have criticised his treatment of women have missed the point entirely, in this and in subsequent books. By showing folly its own image, whether in man or woman, he has labored since the publication of that book for the advancement of men and women alike. He studied American life as few men ever study life, and the results were seen in each new volume.

In each succeeding work his canvas thickened with figures, as his insight grew keener and his range of life broader. *A Modern Instance* came as a magnificent surprise, even to those who knew the writer best, so great was the advance in scope and power. It had a motive, and though the author remained artistically out of sight behind the characters, one felt that a master hand had stated the problem. *A Modern Instance* was a superb book. It had all the grace of humor which his readers had learned to look for, and it had moments of new and surprising force. . . .

That Mr. Howells thus caught and recorded unprecedentedly well a part of the social questioning of our day is not a decline, but an advance in his art. Social regeneration is a living issue—it is in the air, and as a living, present problem is the properest of all subjects for the pen of our greatest novelist. He would have been false to his theories and blind to the world he is depicting had he not taken up the question of progress and poverty, which is alarming and confusing so many minds. It is impossible to go into any town alive to the world without finding Mr. Putney and Mr. Gerrish discussing the question of poverty. It is the theme of every speech; the magazines are full of special articles upon it. The tax-dodger is a reality, the laborers in mills are crying out, orators are going about advocating free trade and free land, the whole of England and America being in a foment. We are living in great days, and the novelist should rightfully be he who has keenest ear, subtlest art of representation, and clearest head. He should teach, but concretely, objectively, not by stopping in the midst of his story to deliver harangues in the manner of the old school. We are no longer children to be fed on pap. Let the novelist give us food—solid bread and meat—and we will chew it for ourselves. This is the aim of such a book as *Annie Kilburn*. The book was full of the most far-reaching questions, and it announced the immense deepening and widening of the author's sympathy. There has been no writing previously in America at once so purposeful and so artistic. It is electric with inquiry. . . .

In the two-volume novel, *A Hazard of New Fortunes*, Mr. Howells ended all question about his supremacy as an American novelist of life,— if the word novel needs any such addenda. In it he reaches his greatest breadth and his deepest research. He seizes upon the serious social problems now rising in the great cities, their forms, and their developments. To me the book appears the most impressive and the sanest study of a city ever made, and it as much a product of the times as the electric car. It is the logical sequence of *Annie Kilburn* and *Silas Lapham*.

It is interesting to observe the steady growth in the power to handle masses, which the later books show. . . . To go from *Annie Kilburn* to *A Hazard of New Fortunes* is like leaving the quiet and elm-shaded village roads of Hatboro', and plunging into actual New York. The author, leaving his retirement, has joined the vast currents of human action confluent in our greatest city, a city where the pressure of human life is appalling, where men live two hundred and ninety thousand to the square mile; where they roar through crevasses called streets, and sleep in dens called homes. Into the midst of the splendid, terrible restless city, our novelist cast himself, and the result is a marvellous book that is at once a work of art and a profound criticism. It is a section of real life. In it men live and love and die as in real life. There are strikes, the war called business, and there are beautiful and devoted souls living lives of charity in the hope of repairing the havoc caused by the greed of others. It is full of real individuals, and we comprehend aims, and judge character as in real life.

It is interesting to put this book over against the old-time studies of the city, where the houses were askew, doors battered and swinging, blinds squeaking in the blast, trap-doors and cellars full of spooks; cities filled with caricatures mainly, streams of men with wooden legs or horrible noses, women too short or too thin, warty, beery—bloodless exaggerations and grotesque peculiarities doing duty as characters, and walking the Rembrandtesque shadows of ram-shackle, perilous, and endless streets; impossible cities filled with impossible beings, arranged in symmetrical groups of good and bad; the city of the humorist and the satirist, but not the reality. Here there is no concealing the misery and the crime of life; on the contrary, the blessed sunlight falls upon the filth and grime of the streets, making the contrast still more hideous and complete. The romantic glooms are stripped from the haunts of vice and poverty, and the terrible squalor appalls by its very commonness and nakedness. The reader walks its streets with the author and studies its life while the sun is shining; there is no mystery but the mystery of misery and fruitless labor, no romance beyond the romance of men and women trying to be good and just under conditions which tempt them to be mean and selfish.

As the author's canon of art is to perceive and state as he perceives, and because the question concerning the persistence of poverty in the midst of abounding wealth is everywhere being asked, and social life is full of reformers, therefore in the book of the present we have an elaborate and impartial study of the reform spirit of the day. It will undoubtedly alienate him completely from the ultra conservative class, but it must as certainly win the regard and admiration of all those whose sympathies are broadening with the growing altruism of the age, and deepening with the intellectual perception of the art-value of the infinite drama of our common life.

This book, like *Annie Kilburn*, is artistic in that, while it is filled with the fear and wonder of a great and sympathetic nature when facing the life of the city, it also never preaches. The writer speaks through his characters. It is full of thought that makes the flesh tingle and the breath quicken. There are dramatic episodes treated with perfect freedom from "effectism." It has everywhere the great corrective humor, which forbids exaggeration and fanaticism. Yet it is unswerving in its criticism of things as they are. . . .

Personally one of the most genial and lovable of men, Mr. Howells is the last person to be taken as a controversialist. His ready laugh and inexhaustible fund of humor make the casual acquaintance wonder if this can be the author of *A Hazard of New Fortunes* and the target of all the conservative criticisms. But there come moments when the head droops and the strength of the face comes out, and the eyes deepen and darken, till the visitor sees before him one of the greatest personalites in America,—a personality so great that it is content to become the humble percipient and recorder of realities, and so sure of itself as to bow to no criterion but truth.

Mr. Howells carries the sturdy figure and the direct and simple bearing of the man whose boyhood held many a hardship, and who has fought his way to where he is against poverty and discouragement. No man could be more democratic, more approachable, more sympathetic. He has the poet's love for nature, for color, but above all, love for humanity. As one writer has well put it, Mr. Howells "knows how it is himself." This is the quality which makes the author of *Annie Kilburn* and *A Hazard of New Fortunes*. It is a quality that is endearing him daily to new circles of readers, who feel that he is stating their case, is voicing their hopes and defeats and longings. The *dilettante* reader may reject Mr. Howells, but earnest, thinking, suffering men and women find him greater and deeper and truer every day.

As the art which Mr. Howells represents declines to be held accountable to any age, or land, or individual, so it discourages discipleship. It says to the young writer: "Look to nature and to actuality for your model—not to any book, or man, or number of men. Be true to yourself. Write of that of which you know the most and feel the most, and follow faithfully the changes in your feeling. Put yourself down before common realities, common hopes, common men, till their pathos and mystery and significance flood you like a sea, and when the life that is all about you is so rich with drama and poetry, and the vista of human thought and passion so infinite that you are in despair of ever expressing a thousandth part of what you feel, then all idea of discipleship will be at an end. Your whole aim will be to be true to yourself and your infinite teacher, nature, and you will no longer strive to delineate beauty, but truth, and at last truth will be beauty."

The realist of the stamp of Valdes and Howells, so far from being "materialistic," is really a mystic. He reaches at last the mysticism of the philosopher, to whom matter is as mysterious as spirit; of Whitman, who says that "every cubic inch of space is a miracle." "In nature," says Valdes, "there is nothing great or small; nothing is trivial absolutely. All depends upon the mind perceiving; and values are relative in art as in all else." So that to call the work of these realists vulgar or material is to beg the question. To whom are they vulgar or trivial? To say that the modern novel deals largely with the particular is true; that is its distinction. This has been superbly stated by Véron: "We care no longer for gods or heroes, we care for men. . . ."

Only when the development of literature and art, the incessant change of ideals from age to age, is recognized, as the comparative critic sees it, can full justice be done to the group of young writers now rising in America, who represent this new tendency, and of whom Mr. Howells is the champion and the unquestioned leader.

Mr. Howells's Latest Novel

Annie R. M. Logan*

'A Hazard of New Fortunes' differs essentially from those novels by Mr. Howells which might be arranged in a series appropriately entitled 'Boston Under the Scalpel,' or 'Boston Torn to Tatters' or 'The True Inwardness of Boston.' The difference is not in motive, for, from the beginning, he has adhered uncompromisingly to the only motive which he considers worthy, that of depicting life as he sees it, as it appears to his outward and inward vision; it is shown in a wider outlook, a deeper insight, an expansion of sympathy, and especially in a sensitiveness to emotional tragedy the actuality of which he has hitherto almost denied. The novel is perhaps no cleverer than 'Silas Lapham' or 'A Modern Instance,' but it is greater in just the same way that Mr. James's 'Princess Casamassima' is greater than his sharpest satire of Boston society or wittiest international episode. Both novels are the expression of observation of the multiform life of great cities, and of sufficient self-identification with it to produce a faithful and vivid picture. In London Mr. James heard and understood the cry of humanity for something better than it has or knows—a cry that gathers volume from age to age, and tones from the four winds of heaven. Mr. Howells has heard the same cry in New York; he has caught its shrill notes, its weak notes, its false notes, and has recognized the unbroken undertone of tragedy and sorrow.

*Reprinted from the *Nation*, 50 (5 June 1890), 454–55.

Mr. Howells's Literary Creed

Horace E. Scudder*

It was somewhat of a shock to Mr. Howells's readers, and therefore to his friends, for all his readers are his friends, when in one of his novels two or three years ago they came upon a light and trifling reference to his own fiction. In spite of its playfulness it jarred on the ear; it was something to be accounted for, to be excused, to be defended. But this new *Apologia pro Arte mea*[1] is so aggressive in tone, so shrill almost in its pitch of voice, that the reader is compelled to listen

*Reprinted from *Atlantic Monthly*, 68 (October 1891), 566–69.

attentively, and possibly to readjust his notions regarding this writer. May it not be, one asks, that the change of subject noticeable in Mr. Howells's recent work is consentaneous with a new outlook on his part? If there is a wider scope and more generous humanity in A Hazard of New Fortunes than in The Lady of the Aroostook, ought we not to look for a note in his criticism as gathered in this little book different from, or rather fuller and richer than, that which sounded in the book notices to which one turns with pleasure still as one looks over old files of The Atlantic, *consul Planco*?

Far be it from us to set out on a study of Howells in his first and second periods. How do we know that there will not be a third which will offer even a better vantage-ground for observing the intellectual path made by him? Rather, we postpone to the days of our children this interesting task of historical analysis, and leave to them the thesis of establishing his identity by means of his successive developments. We have something better to do with a contemporaneous author. Imaginary perspectives are illusory, and we must accept whatever disadvantage there may be in using our own angle of observation when on the same parallel line with this novelist and critic. The views which he sets forth are working views; they concern his neighbors and friends who are engaged in the same pursuit, and we cannot treat them merely as an interesting contribution to nineteenth-century criticism which we in the twentieth are classifying and reducing to order in our history of the development of literature.

This being so, we cannot fail to be struck with the sincerity of the utterance. Whether or not we agree with the conclusions reached by Mr. Howells, we must admit that the very intemperateness of his zeal, the almost incoherence of his protestations, bears witness to the fact that his literary creed as regards criticism and fiction is not a cool intellectual dogma, but a belief *quicunque vult*. His playfulness does not altogether desert him,—indeed, it betrays him into expressions which his critics, willfully or not, seize upon as fresh illustrations of his supposed arrogance; but for the most part he is too much in earnest to catch up any lighter weapons than sarcasm and irony. Nor does he look to his defenses, and with a carelessness which is born, not of confidence, but of zeal, troubles himself little with consistency, and accentuates his doctrines by personal illustrations which he makes sweeping that he may not weaken the force of his argument by too many modifications. One is not tempted to liken him to Proudhon, who, when he was expostulated with for his extravagant assertion Property is Robbery, replied that he put his price high because he know he should be beaten down. There is no note of audacious exaggeration in Mr Howells's vehment assertions; he almost forgets the humorist in him as he strikes his blows and invites his opponents to come on.

It is easy, therefore, to find weaknesses in his position; to divert attention from the main question by indignantly declaring that he is slandering Scott and Thackeray, and setting up a Russian idol in place of our native gods. A juster view discovers that his contention is for art in its relation to human nature and human history; that the figures whom he uses are not so much directly the subjects of his criticism as they are concrete examples of artistic tendencies. In his eagerness to preach his doctrines he ignores the offenses of those whom he holds to have the true faith at heart, and overlooks the shining virtues of those who are to him worshipers of false gods. The dreariness of Ibsen, the false proportions of Margaret Fleming, may be forgiven; the fine honor, the noble recognition of service, displayed in Scott's characters are forgotten.

Yet is not this narrowness of intention a defect in a critic? Does it not argue the mind of a special pleader rather than of a judge? Unquestionably, and this admission would damage our estimate of Mr. Howells as a critic, if his book in its very fibre did not renounce pretensions to criticism as that word is generally understood It would indeed be a *reductio ad adsurdum* if we could suppose Mr. Howells savagely girding against critics for the purpose of demonstrating that he is himself a critic. It is true that now and then he takes his place in the prisoners' dock along with these literary criminals, but there is a mockery in this suppositious attitude which precludes deceit. No, wherever else he may deliberately discriminate, and divide, and seek with the self-effacement which belongs to the genuine critic to get at the bottom of the well, the patience which such study demands is not to be found in this little book. Here he is an apostle ardently declaring his gospel; a crusader who knows only two classes of men, believers and paynims. It is in this light only that one can view his book.

What, then, is the truth for which Mr. Howells contends, and counts all else as dross? What is the central idea about which all his deliverances gather? What does he want of us,—especially what does he want of his fellow-craftsmen? In looking through his book for some single expression of his belief we find it somewhat difficult to settle upon any one phrase; for if we content ourselves with his final statement, that "neither arts, nor letters, nor sciences, except as they . . . tend to make the race better and kinder, are to be regarded as serious interests, . . . and they cannot do this except from and through the truth;" or take his initial proposition "that moods and tastes and fashions change, . . . but what is unpretentious and what is true is always beautiful and good, and nothing else is so," we find truisms not to be quarreled with; yet we are only at the threshold of our inquiry, for the question forces itself upon us, to be asked in no spirit of mockery, What is Truth? The most fatal error a critic could make would be to assume that the only truth in art is what commends itself to him as truth. Here are words which bring us a little closer to Mr. Howells's mind:—

"I believe that, while inferior writers will and must continue to imitate them"—great writers, that is, who have sinned against the truth—"in their foibles and their errors, no one hereafter will be able to achieve greatness who is false to humanity, either in its facts or its duties. The light of civilization has already broken even upon the novel, and no conscientious man can now set about painting an image of life without perpetual question of the verity of his work, and without feeling bound to distinguish so clearly that no reader of his may be misled between what is right and what is wrong, what is noble and what is base, what is health and what is perdition, in the actions and characters he portrays. . . . I confess that I do not care to judge any work of the imagination without first of all applying this test to it. We must ask ourselves before we ask anything else, Is it true?—true to the motives, the impulses, the principles, that shape the life of actual men and women? This truth, which necessarily includes the highest morality and the highest artistry,—this truth given, the book cannot be wicked and cannot be weak; and without it all graces of style and feats of invention and cunning of construction are so many superfluous of naughtiness. It is well for the truth to have all these and shine in them, but for falsehood they are merely meretricious, the bedizenment of the wanton; they atone for nothing, they count for nothing. But in fact they come naturally of truth, and grace it without solicitation; they are added unto it. In the whole range of fiction we know of no true picture of life—that is, of human nature—which is not also a masterpiece of literature, full of divine and natural beauty. It may have no touch or tint of this special civilization or that; it would better have this local color well ascertained; but the truth is deeper and finer than aspects, and if the book is true to what men and women know of one another's souls it will be true enough, and it will be great and beautiful."

If we read this passage aright, Mr. Howells believes that a new era has dawned in fiction so radically different as to render all the achievements of the past at once antiquated; that the distinction between the old and the new is as wide as between artificiality and naturalness that whereas the novel of the past was false to human nature, the only test to be applied to contemporaneous and future fiction is its fidelity to truth. There is no doubt that the range of fictitious writing has broadened and taken in subjects which once were treated only in the drama, in history, or in essays, and we agree with Mr. Howells in a remark elsewhere made that they "form the whole intellectual life of immense numbers of people;" there has been a development likewise in the form of the novel, so that it requires some training or historical imagination to enjoy early examples, and with the greater freedom and flexibility which the novelist has attained there is greater opportunity for the full expression of individual genius; the bounds of fiction have been extended greatly. But what proof can he allege that this development, which has been steady and normal, has suddenly become a cataclysm? It would have been a more tenable position to hold that Walter Scott's romances marked a new era in fiction, and that all behind belonged to the dark ages.

In Mr. Howells's creed there is an assumption that the present generation is possessed of finer perception and is more acutely sensitive to truth in fiction, but it is incredible that men's judgments as to truth in one form of literature should vary with the generations. There are many persons now who are misled by the false notes in Ibsen and Tolstoi, but it does not therefore follow that they would have been quick to respond to the healthy, generous sentiment of Scott. The apprehension of truth, like the expression of truth, is fundamental in human nature, and not the fortune of one favored generation. Fashions change, and it is entirely possible that the form of fiction which once was acceptable should now seem tiresome; but if our ancestors could read some of the microscopic fiction of the present day, we suspect they would cry out for something more in mass, less in detail. "The touch of nature is there," they might say, "but we prefer nature in larger form. Grasshoppers do not interest us, no matter how truthful. We prefer leopards." That truth is the test of art in fiction as in all forms of literature is undeniable; but then the test has always been applied; it is no new discovery.

There is again in Mr. Howells's creed an assumption that literary art is of necessity false; that art is a foe to the best fiction. It is true that he understands by art something that is derivative and not in itself original, but there is throughout his book a latent distrust of any art of fiction. "Graces of style, feats of invention, cunning of construction," these come near contempt, yet they are notes of art which, whether in fiction or poetry, has served to keep alive one work, when its neighbor, though it may have been true to fact, has perished ignominiously. We are entering, some of us think, upon a period when almost every one will write fiction, and there would be little comfort for the few of us left to read and not write if we did not believe that grace of style, feats of invention, and cunning of construction would separate some of the productions and make them worth reading. Art is the interpreter of nature, not its traducer, and in fiction as in all literature he who sees wholes and not fragments is the master. It is a mere gloss of the scholiast which makes creation to be the production of something out of nothing; in genuine theology as in genuine art the creator shapes and fashions forms of chaotic material and breathes into them the breath of life.

With the passionate demand for truth in fiction and the denunciation of all artificiality which are prevalent notes in Mr. Howells's book one may be in entire sympathy, without in the least believing that the portrayers of human life who are using fiction as a vehicle for conveying their diseased or hopeless views upon the character of our civilization and the destiny of man are any more close to the truth than men and women who, taking great delight in life, and unvisited by dreadful visions of the future, have built in their imagination from the materials lying about them beautiful palaces of art. A king is no doubt an obsolete sort of a creature, and the Pretender was a dismal failure, but loyalty is not a democratic invention, though it has been improved upon by democracies. Young people may safely be left in the company of paper courtiers if the man behind the courtier has not been obliterated, and something less than an historic imagination will long continue to be touched by the creations of the past.

In short, the difficulty with Mr. Howells's literary creed is the difficulty which attaches to many religious creeds. The fundamental truth may be there, but the creed is dreadfully contemporaneous and hopelessly individual. Because one is vividly impressed by existing conditions, and discovers, it may be, here one and there one whose cry is like his own, he mistakes the accidental for the permanent, and straightway insists that the truth, though admittedly universal, must be stated in certain formulas. We are more disposed to think that what is technically known as realism is a phase of literature which corresponds with much that is contemporary in science and religion, but that, so far from being the final word in literature, it will simply make its contribution to art and give place to purer idealism.

Notes

1. W. D. Howells, *Criticism and Fiction* (New York: Harper & Brothers, 1891).

Recent Essays in Criticism

Brander Matthews*

Mr. Howells's little volume is substantially a selection of the papers which he has been publishing monthly in the "Editor's Study," stripped of all special criticism of individual books and limited to the discussion of general principles. In other words, it is a coördinated code of criticism—the body of doctrine which Mr. Howells believes and declares, and by which he is willing to stand his trial. It is apparently a complete and adequate presentation of the subject, free and direct and unencumbered by any digression or excursus. As a critic, Mr. Howells's attitude has often been combative, not to say aggressive; sometimes it seemed almost as though he longed to see all mankind wearing one coat that he might tread on the tail of it. Now, a good critic is not known by the chips on his shoulder; suavity is the badge of all his tribe—or should be. But there is such a thing as militant criticism—what else are Schlegel's Lectures on Dramatic Literature? When M. Zola gathered together into a volume the polemical papers he had been contributing to the Figaro, he called the book Une Campagne. And this is what Mr. Howells's tiny tome might also be called; it is a sortie against those who are besieging the citadel of literary art. There are those who have said that Mr. Howells lacked the breadth of equipment which the ideal critic should possess, and that he did not carry about in his hand a sufficiency of standards of comparison. No doubt there is a basis for this charge; but it is true also that Mr. Howells has brought the zest of discovery to his new appreciation of certain of the classics which other critics toiled over in college classrooms. And this freshness of taste is not without compensating advantages. Mr. Howells's writing was never perfunctory, and even when it seemed most arbitrary it was unfailingly stimulant. It performed the most useful office of forcing those who did not agree with him and those whom his criticism arided to formulate their views in opposition.

One of Mr. Howells's chief titles to gratitude is that he has done not a little toward destroying the tradition of deference toward British criticism. Here in America respect for contemporary British criticism is a survival of colonialism. In its judgments of America and of Americans the British criticism of this last quarter of the nineteenth century is insular almost always, and ignorant very often. It is inspired by that contemptuous hostility which the Greek had for the Barbarian, the Jew for the Gentile and the Englishman for the Foreigner; and despite all external similarities, we Yankees are to the British the most foreign of foreigners. A typical instance of British criticism of this sort is to be

*Cosmopolitan Magazine, 12 (November 1891), 124–26.

found in a volume of Essays in English Literature 1780–1860, put forth
in London last winter by one of the most industrious contributors to the
periodicals of London. In an introductory essay on The Kinds of Criticism, the writer holds up Mr. Howells and Mr. Howells's method of
criticism as an awful warning. "Some of my friends jeer or comminate
at Mr. Howells," says this British critic, "for my part I only shudder,
and echo the celebrated, 'There, but for the grace of God.'" A fling
like this may seem to some arrogant and to others impudent; to me it
seems chiefly conceited, as though it needed the interposition of heaven
to prevent an Englishman of this sort from resembling an American like
Mr. Howells: ne fait ce tour qui veut.

Other instances of personal criticism closely akin to this could be
collected from the pages of the London Athenaeum and of the Saturday
Review. Perhaps the Saturday Review is the chief offender. And I say
this with no personal dislike of the Saturday Review, to which journal,
indeed, it has been my privilege to contribute now and again, during
the past eight or ten years; its editor is an ancient ally of mine—we have
written short stories together; and two of its chief contributors are among
the very best friends I have. But the Saturday Review is the typical
organ of "The Poor Islanders"—a delightful and undying nickname, for
which they will not readily pardon Mr. Howells. It dislikes all foreigners
and especially all Americans; it has the bad manners which generally
accompany unreasoning dislikes; and in literature it is wedded to false
idols. In literature as in politics it is obstinately conservative, Tory,
reactionary. It sets its face resolutely towards the past, and any stray
glance it may venture towards the future brings an instant frown upon
its brow. It did not like Thackerary when that great novelist was alive.
It does not like Mr. Howells when he advocates the views which one
may hazard a guess that Thackeray would hold if he were now alive.
Without espousing all of Mr. Howells's opinions, I confess that a perusal
of his collected essays has left me with the belief that he is not far wrong
in the main question however widely he may err in matters of detail.

Mr. Howells's book is little more than a plea for truth in fiction.
It is a request that literature shall be judged by life and not by the
library. He quotes with approval Burke's assertion that "the true standard
of the artist is in every man's power" already; and he agrees with Michael
Angelo that the "light of the piazza," the glance of the common eye,
"is and always was the best light on a statue." He is a true democrat of
literature and puts his trust in the common people, as did Abraham
Lincoln. He is a good American, and he calls us to consider our own life
and not the pale reflection of foreign life as we find it in the ordinary
English novel. He tells us that "an English novel, full of titles and rank,
is apparently essential to the happiness" of some people who like hash

many times warmed over because this calls for no effort of mental mastication. "Whereas a story of our own life, honestly studied and faithfully represented, troubles them with varied misgiving. They are not sure that it is literature; they do not feel that it is good society; its characters, so like their own, strike them as commonplace; they say they do not wish to know such people."

In urging these truths with unfailing felicity, if at times with undue force, Mr. Howells has deserved well of all who love letters and who abhor the cut-and-dried, the ready-made, the artificial. But in his fight for truth, for nature, even if it be raw, perhaps Mr. Howells is unduly negligent of form. "Life is not rounded in an epigram," as George Eliot said, and art must needs be selection. The masterpieces of literature are not mere fragments of human existence seized at haphazard; they have a beginning, a middle and an end. They are composed as a picture is composed. To say this is not to ask for a so-called "plot," any more than one would expect to find in the Paris Salon of this year a picture with composition according to the formulas of the Bolognese school. It is to ask for the harmonious and complete presentation of the subject, such a presentation as one found in Their Wedding Journey and in The Rise of Silas Lapham, such as one failed to find in A Hazard of New Fortunes, in which certain episodes seemed disproportionate.

A graver failing of Mr. Howells's is his unfairness to Thackeray. Dickens we may abandon to him; Dickens is the delight of those who like their humor cut thick and their pathos laid in slabs; Dickens was rarely an artist, and we file no protest when Mr. Howells declares that Dickens's "literary principles seem almost as grotesque as his theories of political economy." But Thackeray, with all his defects, was an artist at heart. There is no more rigorous artistic work in the whole history of English fiction than Barry Lyndon and Henry Esmond. When he chose, Thackeray was an artist of the strictest sect. That he did not always choose may be admitted; that he was lazy and procrastinating he confessed; and that he filled up the monthly part of his periodical novel as best he could at the last minute, with the printer's devil at the door, is unfortunately obvious enough. But to speak of him as a caricaturist merely, is to use language carelessly; and to praise Trollope at Thackeray's expense is an abuse even of the privileges of polemical criticism. Mr. Howells has not here reprinted the passage in which he compared Charles Reade from afar with George Eliot, but it will be present in the minds of many readers who think that the same difference separates Trollope from Thackeray. On more than one page Mr. Howells is more forcible than suave, and he is at his best when he is most urbane.

Literary Notes

Laurence Hutton*

Mr. Howells's *An Imperative Duty* is a work of a very different kind, and it treats of a social problem much more serious than the conundrums is a man a gentleman because he wears a "stove-pipe hat," and is a woman a lady, no matter who she is, or what she does, or how much she knows? The story turns upon that peculiar condition of our mixed population in this country, which, as Mr. Howells observes, "vexes our social question with its servile past, and promises to keep it uncomfortable with its civic future"; and the chapter in which he describes the momentous interview between the niece and the aunt, where the girl learns for the first time that her grandmother was a slave, and that she herself has black blood in her veins, is as powerful as anything in modern fiction.

Mr. Howells does not attempt to solve the Negro Problem, as it is called. He does not try to explain why a man who would not think of sitting at table with his white servants is considered inconsistent because he does not sit at table with his servants who are black. He does not even affirm that all negroes are *not* servants. He simply asks in an indirect way why a man who is one-eighth African, is not as good as a man who is one-quarter European, or one-half Asiatic, or all American Indian. He simply wonders if the soul of a negro Bishop of Georgia is not as white as the soul of the newly elected Bishop of Massachusetts. He only wants to know why a good, pure, intellectual girl, who is in every respect a lady, but who has inherited a small percentage of negro blood, should not marry the whitest man that ever lived in Boston.

When Mr. John L. Sullivan goes through the Southern States upon a professional tour, he is lodged in the best apartments of the best hotels, and he rides in parlor cars; when Mr. Frederick Douglass travels over the same roads and visits the same towns a few days later, he is compelled to accept second-class accommodation (upon a first-class ticket), and to dine, like a leper, in a pen set apart for a contaminated and a contaminating race. The former is the prophet of brutality, but he is white. The latter is an educated and refined gentleman, whose name will live in the history of the nation as a heroic figure, but his mother was a slave. These are not extreme cases. There are scores of negroes in America treated, of course, as Mr. Douglass is treated, who are in no sense inferior to him; while most of the pure Caucasians who encourage the prize-fighter by their applause and their support are quite as low and quite as brutal as is Mr. John L. Sullivan himself. This is "The

*Reprinted from *Harper's Monthly*, 83 (November 1891), 2.

Color Line" which Mr. Howells draws in his latest story. And he draws it finely, although not too fine. Rhoda Aldgate is quite unlike any of the women Mr. Howells has previously pictured. Her aunt, Mrs. Meredith, on the other hand, belonged to the regulation type. She had nerves, and she lived on them; like Mrs. Marsh (sic), she was amusingly illogical; she was also intense, and she would have left her husband alone in the Albany Depot to solve the problem of a new cook and a dozen bundles as fearlessly and as placidly as she lied to her stricken niece when asked if she had ever revealed the secret of that niece's birth to anybody else.

"An Imperative Duty" is, perhaps, taken all in all, the strongest piece of work Mr. Howells has done since the appearance of "A Foregone Conclusion."

1892-1894

Mr. Howells's Plans

Hamlin Garland*

The announcement that Mr. Howells had decided to give up "The Study" in Harpers and that he had accepted an editorial position with the Cosmopolitan is a significant literary event. Mr. Howells has come to stand for the most vital and progressive principle in American literature and to have him again assume editorial charge of a magazine means a great deal to the conservative as well as to the more radical wing of our literary public.... There is a field for a magazine that shall be American to the "rine," as Whitcomb Riley puts it. That is to say, a magazine that reflects the most characteristic and progressive art and criticism in America. That shall add to truth in criticism and to sincerity and freedom in poetry, fiction, and the drama. Mr. Howells imparted this quality to the *Atlantic* years ago, and now with riper judgment and larger powers, and with a wider freedom of action, he allies himself with a magazine with ample resources, to do a more important literary work possibly than has ever been done by a moderate priced magazine.

He has always taken the deepest interest in young writers who struck out in lines of expression native and sincere, and many struggling novelists can show encouraging, inspiring letters from his unhesitating hand. He enjoys keeping an eye upon the whole field of fiction and the drama; and this part of his editorial work will not be any great addition to his reading, and it will be entirely congenial....

He will not begin going down to the office for some time. His forenoons will be reserved as usual for his own writing. The May issue will be the first number of the magazine made up under his charge. No immediate change need be looked for, as any one familiar with magazine work knows. An illustrated journal like the Cosmopolitan is necessarily made up months in advance. In the May issue, however, very considerable changes will be introduced. This number Mr. Howells will set to

*Reprinted from *Boston Evening Transcript*, 1 January 1892, p. 6.

work upon soon, and it will be a very notable one, and will forecast
the work of the year. Unquestionably Mr. Howells will be a greater
power than ever in the radical wing of American literature, and do his
great work at less cost to himself.

Mr. Howells's
Agreements with Whitman

John Burroughs*

The choicest and most satisfying literary treat I have had for a long
time came to me when I brought home from the book-store Mr. Howells's
little volume on "Criticism and Fiction." That literary criticism had been
making such strides in my own time, that it had placed itself in the
great modern current of the comparative method of treatment of all
subjects as opposed to the old dogmatic method, was a surprise to me.

I had become more or less familiar, as every reader must have become, with the comparative method as applied to nearly all provinces
of thought and inquiry—to science, to ethics, to theology, and even to
business and politics; now I was to see the same method applied to
literary criticism. The difference between the two methods is mainly
this: one is based upon principles, the other upon standards, and this
difference is more radical than at first might appear. A principle is flexible, elastic, vital, assimilative; standards are fixed, settled, arbitrary,
exclusive. In life he who has only standards is tethered and never master
of himself; he is bewildered by a new situation. Think of an architect or
civil engineer who should work from models instead of principles. The
dogmatic method in religion—we know what that has given us and we
know how strongly the currents are setting the other way. As soon as
we begin to compare religions, and get at the principles that underlie
them, we are not so sure that one system, one creed holds the final
truth, or all truth. Science discloses the relativity of things, how they
defer and refer, how fleeting is form, how permanent is substance, how
protean is force.

Mr. Howells, it seems to me, has given the dogmatic method in
criticism, or the rigid adherence to standards and models, the severest
blow it has received in our day. He shows us how the critic, to keep
himself free and untrammelled, and ready to receive and do justice to a
new thing, must follow principles, the principles of nature and life, and
not criterions and measurements deduced from accepted works, however

*Reprinted from the *Critic*, NS 17 (6 February 1892), 85–86.

great. The original mind, he says, cannot conform to models; "it has its norm within itself. It can work only in its own way and by its self-given laws." Current criticism, he says, "does not inquire whether a work is true to life, but tacitly or explicitly compares it with models and tests it by them." Criticism cannot give laws: its business is to observe, record, and compare, "to analyze the material before it and then synthetize its impressions." This, one sees, is only the inductive and comparative method of the scientist. The critic can only give laws to the imitative, and never to the creative mind. Mr. Howells avers that it has always fought the new-good thing in behalf of the old-good thing. The man with principles is always ready for a new case, a new problem: the man with standards is always suspicious of a new thing lest it discredit his idols.

Before I saw Mr. Howells's book (and this was probably the reason why I sought it out) I had read his "Editor's Study" paper in a late *Harper's*, in which he replies in such a felicitous strain to the reiterated demands of English critics for an American literature. I noted what he said in that study of our old poet, Walt Whitman, the half-hearted praise, etc., that "he was on the way to the way we should all like to find, but that his way was not the way," etc.

But in reading his book it seemed to me as if he might have taken courage, in uttering many of his trenchant sayings, from Whitman's example. At least Whitman kept constantly running in my mind, and I said, as one after another of these banners of revolt against the dogmatic method of current criticism was unfurled and waved, not defiantly but smilingly and significantly, how well that fits his case, and that, and that. At the very outset he quotes with approval a passage from Mr. John Addington Symonds, one of Whitman's most ardent European admirers, in which that able critic says in effect that the excellence of any work of art consists in what there is "of truth, sincerity, and natural vigor in it." Then he quotes with approval Burke's saying that the rules that make an art can never be learned from art, but must be sought in nature, that "The true standard of the arts is in every man's power; and an easy observation of the most common, sometimes the meanest things in nature will give the truest lights." Howells adds very justly that "hitherto the mass of common men have been afraid to apply their own simplicity, naturalness and honesty to the appreciation of the beautiful." "Especially if they have themselves the artistic impulse in any direction they are taught to form themselves, not upon life, but upon the masters who became masters only by forming themselves upon life." All these things are bold and strong and are calculated to give aid and comfort to the readers of Whitman. This, too, that he says about the new school of American novelists:—"I find in nearly every one of them a disposition to regard our life without the literary glasses so long thought desirable, and to see character, not as it is in other fiction, but as it abounds outside of all fiction." This is very like a passage in *Leaves of Grass* wherein the poet gives a hint as to what the reader will find in that book.

You shall no longer take things at second or third hand, nor look through the eyes of the dead, nor feed on the spectres in books . . .
You shall not look through my eyes either, nor take things from me. You shall listen to all sides, and filter them for yourself.

Of course we do see things through the poet's eyes, and want to so see them. It is his quality as poet that makes all the difference. By the last line he would seem to mean that we are not to be influenced by his preferences or opinions: we are to see and hear, and judge for ourselves.

It would seem then that Walt Whitman is not merely on the way to the way that Mr. Howells is so fond of, but that he is actually on the way itself—the way of realism in art, the way that leads through the actual life and conditions immediately about us. "Creeds and schools in abeyance," says Whitman; and creeds and schools in abeyance, says Mr. Howells. Whitman declares, in one of his latest prose pieces, that the true use for the imaginative faculty of modern times is to give ultimate vivification to facts, to science, and to common lives, endowing them with the "glows and glories and final illustriousness which belong to every real thing, and to real things only." Mr. Howells is preaching the Whitman gospel when he says, the true realist "cannot look upon human life and declare this thing or that thing unworthy of notice, any more than the scientist can declare a fact of the material world beneath the dignity of his inquiry. He feels in every nerve the equality of things and the unity of men; his soul is exalted, not by vain shows and shadows and ideals, but by realities in which alone the truth lives." Whitman says in one of his poems

What is commonest, cheapest, nearest, easiest, is Me;

and Mr. Howells says:—"It is only the extraordinary person who can say with Emerson: 'I ask not for the great, the remote, the romantic. * * * I embrace the common; I sit at the feet of the familiar and the low.'" I know the real rub is whether Whitman succeeds in making poetry out of the common, the near, the easy. Mr. Howells thinks that for the most part his effort is a failure, and many other good judges think the same. That he fails sometimes I should freely admit, notably in many of the pieces written since the beginning of his illness in 1873, but that his work as a whole constitutes one of the master poetic currents of the world is my full conviction.

Why Whitman has made way so slowly with readers of poetry is not hard to discover. Mr. Howells says that the recognition of such poets

as Wordsworth and Browning was delayed so long by "something unwonted, unexpected," in the quality of each; "each was not only a poet,
he was a revolution, a new order of things, to which the critical per-
ceptions and habitudes had painfully to adjust themselves." How much
more is this true of Walt Whitman; how much more truly is he a revolution, a new order of things. There is not only something unwonted and
forbidden about him, there is at times an unconventionality that is appalling and that almost raises the goose-flesh. It will probably take us
a hundred years to get used to it. Nothing but a long stretch of time
can supply the necessary illusion. Nothing but a long stretch of time
can efface a disagreeable element from the portrait of himself which
he appended to the first thin quarto volume of "Leaves of Grass," and
which he retains in the edition of his poems just issued, and which he
undoubtedly meant to be typical of his attitude toward the world of
literature and art. The face is strong and serious and interesting, but
the pose, the dress of shirt and trousers, the hat on one side—what shall
we say of all this? Has not this man come to shoe our horses or chop
our wood, rather than to write poems? But time and distance will correct
all that, and we shall be no more disturbed by it than one would be by
seeing a picture of Cervantes in the habit of a soldier, or Michael Angelo
with his cap and apron on. We shall see that he indeed meant a revolution, a new order of things, and that his workman's garb signified more
than at first appeared.

The Editor's Study

Charles Dudley Warner*

III

The flight of Northwick through Canada, in Mr. Howells's *The
Quality of Mercy*, is an episode which would make the reputation of
a new writer, and, indeed, the author has never done anything else that
exhibited more subtle power. It does not set out to be dramatic or
thrilling; the fugitive is in no danger; the journey has the ordinary
incidents of travel; and nature is not called on to exhibit unusual por-
tents. It is never the author's habit to use nature much as a background,
or to attempt to carry on a story by elaborate descriptions of her aspects
and moods. The reader, like the fugitive, takes little account at first of
the inhospitable winter, the increasing cold, the drifting snow. The

*Reprinted from *Harper's Monthly*, 85 (July 1892), 316–17.

hardships of the journey are even stimulating. Presently, however, these things intensify the loneliness and the torpor of the fleeing man. He is not a person of sentiment, and although he has a New England conscience, it has never given him much trouble. But now he begins to waver. He is conscious of a dual action of the mind; he makes bargains with the Lord, with a cunning notion that he can propitiate fate; and he is conscious of a failure of the power of his will. Is it the cold? Is it coming illness? Is it a creeping sense of guilt? Perhaps the inhospitable region really affects his imagination. He goes on in a dream. He is full of projects when his mind will work, and he has flashes of energy and courage in his restlessness and sleeplessness; but the reader begins to perceive that this is an aimless journey. In all this drive and haste and eagerness to get on, the man is going nowhere. In fact, this winter Canada is only a phantasmagoria of things to be evaded, of objects to be sought. The flight is an internal one. The man is fleeing from himself, and this double action, the reality of movement with this dodging of a psychological spectre, rises into the most pitiful tragedy. Physically the man is not hunted; there is no danger of pursuit; he knows that he is absolutely safe. Nor is he the prey of remorse. What he needs is time to adjust his affairs. In certain moments he clearly sees his way to do this. What has he done that others are not daily doing? Yet something had gone wrong with him. Fatigue he does not mind, or would not ordinarily, but it is queer that he is so baffled in his mental operations. Decision has given place to irresolution, enterprise to a mere effort to hide himself and his stolen money, and the one thing remaining to the man is the dull instinct of going on. Was it the hardship of the journey or was it a moral struggle that finally landed him in helplessness? The author does not explain. He simply narrates events with singular fidelity to the common aspects of life, and yet the power of all this is in an apprehension of the unseen and the spiritual that makes this flight a high achievement of the artist. The man sets out full of vigor, ingenuity, self-confidence, and purpose. There arrived at the end of the journey the wreck of a human being. It is absolute and remediless. Even in Northwick the mainspring of life, self-respect, had snapped. The author does not need to moralize on the sort of company a thief is to himself.

It is perhaps wrong to call this flight an episode, since it is the illumination of the novel, but it is a complete tragedy by itself.

Real Conversations.—I. A Dialogue Between William Dean Howells and Hjalmar Hjorth Boyesen.

Hjalmar Hjorth Boyesen*

When I was requested to furnish a dramatic biography of Mr. Howells, I was confronted with what seemed an insuperable difficulty. The more I thought of William Dean Howells, the less dramatic did he seem to me. The only way that occurred to me of introducing a dramatic element into our proposed interview was for me to assault him with tongue or pen, in the hope that he might take energetic measures to resent my intrusion; but as, notwithstanding his unvarying kindness to me, and many unforgotten benefits, I cherished only the friendliest feelings for him, I could not persuade myself to procure dramatic interest at such a price.

My second objection, I am bound to confess, arose from my own sense of dignity which rebelled against the *rôle* of an interviewer, and it was not until my conscience was made easy on this point that I agreed to undertake the present article. I was reminded that it was an ancient and highly dignified form of literature I was about to revive; and that my precedent was to be sought not in the modern newspaper interview, but in the Platonic dialogue. By the friction of two kindred minds, sparks of thought may flash forth which owe their origin solely to the friendly collision. We have a far more vivid portrait of Socrates in the beautiful conversational turns of "The Symposium" and the first book of "The Republic," than in the purely objective account of Xenophon in his "Memorabilia." And Howells, though he may not know it, has this trait in common with Socrates, that he can portray himself, unconsciously, better than I or anybody else could do it for him.

If I needed any further encouragement, I found it in the assurance that what I was expected to furnish was to be in the nature of "an exchange of confidences between two friends with a view to publication." It was understood, of course, that Mr. Howells was to be more confiding than myself, and that his reminiscences were to predominate; for an author, however unheroic he may appear to his own modesty, is bound to be the hero of his biography. What made the subject so alluring to me, apart from the personal charm which inheres in the man and all that appertains to him, was the consciousness that our friendship was of twenty-two years' standing, and that during all that time not a single jarring note had been introduced to mar the harmony of our relation.

*Reprinted from *McClure's Magazine*, 1 (June 1893), 3–11.

Equipped, accordingly, with a good conscience and a lead pencil (which remained undisturbed in my breastpocket) I set out to "exchange confidences" with the author of "Silas Lapham" and "A Modern Instance." I reached the enormous human hive on Fifty-ninth Street where my subject, for the present, occupies a dozen most comfortable and ornamental cells, and was promptly hoisted up to the fourth floor and deposited in front of his door. It is a house full of electric wires and tubes—literally honeycombed with modern conveniences. But in spite of all these, I made my way triumphantly to Mr. Howells's den, and after a proper prelude began the novel task assigned to me.

"I am afraid," I remarked quite *en passant*, "that I shall be embarrassed not by my ignorance, but by my knowledge concerning your life. For it is difficult to ask with good grace about what you already know. I am aware, for instance, that you were born at Martin's Ferry, Ohio, March 11, 1837;[1] that you removed thence to Dayton, and a few years later to Jefferson, Ashtabula County; that your father edited, published, and printed a country newspaper of Republican complexion, and that you spent a good part of your early years in the printing office. Nevertheless, I have some difficulty in realizing the environment of your boyhood."

Howells. If you have read my "Boy's Town," which is in all essentials autobiograhical, you know as much as I could tell you. The environment of my early life was exactly as there described.

Boyesen. Your father, I should judge, then, was not a strict disciplinarian?

Howells. No. He was the gentlest of men—a friend and companion to his sons. He guided us in an unobtrusive way without our suspecting it. He was continually putting books into my hands, and they were always good books; many of them became events in my life. I had no end of such literary passions during my boyhood. Among the first was Goldsmith, then came Cervantes and Irving.

Boyesen. Then there was a good deal of literary atmosphere about your childhood?

Howells. Yes. I can scarcely remember the time when books did not play a great part in my life. Father was by his culture and his interests rather isolated from the community in which we lived, and this made him and all of us rejoice the more in a new author, in whose world we would live for weeks and months, and who colored our thoughts and conversation.

Boyesen. It has always been a matter of wonder to me that, with so little regular schooling, you stepped full-fledged into literature with such an exquisite and wholly individual style.

Howells. If you accuse me of that kind of thing, I must leave you to account for it. I had always a passion for literature, and to a boy with a mind and a desire to learn, a printing office is not a bad school.

Boyesen. How old were you when you left Jefferson, and went to Columbus?

Howells. I was nineteen years old when I went to the capital and wrote legislative reports for Cincinnati and Cleveland papers; afterwards I became one of the editors of the "Ohio State Journal." My duties gradually took a wide range, and I edited the literary column and wrote many of the leading articles. I was then in the midst of my enthusiasm for Heine, and was so impregnated with his spirit, that a poem which I sent to the "Atlantic Monthly" was mistaken by Mr. Lowell for a translation from the German poet. When he had satisfied himself, however, that it was not a translation, he accepted and printed it.

Boyesen. Tell me how you happened to publish your first volume, "Poems by Two Friends," in partnership with John J. Piatt.

Howells. I had known Piatt as a young printer; afterwards when he began to write poems, I read them and was delighted with them. When he came to Columbus I made his acquaintance, and we became friends. By this time we were both contributors to the "Atlantic Monthly." I may as well tell you that his contributions to our joint volume were far superior to mine.

Boyesen. Did Lowell share that opinion?

Howells. That I don't know. He wrote me a very charming letter, in which he said many encouraging things, and he briefly reviewed the book in the "Atlantic."

Boyesen. What was the condition of society in Columbus during those days?

Howells. There were many delightful and cultivated people there, and society was charming; the North and South were both represented, and their characteristics united in a kind of informal Western hospitality, warm and cordial in its tone, which gave of its very best without stint. Salmon P. Chase, later Secretary of the Treasury, and Chief Justice of the United States, was then Governor of Ohio. He had a charming family, and made us young editors welcome at his house. All winter long there was a round of parties at the different houses; the houses were large and we always danced. These parties were brilliant affairs, socially, but besides, we young people had many informal gayeties. The old Starling Medical College, which was defunct as an educational institution, except for some vivisection and experiments on hapless cats and dogs that went on in some out-of-the-way corners, was used as a boarding-house; and there was a large circular room in which we often improvised dances. We young fellows who lodged in the place were half a dozen journalists, lawyers, and law-students; one was, like myself, a writer for the "Atlantic," and we saw life with joyous eyes. We read the new books, and talked them over with the young ladies whom we seem to have been always calling upon. I remember those years in Columbus as among the happiest years of life.

Boyesen. From Columbus you went as consul to Venice, did not you?

Howells. Yes. You remember I had written a campaign "Life of Lincoln." I was, like my father, an ardent Anti-slavery man. I went myself to Washington soon after President Lincoln's inauguration. I was first offered the consulate to Rome; but as it depended entirely upon perquisites, which amounted only to three or four hundred dollars a year, I declined it, and they gave me Venice. The salary was raised to fifteen hundred dollars, which seemed to me quite beyond the dreams of avarice.

Boyesen. Do not you regard that Venetian experience as a very valuable one?

Howells. Oh, of course. In the first place, it gave me four years of almost uninterrupted leisure for study and literary work. There was, to be sure, occasionally an invoice to be verified, but that did not take much time. Secondly, it gave me a wider outlook upon the world than I had hitherto had. Without much study of a systematic kind, I had acquired a notion of English, French, German, and Spanish literature. I had been an eager and constant reader, always guided in my choice of books by my own inclination. I had learned German. Now, my first task was to learn Italian; and one of my early teachers was a Venetian priest, whom I read Dante with. This priest in certain ways suggested Don Ippolito in "A Foregone Conclusion."

Boyesen. Then he took snuff, and had a supernumerary calico handkerchief?

Howells. Yes. But what interested me most about him was his religious skepticism. He used to say, "The saints are the gods baptized." Then he was a kind of baffled inventor; though whether his inventions had the least merit I was unable to determine.

Boyesen. But his love story?

Howells. That was wholly fictitious.

Boyesen. I remember you gave me, in 1874, a letter of introduction to a Venetian friend of yours, named Brunetta, whom I failed to find.

Howells. Yes, Brunetta was the first friend I had in Venice. He was a distinctly Latin character—sober, well-regulated, and probity itself.

Boyesen. Do you call that the Latin character?

Howells. It is not our conventional idea of it; but it is fully as characteristic, if not more so, than the light, mercurial, pleasure-loving type which somehow in literature has displaced the other. Brunetta and I promptly made the discovery that we were congenial. Then we became daily companions. I had a number of other Italian friends too, full of beautiful *bonhomie* and Southern sweetness of temperament.

Boyesen. You must have acquired Italian in a very short time?

Howells. Yes; being domesticated in that way in the very heart of that Italy, which was then *Italia irridente*, I could not help steeping myself in its atmosphere and breathing in the language, with the rest of its very composite flavors.

Boyesen. Yes; and whatever I know of Italian literature I owe largely to the completeness of that soaking process of yours. Your book on the Italian poets is one of the most charmingly sympathetic and illuminative bits of criticism that I know.

Howells. I am glad you think so; but the book was never a popular success. Of all the Italian authors, the one I delighted in the most was Goldoni. His exquisite realism fascinated me. It was the sort of thing which I felt I ought not to like; but for all that I liked it immensely.

Boyesen. How do you mean that you ought not to like it?

Howells. Why, I was an idealist in those days. I was only twenty-four or twenty-five years old, and I knew the world chiefly through literature. I was all the time trying to see things as others had seen them, and I had a notion that, in literature, persons and things should be nobler and better than they are in the sordid reality; and this romantic glamour veiled the world to me, and kept me from seeing things as they are. But in the lanes and alleys of Venice I found Goldoni everywhere. Scenes from his plays were enacted before my eyes with all the charming Southern vividness of speech and gesture, and I seemed at every turn to have stepped at unawares into one of his comedies. I believe this was the beginning of my revolt. But it was a good while yet before I found my own bearings.

Boyesen. But permit me to say that it was an exquisitely delicate set of fresh Western senses you brought with you to Venice. When I was in Venice in 1878, I could not get away from you, however much I tried. I saw your old Venetian senator, in his august rags, roasting coffee; and I promenaded about for days in the chapters of your "Venetian Life," like the Knight Huldbrand, in the Enchanted Forest in "Undine," and I could not find my way out. Of course, I know that, being what you were, you could not have helped writing that book, but what was the immediate cause of your writing it?

Howells. From the day I arrived in Venice I kept a journal in which I noted down my impressions. I found a young pleasure in registering my sensations at the sight of notable things, and literary reminiscences usually shimmered through my observations. Then I received an offer from the "Boston Daily Advertiser," to write weekly or bi-weekly letters, for which they paid me five dollars, in greenbacks, a column, nonpareil.

By the time this sum reached Venice, shaven and shorn by discounts for exchange in gold premium, it had usually shrunk to half its size or less. Still I was glad enough to get even that, and I kept on writing joyously. So the book grew in my hands until, at the time I resigned in 1865, I was trying to have it published. I offered it successively to a number of English publishers; but they all declined it. At last Mr. Trübner agreed to take it, if I could guarantee the sale of five hundred copies in the United States, or induce an American publisher to buy that number of copies in sheets. I happened to cross the ocean with Mr. Hurd of the New York firm of Hurd & Houghton, and repeated Mr. Trübner's proposition to him. He refused to commit himself; but some weeks after my arrival in New York, he told me that the risk was practically nothing at all, and that his firm would agree to take the five hundred copies. The

book was an instant success. I don't know how many editions of it have been printed, but I should say that its sale has been upward of forty thousand copies, and it still continues. The English weeklies gave me long complimentary notices, which I carried about for months in my pocket like love-letters, and read surreptitiously at odd moments. I thought it was curious that other people to whom I showed the reviews did not seem much interested.

Boyesen. After returning to this country, did not you settle down in New York?

Howells. Yes; I was for a while a free lance in literature. I did whatever came in my way, and sold my articles to the newspapers, going about from office to office, but I was finally offered a place in "The Nation," where I obtained a fixed position at a salary. I had at times a sense that, by going abroad, I had fallen out of the American procession of progress; and, though I was elbowing my way energetically through the crowd, I seemed to have a tremendous difficulty in recovering my lost place on my native soil, and asserting my full right to it. So, when young men beg me to recommend them for consulships, I always feel in duty bound to impress on them this great danger of falling out of the procession, and asking them whether they have confidence in their ability to reconquer the place they have deserted, for while they are away it will be pretty sure to be filled by somebody else. A man returning from a residence of several years abroad has a sense of superfluity in his own country—he has become a mere supernumerary whose presence or absence makes no particular difference.

Boyesen. What year did you leave "The Nation" and assume the editorship of "The Atlantic"?

Howells. I took the editorship in 1872,[2] but went to live in Cambridge six or seven years before. I was first assistant editor under James T. Fields, who was uniformly kind and considerate, and with whom I got along perfectly. It was a place that he could have made odious to me, but he made it delightful. I have the tenderest regard and the highest respect for his memory.

Boyesen. I need scarcely ask you if your association with Lowell was agreeable?

Howells. It was in every way charming. He was twenty years my senior, but he always treated me as an equal and a contemporary. And you know the difference between thirty and fifty is far greater than between forty and sixty, or fifty and seventy. I dined with him every week, and he showed the friendliest appreciation of the work I was trying to do. We took long walks together; and you know what a rare talker he was. Somehow I got much nearer to him than to Longfellow. As a man, Longfellow was flawless. He was full of noble friendliness and encouragement to all literary workers in whom he believed.

Boyesen. Do you remember you once said to me that he was a most inveterate praiser?

Howells. I may have said that; for in the kindness of his heart, and his constitutional reluctance to give pain, he did undoubtedly often strain a point or two in speaking well of things. But that was part of his beautiful kindliness of soul and admirable urbanity. Lowell, you know, confessed to being "a tory in his nerves;" but Longfellow, with all his stateliness of manner, was nobly and perfectly democratic. He was ideally good; I think he was without a fault.

Boyesen. I have never known a man who was more completely free from snobbishness and pretence of all kinds. It delighted him to go out of his way to do a man a favor. There was, however, a little touch of Puritan pallor in his temperament, a slight lack of robustness; that is, if his brother's biography can be trusted. What I mean to say is, that he appears there a trifle too perfect: too bloodlessly, and almost frostily, statuesque. I have always had a little diminutive grudge against the Reverend Samuel Longfellow for not using a single one of those beautiful anecdotes I sent him illustrative of the warmer and more genial side of the poet's character. He evidently wanted to portray a Plutarchian man of heroic size, and he therefore had to exclude all that was subtly individualizing.

Howells. Well, there is always room for another biography of Longfellow.

Boyesen. At the time when I made your acquaintance in 1871, you were writing "Their Wedding Journey." Do you remember the glorious talks we had together while the hours of the night slipped away unnoticed? We have no more of those splendid conversational rages now-a-days. How eloquent we were, to be sure; and with what delight you read those chapters on "Niagara," "Quebec," and "The St. Lawrence;" and with what rapture I listened! I can never read them without supplying the cadence of your voice, and seeing you seated, twenty-two years younger than now, in that cosey little library in Berkeley Street.

Howells. Yes; and do you mind our sudden attacks of hunger, when we would start on a foraging expedition into the cellar, in the middle of the night, and return, you with a cheese and crackers, and I with a watermelon and a bottle of champagne? What jolly meals we improvised! Only it is a wonder to me that we survived them.

Boyesen. You will never suspect what an influence you exerted upon my fate by your friendliness and sympathy in those never-to-be-forgotten days. You Americanized me. I had been an alien, and felt alien in every fibre of my soul, until I met you. Then I became domesticated. I found a kindred spirit who understood me, and whom I understood; and that is the first and indispensable condition of happiness. It was at your house, at a luncheon, I think, that I met Henry James.

Howells. Yes; James and I were constant companions. We took daily walks together, and his father, the elder Henry James, was an incomparably delightful and interesting man.

Boyesen. Yes; I remember him well. I doubt if I ever heard a more brilliant talker.

Howells. No; he was one of the best talkers in America. And didn't the immortal Ralph Keeler appear upon the scene during the summer of '71 or '72?

Boyesen. Yes; your small son "Bua" insisted upon calling him "Big Man Keeler" in spite of his small size.

Howells. Yes, Bua was the only one who ever saw Keeler life-size.

Boyesen. I remember how he sat in your library and told stories of his negro minstrel days and his wild adventures in many climes, and did not care whether you laughed with him or at him, but would join you from sheer sympathy, and how we all laughed in chorus until our sides ached!

Howells. Poor Keeler! He was a sort of migratory, nomadic survival: but he had fine qualities, and was well equipped for a sort of fiction. If he had lived he might have written the great American novel. Who knows?

Boyesen. Was not it at Cambridge that Björnstjerne Björnson visited you?

Howells. No; that was in 1881, at Belmont, where we went in order to be in the country, and give the children the benefit of country air. When I met Björnson before, we had always talked Italian; but the first thing he said to me at Belmont, was: "Now we will speak English." And when he had got into the house, he picked up a book and said in his abrupt way: "We do not put enough in;" meaning thereby, that we ignored too much of life in our fiction—excluded it out of regard for propriety. But when I met him, some years later, in Paris, he had changed his mind about that, for he detested the French naturalism, and could find nothing to praise in Zola.

Boyesen. I am going to ask you one of the interviewer's stock questions, but you need not answer, you know: Which of your books do you regard as the greatest?

Howells. I have always taken the most satisfaction in "A Modern Instance." I have there come closest to American life as I know it.

Boyesen. But in "Silas Lapham" it seems to me that you have got a still firmer grip on American reality.

Howells. Perhaps. Still I prefer "A Modern Instance." "Silas Lapham" is the most successful novel I have published, except "A Hazard of New Fortunes," which has sold nearly twice as many copies as any of the rest.

Boyesen. What do you attribute that to?

Howells. Possibly to the fact that the scene is laid in New York: the public throughout the country is far more interested in New York than in Boston. New York, as Lowell once said, is a huge pudding, and every town and village has been helped to a slice, or wants to be.

Boyesen. I rejoice that New York has found such a subtly appreciative and faithful chronicler as you show yourself to be in "A Hazard of New Fortunes." To the equipment of a great city—a world-city as the Germans say—belongs a great novelist; that is to say, at least one. And even though your modesty may rebel, I shall persist in regarding you henceforth as *the* novelist *par excellence* of New York.

Howells. Ah, you don't expect me to live up to *that* bit of taffy!

Notes

1. The correct birth date for Howells is 1 March 1837.
2. 1 July 1871.

Literary Notes

Laurence Hutton*

For some reason we seem to associate Mr. James with Mr. Howells, despite the fact that their matter and even their method are not always alike. That Mr. Howells has inherited no small portion of the raiment of short stories which Irving dropped there can be no question. In the present instance the garment is a dresscoat which its author's genius will

*Reprinted from *Harper's Monthly*, 87 (October 1893), 377.

cause to survive several fashions. Lowell said to one of his correspondents a good many years ago: "Howells is going to last. He knows how to write." That he knows how to write amusing little comedies as well as serious short stories, and sometimes almost tragic long stories, Mr. Lowell lived to see. While his comedies will not last so long, perhaps, as his other works, they have their place in literature, they play as well as they read, and Mr. Roberts will be, for some time, a popular leading-man. He is an entertaining person whether we find him hiring a cook in "The Albany Depo'," reading "A Letter of Introduction" in his own apartment, or trying to settle the question of *Evening Dress*, as Mr. Howells now exhibits him to us. In the earlier episodes of Mr. Roberts's stage-life with which we are familiar, Mr. Roberts seems to have deserved a good deal of the trouble he brought upon himself. In this latest incident the sympathy of all masculine readers will certainly be with Mr. Roberts. He did not want to go to Mrs. Miller's musical in the first place; he was very tired in the second place; and in the last place, Mrs. Roberts forgot to tell him that she had pressed his dress suit, had folded it up in tissue-paper, had wrapped it up in her white chuddah shawl, and had put it "away back" on the top shelf of the closet, where, of course, Roberts could not possibly find it. All of which was very like Mrs. Roberts, and very aggravating to her husband.

To the charge, frequently made by his critics, that he has never yet created "a noble, perfect woman," Mr. Howells is credited with having told a recent newspaper interviewer that he is waiting to find "a noble, perfect woman" who has appeared in the flesh. Mrs. Roberts is not noble, and she lays no claims to nobility, but if she is not a *perfect* woman, she is almost a perfect *woman*, to assume the italic form of speech of which she is herself so fond. Her performances with her husband's clothes were perfectly womanlike, while her remarks about Roberts's supposed attack of the grippe have rarely been equalled in that respect. "Jump into bed, and cover up warm, and keep up the nourishment with the whiskey," she said; "there's another bottle in the sideboard; and perhaps you'd better break a raw egg in it. I heard of one person that they gave three dozen raw eggs a day to in typhoid fever, and even *then* he died."

Observe the Robertsy emphasis upon the word *then!*

With William Dean Howells

[Frances Whiting Halsey]*

The eyes of William Dean Howells, which are large and blue, with silvery reflections, sudden as the breath of wave, or faint refractions indicative of serious interior vision, contain in their clear pupils something infinite and vague as the tranquil sea.

He lowers his head that it may the better listen to the voice of reverie, and his vast forehead appears in the majestic simplicity of its pure design. It is a creator's forehead.

He talks, and his face, which is expressive, when in repose, of serenity, certitude, and invincible faith, reproduces all the shades of his thoughts in their sadness and in their gayety.

He is observation itself. Those who have really interviewed him know that he has penetrated them.

His destiny is clearly legible. In the paradise where he shall go in a direct line, as a good workman, he will enumerate the worlds, the constellations, the stars, the cherubim, the angels, and the souls. Then he will suggest that huts of azure be demolished in order that the blue facade of the celestial palaces may be enlarged and rendered more consonant with modern ideas.

He is profoundly sympathetic. Men of letters and artists, even those whom all opinions divide, are united in affection for his personality. When one reads in the margin of a magnificent etching by Rajon, which is in his drawing room, the words, "To my dear Howells," one feels that they were not written as a conventional formula.

The inscription is in the handwriting and with the signature of L. Alma Tadema, artist of the painting etched by Rajon. . . .

The long library table, made after a design by Mrs. Howells, is graceful and delicately ornamented with its severely artistic carvings. It is unincumbered with books or papers, as are usually tables of writers. The inkstand reproduces in bronze the wild boar of the great fountain which is at Florence. . . .

"I would give the palm to Hawthorne among all the prose writers," he said in one of his replies. "Hawthorne wrote pure romance. This is perfectly legitimate in fiction, and not to be confounded with the mixture known as the romantic novel.

"I think that 'Evangeline' is the great poem of the century. It is the tragedy of pathos," he said. "I have been passionately fond of Longfellow, then of Tennyson, but my first love was Heine. I read Heine, at seventeen, in the little village where my father had his printing press.

*Reprinted from *New York Times*, 26 November 1893, p. 23.

A German bookbinder, who had gone into exile after the Revolution of 1848, had the works of the poet, and I learned German with him in my ardor to read them. I shall never lose the impression which they made on me. It was Heine who freed my hand in writing."

"I prefer the 'Intermezzo' rather than 'Romeo and Juliet,'" the young man said, with an apologetic air, "because Heine's work is a pure poem without a story."

"Heine," Mr. Howells said, "never had to give a reason for his lyrical emotion. He had the wisdom never to render an account."

"Could you not be persuaded to become a partisan of the theory of art for art's sake?" the young man asked.

"No," Mr. Howells answered, very decidedly. "The theory is excusable only on the plea of a necessary protest against too materialistic surroundings."

To a question about the works of Poe, Mr. Howells replied that they had not impressed him and that he could not understand why the French were enthusiastic about them. Of Walt Whitman, he said:

"He was like Columbus. He discovered an island, instead of the continent. He knew the slavery of the poetic form, but he made his work formless. Form is indispensable to poetry. I think it should not be everything, but the true art is in a middle ground. At a sublime height in his work, Whitman had form. Then he ceased to be nebular, and became stellar."

"People say that you are a Socialist. . . ."

"I should not care to wear a label," Mr. Howells replied. "I do not study the question, the question studies me. In great cities one does not easily avoid it. But Socialism is not imminent. If the people wanted it they would have it, and without any revolution."

"Have you noticed that in our civilization the artist, who is the only person in the right, is apparently the only person in the wrong?" he said, when his questioner quitted with a bewildered air.

A Great American Writer

Edward Marshall*

William Dean Howells, novelist, poet, playwright, however divided critics may be concerning the merit of his books, has been put by the public into place with James Fenimore Cooper, Washington Irving, Longfellow, Whittier and Holmes, the only other Americans whose literary work has been deemed bright and clear enough to fit them to shine

*Reprinted from the *Philadelphia Press*, 15 April 1894, p. 27.

among the world's first literary lights. The most important man is the man who forces from the public the most extensive recognition. The sale of Mr. Howells' novels grows greater with each year. The most important bookseller in New York told me the other day that the call for "Their Wedding Journey"—the first of Mr. Howells' novels—had been heavier during the last twelve months than during the same period in 1892–93, and that should the publishers see fit to issue a worthy edition of the book a steadily increasing sale might be expected. The present edition is printed from half worn-out plates, and with illustrations so bad that there might better be no pictures at all. Of "The Rise of Silas Lapham," "A Hazard of New Fortunes," "The Minister's Charge" and "A Modern Instance," he said that no other novels in his store, printed at an equally remote date and written by any American, save General Lew Wallace's "Ben-Hur," had so steady and large a sale.

So much for the popularity of Mr. Howells' fiction. A word should be said of its unpopularity. That is scarcely less marked in its character-istics. The remark of a critic to me a few weeks ago was: "There is no middle ground with Howells—people think him either a master or an ass." That is literally true. The very large reading public which dislikes his books can see no good in them whatever. One of the most cultivated and mentally fine grained men I ever knew said to me the other day: "I don't like Howells. I read the first half of 'The Rise of Silas Lapham' as it appeared in the *Century* Magazine and stopped, greatly comforted by the fact that while I might be forced to go out on rainy days, lie for some portion of my life ill in bed, serve on juries and deny myself many good things, nothing could ever make me finish 'The Rise of Silas Lap-ham.'" Perhaps this is as good an evidence of the novelist's importance as the other. Everybody that reads in America knows something about Howells and likes or dislikes him. There is none to whom he is unknown.

NOT AN IMPOSING FIGURE.

The man who has aroused all this literary sentiment is not physically impressive. He is slightly below the average height, and to use an artist's term which he utilizes frequently in describing characters in his stories, his figure is "out of drawing." His head and shoulders are much too large for the lower part of his body. The first time I ever saw Mr. Howells he was sitting in a theatre box. Only the upper third of the novelist was visible. From it I imagined that he was a man very little less than six feet tall. After the play had ended I delayed my departure so that I might see him as he went out. As he stepped through the door of the box into the auditorium his small stature, after my expectations of might, was a genuine shock to me.

But however disappointing the legs of Mr. Howells may be, there is no question about his head. It is magnificent. Its splendid massiveness is a great comfort to his admirers. The thin, gray hair, carefully combed, does not hide, but accentuates its gratifying outlines. It droops forward a little, as if from its own weight.

The face is less easy to describe. The years have cut deep lines into it. The brow is overhanging and the cheeks come up to meet it so that most of the time his eyes seem more deeply set than they really are. It is an embarrassing face and one which it is very hard to arouse to animation. Most of the time that I have seen it, it has worn a look of disconcerting weariness, which I am told is habitual. . . .

POLITICS AND RELIGION.

The trend of his recent thought seems to have been political. His "Letters of a Traveler from Altruria" in the Cosmopolitan Magazine and one or two review articles have shown that, and various newspaper articles attributing socialistic and even anarchistic theories to him have been written. To guess that he believes that the ideal political development is along socialistic lines is reasonable, because of what he has written himself. But to say that he is anarchistic is as sensible as was the theme of an article lately printed which claimed that Mr. Howells' literary ambition had been fired—even originated—by Henry James. Mr. Howells had laid the foundations of success before he had ever read anything by Mr. James, and before anything of importance had been published over that deserting American's name. It was said that Mr. Howells' "Lady of the Aroostook" was an answer to Mr. James' "Daisy Miller," which was nonsense. But, notwithstanding Mr. Howells' evident interest in politics, there is no subject on which he is so unwilling to talk.

Religion, which is a much less attractive theme to most prominent men, Mr. Howells discussed at some length. He was born a Swedenborgian and reared in that peculiar and in America never very popular faith. This, in the country communities in which his family lived during his boyhood, rather cut the Howellses off from a very close social life with their neighbors. They were not frequent church-goers, the father of the family considering it as much to the purpose to spend a profitable and thoughtful day of rest among the fields or woods as to devote it to worship in the church of another doctrine. To the fact that this throwing the family on its own resources drew it closer together than common, Mr. Howells attributes much of the delight of his early home life.

The parents were in full sympathy with their children, and the young folks found father and mother more companionable than the boys and girls with whom they became acquainted. So they read and talked and thought together and there was much of religion in their reading, their talking and their thinking. But afterward, when William Dean left the direct influence of that delightful home life and came first East and afterward went abroad as Consul to Venice, he had the doubts which come to most men. Religion played a smaller part in his life, until finally he slipped into agnosticism. This lasted during what was left of his youth and through such part of his middle age as came before his reading of Tolstoi.

"I believe in Christ, the life," he said to me. "I think that is his whole creed. To wish to follow Christ is what Tolstoi teaches, and it seems to me is all that can be asked of us."

HOPES FOR IMMORTALITY.

"Have you faith in the theory of immortal life, Mr. Howells?"

"As we grow older I think we grow less and less positive about such a belief as that. The young are much more positive than the old. With age comes the blunting of the edge of most things. As we gather years we lose love, joy, grief—everything that makes life, and so, to age, it would not seem so strange if life itself ended forever. I've died and lived so many times! But every time we go to sleep, we die—we become unconscious and pass for the time being out of life. How can we know that we will ever awake from the night's slumber or that we shall not wake from death? I can't say more about it, or more than that I hope for another life, another chance."

It was that delightful home life, the books, the magazines and the semi-literary flavor that ran through it all, because, first, of ingrained tastes, and, second, of the fact that the father was the editor of a country newspaper (this was in Ohio) that gave Mr. Howells his literary bent. From the first his ambitions were all toward writing. They never wavered. He has never engaged in any business. The stories of work for an insurance company in Boston are without fact or foundation. This does away with the pretty theory that March, the ex-insurance agent and afterward editor in "A Hazard of New Fortunes," was Mr. Howells himself described by himself in a book. Mr. Howells never described himself in a book. March was "made out of whole cloth."

In fact, the novelist has drawn but one character directly from life in any of his books.

This character was Fulkerson in that same book, "A Hazard of New Fortunes." He was the inventor and business manager of that unique publication, "Every Other Week," which played so important a part in the story. Fulkerson was a breezy Westerner of good heart, selfish, crudily witty and one of the most entertaining of Mr. Howells' creations. He was mainly studied from Ralph Keeler, one of the queerest characters in Boston seventeen years ago. He finally went to Cuba during the outbreak of '77 and was mysteriously murdered there. . . .

HIS INDIAN SUMMER.

The only story in which Mr. Howells might be supposed to have painted himself to even a slight extent is "Indian Summer." That tells of a middle-aged man—an editor from the West—who longed for his youth to come again. That youth had been partly spent among the soft breezes and under the sunny skies of Italy. So the man thinking of this, and remembering the delight of those past days, made a very human mistake. He thought that the delight was due to Italy and not to youth, and went back to Italy to find it. But somehow the breezes and the skies had changed to him, and finally he found that it had not been in them but in himself—his young blood, young heart and young head—that the deliciousness of those bygone days had been. This was Mr. Howells' own experience. He looked back and yearned for the emotions and enjoyments of twenty years before. He, too, fancied that it was the breezes and the skies that breathed and smiled to him across the gulf of years, and he, too, pursuing them to Italy, found that he was wrong.

"Indian Summer," perhaps because there is so much of himself in it, is his favorite among his own stories. Few of his admirers choose with him. The women in the story are better than the men—that is true, in fact, of all of Howells' novels. In no one of his books has he given us a man whom we can lionize in our minds. He has made several heroines, but no heroes.

"Why is it," I asked of him, "that your women are always so much more admirable than your men?"

The reply came so promptly and truthfully that it staggered me: "Because women are better than men. A good woman is beyond the imagination of even a good man, and a bad woman is as good as the average of the other sex."

But he quickly qualified the statement—that is, he robbed femininity of credit for its own goodness, by adding: "it is because women are mostly outside of our infernal economic system." . . .

HARD TO END STORIES.

The ending of his books has always been the hardest part of the work of writing them for Mr. Howells. This began with the very first story he wrote. That is an interesting episode which has never been told before.

"When I was a boy", said Mr. Howells, in speaking of it, "I worked on my father's paper. Among other things I set type. Those were the days of great struggle for all of us. The paper was not profitable, and ours was a large family. My tastes and ambitions were all literary, and I wanted to write a story. Father gave his consent, so I went to work at it.

Instead of writing it and then setting it up in type, I composed it at the case and put it in type as I invented it. Father printed a chapter of it weekly in the paper, and so it was published as fast as I got it up. I tried to get three or four chapters ready in advance, but I could not do it. All I could possibly accomplish was to have one installment ready every time the paper went to press. This went on for a long while, and that story became a burden to me. It stretched out longer and longer, but I could see no way to end it. Every week I resolved that that story should be finished in the next week's paper; every week it refused to be finished. Finally I became positively panic stricken, and ended it somehow or other.

"The experience discouraged me to some extent. I made up my mind that I could not invent.

"I wrote 'Their Wedding Journey,' without intending to make it a piece of fiction or considering it to be one after I had finished it. It was simply a book of American travel, which I hoped to make attractive by a sugar coating of romance. I was very familiar with the route over which I had taken the bridal couple, and I knew it was beautiful and, like most American scenery, was not appreciated.

"This book was more of a success than I expected it to be. I attributed its success to the descriptions of American scenery and places, I gave it to a family friend and asked her to mark those parts of it which she thought real incidents. I was very much astonished and greatly pleased to find, when she returned it, that she had marked some passages which were purely invention. This made me ask myself if I might not hope to write a novel some day."

LITERARY METHODS.

Mr. Howells' literary methods are simple. There is, in fact, nothing eccentric about him. He is as genuine as are the people in his novels. He has no great love for the unusual. He has a fondness, however, for the queer little foreign restaurants that one finds in the unsuspected corners of New York. The family breakfast occurs at 8 in the morning.

"After that," said Mr. Howells, with a smile, "I put my work off as long as I can. Finally when I begin it, I generally keep at it for about three hours. In that time I can write from 500 to 1000 words of a story, and more than that if the work is not fiction. Yes, I am methodical, I suppose. I map my stories out very carefully in my mind before I begin work on them. I do not write out a synopsis. I arrange what might be called the landmarks of the story, and it generally comes out in the end about as I have at the beginning thought it would. Sometimes when I begin a story the last word, the last look, is plain to me.

"I carry my work in my mind from day to day without difficulty, and each day I try to stop at an interesting point so that my attention will be caught at once the next morning."

"Will there ever be a distinctively American school of literature, Mr. Howells?" I asked.

"Yes, I think so in a measure. As yet we are overborne by European traditions and criticism. The middle class—we have divided ourselves into classes, despite our false claims to the contrary—likes American books, but the highest class—measuring height by wealth—does not. It bows before foreign writers because they are foreign, just as it bows before other things because they are foreign. We have been false to the idea of equality, the only thing that could have made us a really great people, and that will have its depressing effect upon our literature. Anyway, we've come too late to be peculiar. We've come when the whole world is writing on the human idea in literature. But in those things which we have undertaken with a will we have always become important, and that is why I say that I think we will develop a literature that shall be in a measure national. Some day I hope we will have the manhood to put ourselves frankly into literature as we have in politics. We certainly have a distinctly national school of politics."

LEADING AMERICAN WRITERS.

"Mary E. Wilkins, Mark Twain, Sarah Orne Jewett and George W. Cable are probably the most strikingly American writers we have to-day. There is another whom I have great hopes of. His name is Stephen Crane, and he is very young, but he promises splendid things. He has written one novel so far—'Maggie.' I think that as a study of East Side life in New York 'Maggie' is a wonderful book. There is so much realism of a certain kind in it that we might not like to have it lying on our parlor tables, but I hope that the time will come when any book can safely tell the truth as completely as 'Maggie' does."

Stephen Crane, the young writer whom Mr. Howells praises in such an unusual manner, is still in the very early twenties and wrote "Maggie" several years ago. The little book, which is sold by the Arena Company of Boston, is the story of the life and death of a girl of the tenements. It aims at exact truth in painting an unpleasant side of life, and approaches nearer to realizing it than any other book written by an American ever has. . . .

Politics, But a Good Thing

Anonymous[*]

"It is politics, but it is a very good thing," said William Dean Howells last night, in speaking of the Woman's Auxiliary, which is to aid the Rev. Dr. Parkhurst in his municipal housecleaning.

Mr. Howells was one of the strong advocates of woman suffrage when the subject was agitated in the Spring, and a reporter for The *New-York Times* called on him to see if he was equally in favor of women taking an active part in public affairs without the franchise.

"I am glad to see women enter into public life in any way," Mr. Howells said. "As for this particular matter, I could not give an opinion of it, as I have not given it any consideration. I should think that any opinions I should have in regard to woman suffrage would apply, so far as I know, to this.

"Mrs. Lowell is a public woman, doing a noble work. There are some women, of course, who would be always frivolous and light-minded, and who would never do themselves or any one else any good, by entering into affairs of State. Women, I believe, are naturally serious-minded. It would be a good thing for a woman's character and a good thing for public affairs if she were interested in them."

"You think it would purify the Government?" said the reporter, quoting a stock phrase.

"Purify the Government!" said Mr. Howells, with some disgust. "We would have to go back a long way for that. I think it would purify public life. I think the average woman is better than the average man.

"The great body of women are better than the mass of men. There are several reasons why they should be so. A woman is not tempted by money, generally. That is one of the evils of public life. A woman could not be bought. Men, and not the women, are the breadwinners.

"There is altogether too much talk about the inborn differences of men and women. Novelists have been apt to make too much distinction between their characters. At first, in the home, there is no difference between the boy and the girl. Why should not the girl inherit the father's traits of character as well as the mother's? The differences are chiefly owing to habit and environment, I think.

"A woman is better for the interest she takes in politics, and politics is better for her consideration of it.

"But this matter is considered no more a political matter than ordinary home housecleaning," said the reporter.

[*]Reprinted from the *New York Times*, 13 October 1894, p. 9.

"I do not see how it can be anything but politics," said Mr. Howells. "There is not so much difference between home housecleaning and municipal housecleaning as people think."

Fears Realists Must Wait

Stephen Crane*

". . . When a writer desires to preach in an obvious way he should announce his intention—let him cry out then that he is in the pulpit. But it is the business of the novel—"

"Ah!" said the other man.

"It is the business of the novel to picture the daily life in the most exact terms possible, with an absolute and clear sense of proportion. That is the important matter—the proportion. As a usual thing, I think, people have absolutely no sense of proportion. Their noses are tight against life, you see. They perceive mountains where there are no mountains, but frequently a great peak appears no larger than a rat trap. An artist sees a dog down the street—well, his eye instantly relates the dog to its surroundings. The dog is proportioned to the building and the trees. Whereas, many people can conceive of that dog's tail resting upon a hill top."

"You have often said that the novel is a perspective," observed the other man.

"A perspective, certainly. It is a perspective made for the benefit of people who have no true use of their eyes. The novel, in its real meaning, adjusts the proportions. It preserves the balances. It is in this way that lessons are to be taught and reforms to be won. When people are introduced to each other they will see the resemblances, and won't want to fight so badly."

"I suppose that when a man tries to write 'what the people want'—when he tries to reflect the popular desire, it is a bad quarter of an hour for the laws of proportion."

"Do you recall any of the hosts of stories that began in love and ended a little further on. Those stories used to represent life to the people, and I believe they do now to a large class. Life began when the hero saw a certain girl, and it ended abruptly when he married her. Love and courtship was not an incident, a part of life—it was the whole of it. All else was of no value. Men of that religion must have felt very stupid when they were engaged at anything but courtship.

*Reprinted from the New York Times, 28 October 1894, p. 20.

Do you see the false proportion? Do you see the dog with his tail upon the hilltop? Somebody touched the universal heart with the fascinating theme—the relation of man to maid—and, for many years, it was if no other relation could be recognized in fiction. Here and there an author raised his voice, but not loudly. I like to see the novelists treating some of the other important things of life—the relation of mother and son, of husband and wife, in fact all those things that we live in continually. The other can be but fragmentary."

"I suppose there must be two or three new literary people just back of the horizon somewhere," said the other man. "Books upon these lines that you speak of are what might be called unpopular. Do you think them to be a profitable investment?"

"From my point of view it is right—it is sure to be a profitable investment. After that it is a question of perseverence, courage. A writer of skill cannot be defeated because he remains true to his conscience. It is a long, serious conflict sometimes, but he must win, if he does not falter. Lowell said to me one time: 'After all, the barriers are very thin. They are paper. If a man has his conscience and one or two friends who can help him, it becomes very simple at last.' "

"Mr. Howells," said the other man, suddenly, "have you observed a change in the literary pulse of the country within the last four months? Last Winter, for instance, it seemed that realism was about to capture things, but then recently I have thought that I saw coming a sort of a counter wave, a flood of the other—a reaction, in fact. Trivial, temporary, perhaps, but a reaction, certainly."

Mr. Howells dropped his hand in a gesture of emphatic assent. "What you say is true. I have seen it coming, . . . I suppose we shall have to wait."

The New Story-Tellers and the Doom of Realism

William Roscoe Thayer*

Eight years ago, in writing on "Realism in Literature," I called attention to the then recently printed essays of M. Emile de Vogüé. That excellent critic, who has since been admitted to the French Academy, had in the essays referred to pointed out indications that realistic fiction—at least in France—was fast nearing the high-water mark, and he confidently expected that the turn in the tide would

*Forum, 18 (December 1894), 470–80.

be followed by fiction of a purer, different sort. Only eight years have elapsed, yet no one can doubt that, so far as Realism is concerned, M. de Vogüé was a far-seeing observer. M. Zola, the archpriest of the obscene rites of French Realism, has ceased to have any formative influence on French novelists; he has ceased to be called "*maître*," or to be imitated by disciples; his own books are still widely read, for obvious reasons, among which his talent as an advertiser is not the least; but they beget no warfare among critics and their power as literary epoch-makers has vanished. Even the stories of Guy de Maupassant, the Realist who presented his delicately-wrought immoralities to you with silver tongs, instead of Zola's coal-shovel, we were told the other day by another watcher of French literature, have lost their vogue: and yet Maupassant is but two years dead.

I refer first to France because France is still the initiator of novelties, whether in politics, literature, or millinery; and when she does not originate she is usually the first to give world-currency to what others have initiated. But the symptoms observed in France have been widespread, and the change they betoken is working most healthily in England and America. We violate no confidences in declaring that Realism in fiction is passing away. Eight years ago the "Realists"— who ought rather to be called the "Epidermists"—had the cry; to-day you have only to look at the publishers' announcements, or at the volumes in everybody's hand, to see what fiction is popular. Caine, Doyle, Zangwill, Weyman, Crockett, Du Maurier,—not Realists but Romanticists, not analysts but story-tellers,—are writing the novels which the multitude are sitting up late to read. And Stevenson and Crawford, whose reputation dates from the very heyday of Realism, have certainly not lost popularity during the past decade, while— worse and worse!—two separate popular editions of Scott, and new translations of Dumas *père*, have just come out, in spite of the assertions of the Epidermists that not even schoolboys could now be coaxed to read Sir Walter. Above all, Rudyard Kipling, who was so recently characterized by Mr. Howells as merely a young man with his hat cocked over one eye, holds the entire English-speaking world in fee as no other story-teller since Dickens has held it.

Now this change deserves attention, even from those of us who read very little current fiction, but who realize how important a symptom is the popular demand for it. To follow the statistics of the circulation of novels may lead to conclusions not less significant than do the statistics of the annual consumption of malt and fermented liquors. If you found, for instance, that the nation had in the course of ten years given up whiskey and taken to beer, you might be able to demonstrate the close relation between strong drink and crime; and so we may be sure that the change in taste which has led the public back to romantic fiction has for its basis something deeper than caprice. It is too soon to say how deep the meaning really is, or what may come of it, but it is not too soon to look back over the losing fight of Realism and to specify some of its traits.

In the first place, the tide turned much earlier than most of us expected. Ten years ago few of us dared hope that the exposure of Zola's plausible fallacy would so soon be generally agreed to. He had been captivated by the eminent physiologist, Claude Bernard, who found medicine an art and left it a science, and reasoning from analogy, he had concluded that fiction might be subjected to a similar evolution. Observation and experiment, these were the two methods by which the "experimental novelists," subsequently miscalled "Realist," should produce his work. We all know with what vigor and plausibility Zola set forth this doctrine, which had all the more attractiveness in that it seemed to tally with the scientific spirit of the age. Everything was tinctured with science; the very word "scientific" had become a shibboleth: we had "scientific" clothespins, "scientific" liverpads,— why not "scientific" novels?

And in due time "scientific" novels came,—"Nana," "L'Assommoir," and the rest; but I suspect that Zola's literary philosophy would have achieved notoriety much more slowly had he not chosen topics either brutally obscene or horrible, which at once excited the jaded Parisian palate. And as the author of these works proclaimed that he was personally as impartial towards virtue and vice as a chemist is towards acids and alkalies, and that he did not make it his business to correct nature, but simply to photograph her, his aim being scientific truth, many persons read his abomination who could not have been induced to do so but for the seductive catchword "scientific." Many others read, and still read, Zola, regardless of any literary theory, to gratify their pornographic appetite; for it required no keenness to perceive that decency, modesty, sanctity,—conceptions which, after many painful centuries, the more civilized minority of the human race has begun to venerate,—could not protect themselves against the brazen presumptions of Realism. Zola and his fellows, at home and abroad, tore the veil away with an affectation of scientific impartiality even more repulsive than the downright prurience of the avowed worshippers of lubricity. Strenuously have they protested that their goddess is the naked Truth, but we may well ask, as we look at the product of their school, whether it has not been the nakedness rather than the divinity of Truth which has attracted them.

When Realism had thus assumed the proportion of a literary movement, the historians of literature went back to discover M. Zola's precursors. They traced, with what accuracy I know not, the roots of Realism down through Flaubert and Balzac to Stendhal. The disciples of the new school had no scruple in asserting that it was not only the school of the present and future, but that it would utterly supersede previous literature; its novels were to all previous novels as modern invention to old-fashioned handiwork. It would soon make even school-girls ashamed to admit that they enjoyed romances. Poetry, of course, could no more exist in its presence than frost before a blow-pipe. "There shall never be any more plots," was one of the edicts of the new law-givers. Not since the memorable conflict of the Romanticists and the Classicists had so pretentious a movement been seen; a movement, moreover, which affected, or tended to affect, not merely the writing of novels and all imaginative literature, but also our established views of morals.

I fear that we must confess that this Realistic movement has been, on the whole, less memorable than we should have predicted of a revolution which boldly took upon itself the task of creating a new heaven and a new earth. It has certainly been less spectacular, amusing, and attractive than the Romantic movement which culminated sixty-five years ago. Victor Hugo led that, as Zola has led this. Hugo was very human, and abounded in qualities which drew enthusiastic disciples round him. We cannot think of Zola as a man whom anybody can love; we think of him as a coldly calculating doctrinaire, a chemist who has invented a process for making top-dressing cheap and has the shrewdness to sell it at an enormous profit. In France, the quarrel has been rather *banal,* not enlivened by any such scenes as those which signalized the triumph of Hugo's supporters at the production of "Hernani."

In America, however, the warfare has not failed to amuse us, thanks to the wit of Mr. Howells. Yet even his wit has lacked the picturesqueness of Théophile Gautier's famous flaming waistcoat, which glows upon us from the records of the warfare of Romanticism. At the outset, however, Mr. Howells gave promise of being both picturesque and lively. We all remember how, after his first naïf declaration that the art of fiction as practised by Mr. Henry James and himself is a finer art than that of Dickens, Thackeray, and George Eliot, a burst of genial laughter swept over the continent and re-echoed even in England. Mr. Howells did not directly name himself, of course, but the implication was not to be escaped. The public laughed because it thought it had caught a man-of-the-world—one, moreover, who had been publishing books for a quarter of a century—in a perfectly indiscreet bit of egotism. The fact is, however, that Mr. Howells told the plain truth,—the art of fiction as practised by him and Mr. James is a finer art than that of Dickens or Thackeray, just as the art of the cameoist is "finer" than that of the sculptor.

Mr. Howells, being thoroughly in earnest, probably did not mind the laughter. At any rate no convert from one religion to another could be more zealous than he was during five or six years. He bore witness to his faith by example not less than by precept; and as he had the good fortune to be able to use as a mouthpiece a magazine with a very large circulation, he spread the gospel of Realism in a brief time before multitudes who are usually slow to feel the direction of literary currents. Whatever opinion readers might have had of the novel by Mr. Howells in the earlier part of the magazine, they were sure to be informed in a crisp, satirical essay farther on that only fools and old fogies tolerated fiction produced by other than Realistic methods.

A propagandist as witty, resourceful, and assured as he, has not for so many years together and from so conspicuous a pulpit preached any literary gospel, good or bad, in America; and there were many of us who, while we read very little of his novels, never missed one of his monthly essays. They were significant, if only as symptoms; and then, perhaps the doctrine they uttered might be true. At any rate, it was very wholesome, if somewhat bewildering, at the start, to have our venerable idols challenged, and to receive from the lips of an evangelist the message which was to revolutionize literature, casting out its false gods, dethroning its arrogant sovereigns, levelling its exclusive aristocracies, and establishing a Simon-pure democracy which should be run forever on scientific principles. It took fortitude, until custom made us callous, to watch Mr. Howells, like another Tarquin, go up and down the poppy-field of literature, lopping off head after head which had brought delight to millions. The Greeks, of course, were smitten very early: they are always the first to excite the righteous rage of all sorts of reformers, and have been demolished so many times! Artistic principles—symmetry, grace, condensation, beauty —went next: Realism, we perceived, knew not beauty, and despised literary neatness as your true son of the soil is supposed to despise those who indulge in soap and water. Poetry, too, had its death-warrant signed. Even Shakespeare was not spared. At his martyrdom, we knew that genius too must go, and soon the dictum came that "there is no such thing as genius," that what the unscientific foreworld called by that name is only a strong congenital predisposition *plus* indefatigable perseverance.

Incidentally we learned the tenets of Realism, and month by month we were introduced to Spanish and Russian masters of the new creed. A little later than some of us, but earlier than the masses, Mr. Howells discovered Tolstoi, and then we knew why the Greeks and art and Shakespeare had been previously swept away. For the great Russian, though he be in many aspects a master, has certainly no inkling of the Greek conception of art, no spark of Shakespeare's dramatic intensity. The Greek made his effects by selection. Tolstoi makes his by cumulation; the Greek's motto was "Nothing superfluous"; Tolstoi's is, "Put in everything, and then add a little more." If you think of Russia as a vast flat prairie land, in which even a tree or hillock is an important feature, you may be reminded of Tolstoi; if you remember Greece, with its infinite variety of chiselled mountains and valleys, its individual headlands, its islands and lovely bays, with a luminous sky above and beautiful color on all below, you have, in contrast with him, the Greek. No Greek could so have sinned against his instinct for symmetry as to write "War and Peace," a story, or congeries of stories, stretching through twenty-five hundred pages—the equivalent in space of fifty "Antigones" and of seven or eight Iliads. The Iliad is getting well on in years, and yet, if there existed a company for insuring the lives of literary works, some of us think that the Iliad would prove a better risk than "War and Peace": for one good reason, it is only one eighth as bulky as the Russian masterpiece; and bulk is an element which will count more and more in the longevity of books.

I pause at Tolstoi, because Mr. Howells assured us that his works not only form the culminating glory of Realism, but practically render obsolete all other works not produced by that system. So we accepted the reign of Czar Lyoff, although for a while, after the immolation of Shakespeare and the great companions of our youth, the world seemed empty, lonesome. It was as if the sun had been stolen, and the thief had hung up a locomotive headlight in its stead. But, on closer examination of Tolstoi, we were surprised to find that he wrote almost always with a strong moral purpose; and this, we had been so often assured, was one of the foul practices of the old school of novelists which Realism would abolish. For, to the genuine Realist, virtue and vice are what acids and alkalies are to the chemist: therefore, he cannot prefer, cannot have, an ethical purpose.

Reading Mr. Howells's preachments month by month, while we could but admire his versatility in iconoclasm, and his unquestioning zeal,—he swallowed Tolstoi's "Kreutzer Sonata" and Zola's "La Terre," and smacked his lips, bidding us all do likewise,—we saw that we had to do with a very clever disciple and not at all with a master. As certainly as Mr. Howells is a more graceful and clever writer than M. Zola, so certainly is M. Zola profounder and more philosophical than Mr. Howells. The Frenchman had, indeed, thought out and formulated his system, and his essays in "Le roman expérimental" remain the chief document of the theory of Realism. Them, the serious student of literary and spiritual movements may consult, but Mr. Howells's critical writings take on more and more the aspect of being merely the register of the vagaries of a mind alert rather than cultured, and of a generous spirit which cannot resist becoming the champion of crude causes. Not impossibly, therefore, these writings of his will be valued less and less as orthodox Realistic tracts, and more and more as data for studying the psychological development of an interesting personality.

Nevertheless, Mr. Howells had the satisfaction, for the time being, of making Realism the chief topic of discussion, and of encouraging the belief in innumerable crude minds that you have only to report word for word the morning gossip of idle women on a summer hotel piazza, or the rusticities in wit and grammar of the patrons of the corner grocery, in order to produce a work beside which Shakespeare's pages look faded. Perhaps no higher compliment can be paid to Mr. Howells than to state that those who undertake to write about Realism in America will inevitably find themselves dealing with it as though it were his private property, instead of with the doctrines and assertions of a system. And yet for a dozen years a horde of Realists, great and small, have been filling the magazines with their products and turning out an average of two novels a day.

And now Realism—a movement which, but for the deep matters it involves, we might call a fad—is on the wane. It has been the logical outcome of our age, whose characteristic is analysis. Our modern science, abandoning the search for the Absolute, has been scrutinizing every atom, to weigh and name it, and to discover its relations with its neighbors. "Relativity" has been the watchword. Science literally knows neither great nor small: it examines the microbe and Sirius with equal interest; it draws no distinction between beauty and ugliness—having no preference for the toadstool or the rose, the sculpin or the trout: it is impartial; it seeks only to know. By observation and experiment, by advancing from the known to the unknown, science has begun to make the first accurate inventory of the substances, laws, and properties of the world of matter. Its achievements have already been stupendous. Its methods have dominated all the other works in our time; it was inevitable that they should encroach on the sphere of art and of literature.

Arguing from analogy, the Realist persuaded himself that the only means for attaining perfect accuracy in fiction must be experiment and observation, which had brought such rich returns to Science. He disdained anything except an exact reproduction of real life— hence his name, Realist. To him, as to the man of science, there should be, he declared, neither beauty nor ugliness, great nor small, goodness nor evil; he was impartial; he eliminated the personal equation; he would make his mind as unprejudiced as a photographic plate. To Pyrrhonism so thoroughgoing, considerations of interest and charm appealed no more than did considerations of morals or of beauty. The Realist frankly announced that the precise record of the humblest mind was just as important as one of Shakespeare's mind would be. So we have been regaled by our English and American Realists with interminable inspection and introspection of commonplace intellects; and if we have yawned, we have been told that we are still poisoned with Romanticism, and still had a childish desire to read about persons with high titles, moving in the upper circles. Realism, we were assured, was the application of democratic principles to fiction. When, on the other hand, the foreign Realists dealt chiefly in moral filth, we were children for our squeamishness, and informed that, since depravity exists, the Realist is in duty bound to make impartial studies of it.

I need not point out that such doctrines reduce literature, art, and morals to anarchy. The "scientific method," applied in this way, is not the method for portraying human nature. Only the human can understand, and consequently interpret, the human: how, therefore, shall a man who boasts that he has *dehumanized* himself so that his mind is as impartial as a photographic plate, enabling him to look on his fellow-beings without preferring the good to the bad, the beautiful to the ugly,—how shall he be qualified to speak for the race which does discriminate, does prefer, does feel? The camera sees only the outside; the Realist sees no more, and so it would be more appropriate to call him "Epidermist," one who investigates only the surface, the cuticle of life,—usually with a preference for very dirty skin.

And, in truth, he deceives himself as to the extent of his scientific impartiality. He, too, has to select; he cannot set down every trivial thought, cannot measure every freckle. His work is fiction— a consideration which he had forgotten. But since he is forced to select, he cannot escape being judged by the same canons as all other artists. Do they not all aim at representing life? Is *Silas Lapham*, produced by Epidermist methods, more real than *Shylock* or *Hamlet?* Will he be thought so three hundred years hence, or will he seem odd and antiquated, a mere fashion, like the cut of old garments? Only the human can understand and interpret the human; and our Epidermists also will, in time, perceive that not by relying on the phonograph and kodak can they come to know the heart of man. They have mistaken the dead actual for reality, the show of the moment for the essence, the letter for the spirit.

By the imagination have all the highest creations of art and literature been produced, and the general truths of science and morals been discovered: (for the imagination is that supreme faculty in man which beholds reality;) it is the faculty, furthermore, which synthetizes, which vivifies, which constructs. The Epidermist, whose forte is analysis, discarding the imagination, has hoped by accumulating masses of details to produce as sure an effect of reality, as genuis produces by using a few essentials. Yet, merely in the matter of illusion, this is an inferior method: if Mr. Kipling, for instance, can in a paragraph illude his readers to the extent he desires, whereas it takes Mr. Howells or Mr. James ten pages to produce an illusion, the chances are ten to one against Epidermism as a means of literary expression.

That heaping up of minute details which is proper in scientific investigation has influenced immensely all our intellectual processes for the past fifty years. There was a time when theology was the absorbing interest, and even non-theological works of that time, the fiction and poetry, are inevitably saturated with theology. We can detect it plainly and can pronounce it just so far a detriment to the novel or poem in which we find it. So science has permeated our time, encroaching upon, and inevitably vitiating, departments over which it has no jurisdiction. The multitude has been willing to accept the products of Epidermism, because its own imagination has been dulled, and it has come to suppose that observation and experiment were the only methods by which truth can be discovered. Hence the tanks of *real* water and the *real* burglars and the *real* fire-engines in our recent plays, and hence the predominance of Realism in fiction.

But the knell of the Epidermists has sounded. The novels that are everywhere in demand are the novels with a story. Individually, they may be good or bad—it matters not: the significant fact is that the public taste has turned, and that that instinct which is as old as the children of Adam and Eve, the instinct for a story, has reasserted itself.

Realism, therefore, has been a phase, indicating the decadence of fiction, and not, as the Epidermists themselves believed, its regeneration. It represents the period during which fiction has been enslaved by scientific methods, a period when the imagination has lain dormant, and other—lower—faculties have essayed to do her work. The novels produced by Realism will not, I suppose, occupy the attention of the world sixty years from now to the same extent that the products of Romanticism still occupy our attention. Certainly, the polemics of Realism have produced nothing so striking as Hugo's and Manzoni's and Heine's essays on Romanticism; nothing that has the lasting quality of Wordsworth's prefaces, or of Coleridge's criticism on Wordsworth. I hazard the prediction that our children, if they ever turn the pages of the masterpieces of Realism, will wonder how we could once have read them: and that, not because they will find in those pages much that is nasty (under the plea of "science"), and much that is morbid, and more that is petty, but because the prevailing note is dulness. Against dulness, the gods themselves have no refuge save flight.

Eight years ago all this was less evident than it is now. We could not say with assurance eight years ago that the movement had reached its logical culmination. To-day we can say this. Doubtless its votaries will not abandon it suddenly; but when they find the story-tellers getting all the readers, they will know their doom. Epidermism has already found its true habitat in the sensational daily press: there, the kodak and the phonograph and the eavesdropper have untrammelled play; and moreover, the persons portrayed are really alive—which gives them an advantage against which the make-believe real people of Mr. Howells cannot in the long run compete; for if *realness* be the final test, the really real heroes of the newspapers must excel the make-believe real characters of Epidermist fiction. What chance has *Silas Lapham* with the barber or bootblacks described, with illustrations, any day in the New York "Scavenger"? Another product of Epidermism, the dialect story, will soon, we may hope, be banished from the magazines to the transactions of the dialect societies, which have been providentially springing up. Of the shameless products—the obscenities and filth—we can at least predict that the time for foisting them, and all other matters not pertinent to fiction, upon us, under the plea of scientific impartiality, has passed; though doubtless from time to time some angel of the pit, some new Zola, will come to stir the surface of the cesspools of society.

Realism, or Epidermism, passes; but at least the example of sincerity which many of its devotees have given will not be lost. And now, as the atmosphere is clearing, the dear and venerable masters greet us in their majesty undiminished. Shakespeare—whose laurel has been prematurely claimed so many times by ardent partisans for the brows of ephemeral idols—Shakespeare and Dante, and the spokesmen of antiquity, confer serenely together. Near them, in another group, are Scott and Hawthorne and Thackeray, unconscious that they were so recently ostracized from Olympus. Could their words reach us, assuredly they would confirm the message written through all their books: "The lamp of Art differs from the lamp of Science; confound not their uses. Think not by machine or tool, which is material, to discover the secret of the heart of man, who is spiritual. The Real includes the Ideal; but the Real without the Ideal is as the body without life, a thing for anatomists to dissect. Only the human can understand and interpret the human."

William Dean Howells

Henry C. Vedder*

II

With the publication of "Their Wedding Journey" in 1871, Mr. Howells entered on his real career. Hitherto he had been experimenting, now he had found his vocation. One cannot treat his poems as anything better than the exercises of a clever lad, or the amusements of a versatile man of letters. His critical work is a by-product, a collection of chips from the workshop of a busy writer. From this time on we have to do with a man who is first of all and last of all a novelist. Novel after novel has made its appearance, with the unfailing regularity of the seasons. Yet this fecundity has not been reached at the expense of quality. None of his books bears marks of undue haste, of careless workmanship, of failing powers. On the contrary, if each book published has not surpassed all its predecessors, we can trace in the author from year to year an increase of power, a completer mastery of the resources of this art, a large view, an ampler spirit. One has heard and read that of late years a change has come over Mr. Howells,—that the romance of his earlier books has faded away into a hard, dry, realism, that he has lost the joyousness of youth and has become pessimistic, not to say cynical. This seems an opinion founded on a partial and superficial knowledge of Mr. Howells's writings. There is nothing more romantic or idyllic in the Marches when we first meet them on "Their Wedding Journey" than when after a score of years we renew their acquaintance in "A Hazard of New Fortunes." Such change as is to be noted in his later books is due rather to the influence of the much-admired Tolstoi than to any other cause. "The World of Chance" is quite strongly tinged with the Russian novelist's views of society and religion. It cannot be said, however, that much of the light of hope is thrown on the regeneration of society by a book in which one would-be regenerator becomes a maniac, and commits suicide after unsuccessfully attempting murder, while another dies without having accomplished the great purpose of his life, the publication of a book that was to be the gospel of a new era.

III

Even a casual reader of these books is soon aware that their author is no mere story-teller, content just to amuse the public, regarding their

American Writers of To-Day (New York, 1894), pp. 50–68.

smiling approval as the be-all and end-all of his obligation. He is a thoroughly instructed artist, who works not at haphazard, who succeeds not by lucky strokes of genius, but proceeds according to a well-defined theory of his art,—a theory that we must take pains to understand if we would judge him fairly and sympathetically. We may dissent from the theory, we may find the practice faulty; what we may not do is to judge him in the empirical and *a priori* fashion so common in current criticism.

Both in theory and in practice, Mr. Howells is a realist. He believes, that is to say, that the chief end of the novel is not to tell a story, but to represent life. A story there must be, of course, but not necessarily a plot; the history of the spiritual development of a single personage, for example, is a "story." The novel must tell a story in the sense that a picture tells a story, and in no other sense; in other words, whatever represents a bit of life necessarily tells a story. This fundamental canon requires no debate, for it is not merely truth but truism, or nearly so. Like Captain Cuttle's observation, the bearings of it lie in its application, and it is when Mr. Howells begins to apply his canon, whether in his own practice or in criticism of others, that doubts begin to suggest themselves.

Art is necessarily selective, for the sufficient reason that no man can represent the whole of life. It is only a scrap of landscape that the painter can put on his largest canvas, and only a glimpse of some tiny segment of the social cosmos (or shall we say chaos?) can be afforded the readers of a three-volume novel. This being the case, the question immediately arises whether some principle or principles should not govern the selection of what is to be represented. There are professors of realism in fiction who teach that all possible objects are equally worthy of representation. They do not really believe this, because even they practise selection, and therefore, of course, rejection; but, as children say, they "make believe" believe it when they are challenged. Nay, they virtually affirm that the more worthless and commonplace, the more hideous and repulsive and vile an object is, the more worthy it is of representation.

Now this application of the canon of realism one is certainly entitled to dispute without thereby incurring suspicion of questioning the canon itself. All art has taken it for granted, from its rudest beginnings until now, that some objects in nature, some experiences in life, are better adapted for representation than others. The choice of object has been dictated, in the main, by its capacity to please. Without disputing the fact that there is a place in art for the grotesque, for the painful, even, its chief function is to please and ennoble. The great artists have always appealed to the moral as well as to the aesthetic faculties. One is not convinced, therefore, by any assertions or examples of realists in fiction, that the trivial and the vile furnish proper subjects for the artist. To the healthy mind they give no pleasure; they inspire only *ennui* or disgust.

Mr. Howells cannot be too promptly acquitted of any suspicion of choosing the vile as subject of his art. His one villain, Bradley Hubbard, is so ill done, in comparison with his other work, as to suggest lack of knowledge of this type. The bad woman he has never attempted to draw, though American society is not quite guiltless of Becky Sharps. But the trivial, the commonplace, he has exhibited in season and out, especially in his representations of American women. That, however, introduces a subject so large as to demand discussion by itself. Passing it by for the present, it is pertinent to inquire, Can it be that Mr. Howells gives us in his books a fair representation of life as he has known it? Has his whole experience been of this stale, flat, unprofitable sort? Has he never known anybody who had a soul above buttons? The thing seems difficult to believe. It may be that the people we meet in his novels are those with whom he is most familiar, those that he feels himself most competent to depict, but that they exhaust his experience of life and his knowledge of the world one cannot so easily accept.

Let us be just, however. To Mr. Howells we must award the praise of having done well what he set out to do. Given the propriety of the choice, we must grant that he has made a faithful and lifelike picture of the thing chosen. It is with the choice itself that many of his readers quarrel; or, perhaps one should say, they quarrel with his persistent and exclusive choice of one type of character and one sort of experience for representation in his fiction. Whether he has not known higher types of character among us, or has lacked courage to attempt their portraiture—in either case he has chosen badly for his readers, though possibly prudently for himself.

IV

No examination of the works of Mr. Howells would have any claim to comprehensiveness that failed to take account of his farce-comedies. There is quite a series of these, beginning with "The Sleeping-Car" and ending with the "Unexpected Guests." No American author has given us more admirable fooling than this, at once clever and refined. The humor is free from that element of exaggeration supposed to be peculiarly characteristic of American humor. The humor of Mr. Howells is as well-bred and studiously proper as the elegant Bostonians who are his *dramatis personae*; it is humor in a swallow-tail coat and white-lawn tie, so to say. Those *dramatis personae* deserve a separate word: they are but four,—the real characters, that is to say, though make-weights may occasionally be introduced,—but they have been ingeniously utilized, year after year, in new situations, until they seem to us people whom we have known all our lives. The same idea has been almost simultaneously worked out by several clever writers of short stories; but none of his rivals has succeeded like Mr. Howells in making his people real flesh-and-blood persons.

These comedies bring us again face to face with the chief grievance one has against Mr. Howells, and it is time to have it fairly out with him,—that is, his curiously and indeed exasperatingly inadequate portraiture of American womanhood. This is more or less a fault of all his writing, but it becomes most conspicuous in these farces. Are Mrs. Roberts and Mrs. Campbell fair types of American womanhood? Is the American woman who is both well-bred and well-read usually only one remove from idiocy? * * * *

* * * * *

Enough, with over-measure, of this. Let Mr. Howells, if he will, renounce the critic and all his works, and in the next breath do the same works and greater things also. We do not demand of him that consistency which is the virtue of feeble minds, but are rather grateful to find in him a single redeeming vice. Even though he occasionally aggravate us by his wrong-headedness, as some of us must consider it, Mr. Howells is easily the first living American novelist. We cannot deny him the praise of being faithful to his own ideal, of practising diligently his own canons of art. He himself tells us, with great earnestness and frequent iteration, that he utterly contemns and rejects the

notion that the novel should aim merely to entertain. What we must say to any serious fiction is this, "Is it true? true to the motives, the impulses, the principles that shape the life of actual men and women?" If the answer be in the affirmative, such a work cannot be bad, for this truth "necessarily includes the highest morality and the highest artistry." To realize this ideal, Mr. Howells has earnestly striven. If he has failed in some instances to reach it, his failure is not due to lack of conscientious industry and high resolve. And certainly, within his limitations, of all our American writers none has come nearer to doing in fiction what the greatest master of the drama has declared to be the purpose of the stage, "to hold as 't were the mirror up to nature; to show virtue her own feature, scorn her own image, and the very age and body of the time his form and pressure."

1895-1897

The Great Realists and the Empty Story-Tellers

Hjalmar Hjorth Boyesen*

Who that has read Rousseau's "Confessions" will fail to remember the emphatic avowal that he was unfitted for life by the reading of novels? To be sure, the novels he read were of a highly romantic, or, as it is euphemistically called, "idealistic," kind, which represented a condition of things that never was on land or sea. And it was not an occasional excursion the boy, Jean-Jacques, undertook into this delightful region of high-colored improbabilities; but he took up his residence there and dwelt there, making only reluctant visits to the "sordid" reality which surrounded him. He devoured romances with a ravenous appetite for the intoxication which he craved, and craved more and more. He sought refuge in a fictitious world of resonant speech and mighty deeds from the *petites misères* of a small *bourgeois* existence in Geneva. Like the opium-habit the craving for fiction grew upon him, until the fundamental part of him had suffered irreparable harm.

It is barely possible, of course, that Rousseau, in looking back upon his past life and trying to account for its vagaries and misadventures, exaggerates the effect of his intemperance in the matter of fiction. He may have had a taint from his birth, making him nervously unstrung and liable to excesses. But, even making allowance for this, I find his avowal interesting and significant. He is not the only one who has experienced detrimental effects from dwelling too long in the pleasant land of romance. As soon as a man—and particularly a child—gets acclimated there, he is likely to become of very small account as far as reality is concerned. He becomes less and less able to apply sound standards of judgment to the things of this world; and as the success in life for which we are all striving depends primarily upon this ability to see things straight and to judge them clearly, no one can escape the conclusion

*Reprinted from *Forum*, 18 (February 1895), 724–31.

that a large consumption of romantic fiction tends distinctly to disqualify a man for worldly success. A habit of mind is produced by the frequent repetition of the same or similar impressions; and if, while young, your thoughts move among absurd and lurid unrealities, and your eyes become accustomed to the Bengal illumination of romance, you will be likely to tumble about like a blundering bat in the daylight. Many a time, I will warrant, you have had this very experience of waking, as from a delightful dream, when your novel was finished. The world and all your daily concerns look pale, dreary and vaguely irritating, while your mind is yet vibrating with the courtly speeches of some fascinating d'Artagnan, to whom life was but a stage for gallant adventures, or with the clash of Ivanhoe's sword or the impossible heroism of an impossible Esmeralda. The youth who gets his mind adjusted to these styles of speech and action and the motives which they imply will be severely handicapped in dealing with affairs which require a nice discrimination of practical values. He will find it next to impossible to command that supreme concentration of effort without which no great achievement is accomplished. He will lapse into mediocrity, even though he may have been equipped for distinction.

"But," you will object, "this escape which romance affords us from life's dreary round of cares and duties is not only delightful but beneficial: it refreshes the mind, satisfies a latent craving for the heroic, which we all have, and sends sun-gleams from an ideal world down into our gray, monotonous existence; it is like canvas-back, terrapin, and champagne to a man who is wont to dine on porridge and red herring."

Well, there is a good deal to be said for this view. But, in my opinion, it is unsound. As the world is now constituted, the little margin of superiority by which a man secures survival and success is so narrow, that the very smallest advantage, gained or squandered, may be decisive as to his whole career. Therefore, all education should be primarily directed toward securing as intimate an acquaintance as possible with one's environment, so that one may be able to utilize it most effectively. I freely admit that this is not the aim of our present educational system, which flounders helplessly between the old humanistic curriculum and the new scientific studies. But a new light has dawned upon our darkness, and education is being reformed about as fast as academic conservatism will permit. This by way of a parenthesis, which, however, has a direct bearing upon my contention. The most modern novel—which should not be confounded with the romance—has set itself this very task of exploring reality, and gauging the relative strength of the forces that enter into our lives and determine our own fate....

I am distinctly conscious of being indebted to Thackeray for having led me out of the "moon-illumined magic night" of German romanticism (in which I once revelled) and accustomed me, by degrees, to a wholesomer, though less poetic, light. Vividly do I remember the distaste, the resentment, with which as a youth of twenty I flung away "The Virginians" at the chapter where Harry's calf-love for Maria is satirized. Like a sting to the quick was to me the remark about his pressing "the wilted vegetable" with rapture to his lips, or was it his heart? The delicious, good-natured ridicule with which the infatuation of Pen for Miss Fotheringay is treated in "Pendennis" hurt and disgusted me. I felt as if the author were personally abusing me. For I was then at the age when Pen's madness seemed to verge more nearly on sublimity than on foolishness. Accordingly I had a low opinion of Thackeray in those days.

But for all that, I could not help reading him; and, truth to tell, I owe him a debt of gratitude which it would be difficult to over-estimate. He saved me from no end of dangerous follies by kindling in me a spark of sobering self-criticism, which enabled me to catch little side-glimpses of myself, when I was on the verge of committing a *bêtise*. He aroused in me a salutary scepticism as to the worth of much which the world has stamped with its approval. He blew away a good deal of that romantic haze which hid reality from me and prevented me from appraising men and things at their proper value. Though no crude Sundayschool moral is appended to "Pendennis," "The Newcomes" or "Vanity Fair," he must be duller than an ox to the subtler sense who does not feel in the pervasive atmosphere of these books a wholesome moral tonic. And who can make the acquaintance of Colonel Newcome without having the character of the man stamped on his very soul and feeling a glow of enthusiasm for his nobleness, uprightness and lofty sense of honor? It is because he is so touchingly human, so pathetically true, that he makes so deep an impression. And as for Clive and Rose and the Campaigner, their fates have an educational worth beyond a hundred sermons. Though Thackeray does not often scold his bad and questionable characters (as does, for instance, Dickens), and though he permits an occasional smile to lurk between the lines at Becky Sharp's reprehensible cleverness, there is nowhere any confusion of moral values; and the voice that speaks has a half paternal cadence of genial wisdom and resignation.

Among the other novelists to whom I am indebted for a clearance of vision, I cannot omit Tolstoi. He is a more strenuous and commanding personality than was Thackeray; and the moral he teaches is more direct, insistent, importunate. I am speaking now of his early works, which were written before he became a prophet. Not that—though disagreeing with him—I honor him less in this capacity than in that of a writer of fiction: but his work as a social reformer lies beyond the scope of the present article. It is as the author of "Anna Karénina" that he has his title to immortality. I have heard many good people call this wonderful novel immoral, because they have the notion that every book which touches upon the question of sex is *ipso facto* immoral. Nothing can, to my mind, be sillier than this. The novelist has to take life as he finds it, and he would produce a false, distorted picture if he were to omit a factor which plays so tremendous a part as sex. The morality depends upon the spirit in which the author deals with his subject. "La dame aux Camélias" is immoral, not because the heroine is of the *demi-monde*, but because Dumas *fils* violates the logic of life in representing her as a lovely and sentimental creature, and capable of as pure and exalting a passion as a woman who had never sinned. Likewise Mürger in "Scènes de la vie de Bohême" and Du Maurier in "Trilby," fascinating though they are, extol the grisette, implying that an occasional lapse from virtue is, on the whole, a venial affair and leaves the core of the character unimpaired. Musette in the former novel and Trilby in the latter are rose-colored lies and are the more dangerous because uncritical youth will take them to be types of their kind and will never suspect how untrue they are, how far removed from reality. No, then give me rather Zola's "Nana," which states the unvarnished fact with brutal directness; or even Daudet's "Sappho," which details the whole direful experience, from the first intoxication of the sense through the years of gradual disillusion to the utter blighting of the soul, exhaustion and ruin. No one will feel tempted to embark in so perilous an enterprise, after having received so lucid an exposition of the consequences; while I know more than one young man in whom the seeds of corruption were sown by Dumas and Mürger. These writers are immoral, not because they deal with sin, but because they deal with it untruthfully; while Zola and, in a less degree, Daudet, who give an exact and vivid reflection of an ugly reality, become unintentional, if not unconscious, moralists.

Among these faithful and unflinching chroniclers of life Tolstoi is the foremost. He is the greatest living moralist, because he pierces deeper into the heart of things than any contemporary writer. Nowhere have I found in him an instance of prevarication. Without a word of preaching, he enforces in "Anna Karénina" the inexorable law that all antisocial relations are destructive of character, destructive of happiness, destructive of life itself. When the individual, in pursuing its lawless pleasure, imagines that it is drinking in deep draughts the very fulness of life, it is really engaged in reducing and diminishing its fitness for life—in eliminating itself from the struggle for existence. It is engaged in demonstrating its unfitness for survival. Thus Anna's sin destroys her by a relentless necessity, first, because it brings her upon a war-footing with society, which is founded upon the family and must, in self-protection, resent affinities that controvert this fundamental institution; secondly, because the insecurity of the relation itself and the consciousness of its abnormality induce perpetual excitements, which, by ruining the nerves, upset the mental balance and make sane and tranquil conduct impossible. What profound psychology Tolstoi displays, and what fine reticence, too, in the account of Anna's moral deterioration! How insidiously and gradually she entangles herself in the net which drags her to perdition!

There is something almost appalling in the rigorous veracity of this great and patient Russian with the toil-worn hands and the tragic face. There is a vast murmur of human activities in his novels, a busy clamor of human voices, a throbbing turmoil of human heartbeats,—so much so that one appears to have lived through his books rather than read them. Never did I suspect the closeness of man's kinship to man and the identity of human experience, in spite of race, climate and country, until I read Tolstoi's remarkable autobiography, entitled, "Childhood, Boyhood, and Youth"; and after having finished "Ivan Ilyitch" I actually began to develop the symptoms of the mysterious malady which killed the unheroic hero of that extraordinary novel. To be sure, I had had a fall from my horse the week before, and that may have given color to my illusions.

How unutterably flimsy and juvenile, romantic fiction, such as Stevenson's tales of villainous wreckers and buccaneers, Haggard's chronicles of battle, murder and sudden death, Conan Doyle's accounts of swaggering savagery and sickening atrocities, and S. R. Crockett's sanguinary records of Scotch marauding expeditions, appear to me, compared with Tolstoi's wonderfully vivid and masterly transcripts of the life we all live! Amid all the shouts of the fighters and the clash of arms there is, to me, a deadly silence in the popular novel of adventure. The purely artificial excitement leaves me cold and a trifle fatigued. I see everywhere the hand that pulls the wires. It is a great dead world, whose puppets are galvanized into a semblance of life by the art of the author.

"But," the critics will tell you, "you must be a poor prosaic soul if you do not feel your pulses tingle with delight when you read of heroic adventures and daring deeds." Well, that depends primarily upon what they call heroic. When I read in Rider Haggard of two Englishmen who killed fifty or a hundred or five hundred Zulus, or in Conan Doyle's "The White Company" of four Britishers and a Frenchman keeping an army of six or seven thousand at bay, or in Walter Scott of Ivanhoe's tremendous feat of arms, I am not a particle stirred, first, because the deeds do not seem admirable, and secondly, because neither Ivanhoe nor the Zulu-killing young Britishers are to me alive; for which reason it is of small consequence what they do. When, on the other hand, I read in Tolstoi's "War and Peace" the account of the siege of Sevastopol, during which daring acts were frequent, I am deeply interested, because it all bears the stamp of authenticity, and it is interpenetrated with a warm, red-veined humanity. That is war as it is, written by one who draws upon his own experience, and knows whereof he speaks. But who will pretend that Walter Scott, splendid *raconteur* though he was, represented with even a remote degree of correctness the life of the Middle Ages? And still less can Rider Haggard, or any of his romantic *confrères*, lay claim to verisimilitude or fidelity to anything but their own desire to excite and amuse. The reading of their books tends to the awakening in the young of the feudal ideal which it has cost the world such a deluge of blood and tears, partly to get rid of. For that we have not wholly gotten rid of it the popularity of these very authors sufficiently proves.

I shall probably be charged with exaggeration if I say that the recent aristocratic development in the United States, with its truly mediaeval inequality between the classes, is in no small measure due to this recrudescence of the feudal ideal among us, which is again, in a measure, due to the romantic fiction that our youth of both sexes consume. It is the feudal sentiment of good Sir Walter and his successors which makes our daughters despise the democracy which their fathers founded, and dream of baronial castles, parks and coronets and a marriage with a British peer as the goal of their ambitions. It is the same feudal sentiment which makes their mothers share and encourage their aspirations and equip them, in Paris, with all the ethereal ammunition required for the English campaign. Half the novels they read glorify these things, and it would be a wonder if the perpetual glorification did not produce its effect. For the idea that literature of amusement is a neutral agency which affects you neither for good nor for ill is a pernicious fallacy. What you read, especially in youth, will enter into your mental substance, and will and must increase or impair our efficiency. Much you will outgrow, no doubt; but there always remains a deposit in the mind which you will never outgrow. It is, therefore, of the utmost importance that that which you read should tend to put you *en rapport* with the present industrial age, in which, whether you like it or not, you have to live, rather than with a remote feudalism, whose ideals were essentially barbaric, and certainly cruder and less humane than ours. It is your comprehension of the problems in your own existence and in that of your unheroic neighbors—what the romancers contemptuously call the prose of life—which makes you a useful and influential citizen; while preoccupation with what is wrongfully conceived to be its poetry produces wrecks and failures. It is because the romantic novel tends to unfit you for this prose of life that I condemn it; and it is because the realistic novel opens your eyes to its beauty, its power and its deeper significance that I commend it.

Sense and Sentiment

Clifton Johnson*

I sat at the desk, at Mr. Howells's invitation, and he took a chair and sat just beyond the desk at the back of the room. The question which started the talk was as to whether men and women were different in their temperaments because of environment, or because Nature made them so. Mr. Howells said, substantially:

"I have come latterly to think that the differences we see between men and women are due very largely to their bringing up—to their education. Boys and girls begin to be differentiated when they are small children, and I must say that I think the stress we lay on the proprieties with them is a very mischievous one. The girl is not allowed the freedom the boy has. Many of the things he does she is warned against. Her mother says, 'That is very rude, that is very tomboyish; you mustn't do that;' and her open-air life begins to be curtailed very early; it's our version of the Chinese foot-binding. Up to seven or eight years of age the boys and girls play together with entire abandon, both indoors and out, and their enjoyment and interest in things are almost exactly the same. Yes, there is much more likeness between men and women than people commonly believe.

"But besides the artificial differences between men and women due to their bringing up, there is the artificial variance created in their minds by the romances they read. It is very common in books for writers to treat their women with a cast of irony. You can't understand a woman's motives, they say, or her character. But you can understand them perfectly. There's no mystery in the matter at all. If a woman's motives have remained the motives of a child, it's because of her bringing up. If her motives are sometimes distorted and queer, so would a man's be with her education. The woman who takes care of her house and has serious responsibilities and works honestly for her living has the same sort of sense in thought and action that a man has. Of course the mind of the unoccupied woman, or the one whose occupations are trivial or frivolous, is the nest for all sorts of odd ideas. But such a one is not the normal woman.

"Women are much given to emotions. A woman is not ashamed to be a coward, and a man is. A woman is not ashamed to cry, and a man is. But the women are invited to be timid from childhood up. Men think their fright and their tears rather pretty, and they encourage such exhibitions. Women are apt to be illogical, and their illogical character is very interesting. I have studied it a good deal in my works. There is a

*Reprinted from *Outlook*, 51 (23 February 1895), 304–05.

little difference between men's and women's characters that is real, but
it has been very much exaggerated.

"In savage nations women are treated as slaves. In Oriental countries
they are treated as dolls. It has remained for the northern nations to
give them their true place. Of course, with some men, even among us,
there still cling remnants of the savage or Oriental view. But the tendency grows to take women more and more seriously. The most marked
feature in our American view of women is the idolization of the girl.
She is worshiped—we are charmed with her and all her ways. It is a
pity this should be so. If the worship is prolonged, its effects are very
bad—it spoils the girl.

"I don't think lovers know much about each other's characters. It's
not character that they fall in love with, usually. A man falls in love
with a woman's beauty, or, more than that, her grace. You see a girl
who is graceful and she is a great captivator. A plain face and grace
are much more powerful than beauty without it. It may be grace of manner, movement, carriage of the head or body, or grace of speech—the
girl that has grace is pretty sure to have suitors.

"Marriage has very much the nature of a lottery, and how can it be
otherwise? The conditions of meeting are not such that lovers get to
know each other really. They must have an acquaintance with each other
somewhere else than at parties and in the parlor, or it can't be real.
Only work and serious interests will bring out character. Religion used
to have a place in life that stirred people's inmost feelings, and they
could get to know each other in that. But the interests of life have
multiplied, and the place of religion is relatively less important. I don't
think happiness can ever be looked forward to with assurance in the
average marriage, until the matter becomes more the affair of society—of
the State. The system in the Moravian Church is excellent, where all the
elders take interest in seeing the young people well placed; and so, too,
among the Quakers, undoubtedly, where there is the same oversight and
nothing is done in haste, or heedless of the general good. There should
be more public interest in marriage. The State is quite as much concerned in having marriages wise and happy as the couples are themselves.

"The Swiss have a divorce law that seems to me almost perfect. The
man and wife who think they can't get along together go before a
judge, state their case, and are remanded to their homes as they were
before marriage. Six months later they again come before the judge. If
they are still antagonistic, they are sent away for another six months. At
the end of that time they must again appear before the judge. If they
then are of the same mind as at the beginning, the case is concluded
and they are divorced. What we need is not only the same law about
divorce but a similar law about marriage. If those who intended mar-

riage were obliged to come three times before a court in that way, at intervals of six months, before they were allowed to unite, it would be a great thing. If lovers were compelled to do that, they wouldn't merely feel their love, they would think it, and there would be a comparative safety.

"As we have no such law, perhaps the best safeguard within reach is a long engagement. If it is the fashion now to make the engagements short—so much the worse for the fashion. Two, three, or four months— what a brief time to determine the fate of a life!

"Those who love should have time to get thoroughly acquainted, and, if it seems they have made a mistake, to repair it by breaking the engagement. I think every broken engagement is the best thing that could happen. If it can be broken, it ought to be.

"After marriage the charms and fancies that first drew the two to-gether gradually wear off. They begin to get a true acquaintance with each other. Then they become friends and companions. It isn't desirable that the early, sentimental attraction should continue. They would be fools if it did. If you find married people of middle age showing the same romantic affection that you see among young lovers, it is simply silly. There's no merit in it. In novels it is generally regarded as a great credit to a man if he has a sentimental regard for his wife. But that is a mistake. The early romance must go. It can't last any more than the blossoms on a tree can last.

"I don't think that marrying for money or position is very common in this country. It isn't among the people that I know, though it may be more so outside. Money marries money, as a rule. If one is rich and the other not, they instinctively feel that it is an unequal thing. The situation is not a comfortable one. In ninety-nine cases out of one hundred our marriages are love-marriages—at least they are called so. They often grow out of the silliest triviality, but there is love in them. Yet the fact that one loves does not insure future happiness. The proof that our love-marriages are not inspired is the commonness of our di-vorce. There should be no marriage without love, but there should be common interests and a likeness of tastes and character that will give some deeper bond of union than fancy. There's a hazard and heedless-ness in our nature that are very detrimental to our happiness in mar-riage. It would be better for us if marriages were left more to the parents, as they are in Italy and France. I think the chances are greater for happy unions in such countries than in ours. It is the young people's affair, and in the end they must be given way to. But there is a need of intelligent oversight and suggestion on the part of the older people from the beginning. As things are, marriage is very haphazard. It rests on fancies that young people take for each other, on propinquity, on the fact that they happen to be thrown together. If they had chanced to meet with different people, lived in some other town, they would have loved just the same, only with a change of objects. The belief that there is destiny in it—that there is only one person in the world you could truly love—will not hold water. Then, you know, lovers' heads are full of stuff—all sorts of notions bottled up there from their reading, the plays they've seen, the talk they've heard. Their feelings and sentiments are not their own—they've been absorbed from outside. They expect to be so and so, and they are so and so.

"Do I think it is any discredit to be an old maid? No, indeed—no, indeed! Why should the fact that a woman doesn't marry be a criterion of her worth any more than it is of a man's? I know people joke about old maids, but it's just tradition. It comes out of the emptiness of people's minds. By far the greater number of old maids are sensible, full of thought, and most estimable. They have more time than married women, and on an average have done more studying and reading, and are mentally more controlled and intelligent. I think that very often a foolish and unprofitable marriage is made by a girl for no other reason than her fear of these shallow jokes about old maids.

"Among silly people there is a habit of talking sentimentally with children about their beaux and 'fellows.' Such talk is very pernicious. Why can't these unthinking people let the children alone? The little friendships between the boys and girls are very precious. A little girl has a fancy for a little boy just as she would have for a little girl. Why must the older people step in and spoil all the sweetness of the fancy by giving it a sentimental interpretation?

"For a woman to marry a man who lacks character—that's terrible! It's gross folly for a girl to marry a man who has habits of drink. She'll never reform him. It's foolish, in the same way, for a man to marry a flirt. The instinct is in her, and you can't get rid of it.

"The relation of ages of those who marry is one very seriously to be regarded. Of course there are happy marriages with great disparity of age; but wide difference of age is apt to mean wide difference of feeling and of interests, and in that case you cannot have happiness. What Tolstoi says is true: that in our aging we pass through a succession of consciousness. Age and youth don't meet on common ground. It is usually best that those who marry should be about the same age, for then you are surer of an equality of tastes. That is the great test—that there should be agreement in likings and feelings.

"A likeness of tastes is a strong tie that makes lasting harmony. There's far more variety in similarity than there is in dissimilarity. That's a paradox, but it's true. I think it's best, besides, that there should be equality of circumstances and of origin, that the two should be of the same race and country and religion. I have said before now that a man had better not marry outside his own voting precinct, but that's drawing the line a little too close. It is well that those who marry should be of the same domestic and social traditions. If they are not, they don't understand each other. If they are alike in their inherited habits and feelings, there's more likelihood of their remaining united. If you marry outside your race, it goes very well in youth—there's a charm in strangeness then; but people as they grow old return to their own, and those who are not of the same race grow apart.

"Preferences wear themselves out. There's change in those we love, and there's change in ourselves. We see what becomes of first love. It almost invariably comes to nothing, and yet the affection felt is just the same as that of some later love that does come to something. A certain strain of music strikes your ear; it delights you. You think you want to listen to it forever. The tenth time you hear it with rapture, and the eleventh the same, but the hundredth time you are ready to scream with agony. You meet some one and are charmed, but only time can prove that the charm will be lasting.

"It is the general thought that if a woman loves she should not make her love known. I don't see much sense in that notion. But so far we haven't got beyond it. You find the idea in all races and in all religions, and I suppose there may be some good reason for it. A woman's affections are just as likely to go out as a man's. It's not a very logical love, any more than his is. It's founded on a fancy for him—she likes certain little traits of his. But it's mostly taken for granted that it would be quite immodest for her to let him know she cares for him.

"If a man loves and is refused, the unhappiness of it depends on how deeply his feelings are committed. But no matter how strong the attachment is, the hurt doesn't last; the deepest bereavement doesn't last. Time heals. The romancers like to tell us of men who have been rejected and yet continue to cherish a tender sentiment for the object of their love, and as long as they live they go staggering around under it. There's little truth in such stories, and no virtue in such performances even if they were true. The man who is crossed in love and spends his life in permanent mourning is exceedingly weak; such a character is not interesting. If you will keep right on with the work and duties of every day, you'll outlive almost anything.

"Work ought to be the rule, in trouble or out of trouble, man or woman, married or unmarried. It's our only salvation. It makes character; it keeps character sweet; it makes life real, and crowds out the artificial and the trivial."

Mr. Howells's Literary Passions

Harry Thurston Peck*

What a delightful thing it must be to attain a degree of distinction at which reminiscence becomes as valuable as creation! Then, if one be a novelist, for instance, he need no longer rack his brain over the complexities of plot and the analysis of character, studying proportion, and inventing incident, and polishing dialogue; but, secure of his public, at any odd moment he can sit down in his library and recall miscellaneous details about himself. They need not have any absolute value in themselves; how, when twelve years of age, he was once very homesick at his uncle's house; how he was once taken to a chemist's shop and dosed with camphor as a prophylactic against cholera; details about what he usually had for dinner and the hour at which he had it; and the peculiarities of an organ-builder who used to lend him books. These bits of life history, of which every human being possesses a million scattering fragments, are, to the person who has attained renown, a veritable gold mine. They have no especial pertinence to anything, but they are deeply interesting because they happened to him; and so, after setting them down in detail to the extent of a column or so of print, the Distinguished Personage gives them a little polishing, garnishes them with a few neat phrases, and sends them off to Mr. Bok, who at once remits a delightful cheque, where-with the Personage enlargeth his bank account and arrayeth himself in purple and fine linen, and maketh merry.

To this beatific state has Mr. Howells attained, and the present book is the first clear evidence of it. For, while it is not his first book of personal reminiscence, it is the first one that is personal reminiscence pure and simple, making its appeal to the reader wholly on the basis of Mr. Howells's ego. It may be said that A Boy's Town, which appeared some five years ago, was of the same character; but this is not true. A Boy's Town was, to be sure, the personal experience of Mr. Howells; but it was much more than that. It was a most subtle reproduction of the spirit of boyhood itself—a wonderful piece of psychology, and a perfect miracle of memory. It reproduced exactly and to the last minute detail the whole mentality of Boyhood, its fancies, beliefs, superstitions, morals—in fact, a point of view that not one grown person in ten million ever gets the slightest glimpse of. No man over thirty years of age can read this book without having a thousand strange remembrances crowd upon his mind of things that have passed out of his life and thought as though they had never been, but which the perfectly marvellous art of Mr. Howells wakes to life in him once more until he forgets his maturity

*Reprinted from the Bookman, 1 (July 1895), 400–01.

and passes back into the strange chaotic avatar that we call boyhood. To our mind, *A Boy's Town* is one of the most extraordinary psychologic studies ever put upon paper, but it had no great success when published, because Mr. Howells's successes, as he himself said, depend upon the verdict of women; and no woman could possibly understand *A Boy's Town*, simply because no woman has ever been a boy.

The present volume is, therefore, the first frankly egotistical work of its author; and in saying this, the word egotistical is used in no offensive sense. Nominally, of course, it is a collection of literary criticisms, and there is in it much acute observation with some strange vagaries of judgment; but in the main the literary passions are largely a thread upon which are strung the pearls of personal detail about the author's own career. In the very form of its narrative it differs from *A Boy's Town*. In that book the protagonist was, of course, Mr. Howells; but he was always spoken of in the third person, as "my boy," or "the boy," whereas now it is "I" continually, and the personal pronoun is peppered thickly over every page. This is no cause for criticism, but it accentuates the strong personal note of the whole, which is very marked, also, in the curious assumption that everything relating to the writer must be equally attractive to the reader, and against which assumption we desire to protest. Thus, it is no doubt interesting, even if it be not convincing, to be said that *Vanity Fair* is "the poorest of Thackeray's novels—crude, heavy-handed, caricatured;" and that Mr. J. W. DeForest is one of the very greatest of American writers of fiction; but who is especially concerned to know that Mr. Howells, at the time when he first heard of Don Quixote, was engaged in shelling peas? . . .

Told You So

George Bernard Shaw*

By the way, I have discovered, quite by accident, an amusing farcical comedy. Somebody told me that there was a farce by Mr. W. D. Howells at the Avenue Theatre. I looked in the daily papers, but could find no mention of the name of Mr. Howells. However, it was evidently quite possible that the management had never heard of Mr. Howells, just as they had apparently never heard of me. So I went, and duly found the name "Howels" on the programme. The little piece showed, as might be expected, that with three weeks' practice the American novelist could write the heads off the bunglers to whom our man-

*Reprinted from the *Saturday Review*, 80 (7 December 1895), 761–62.

agers vainly appeal when they want a small bit of work to amuse the people who come at eight. But no doubt it is pleasanter to be a novelist, to have an intelligent circle of readers comfortably seated by their firesides or swinging sunnily in hammocks in their gardens, to be pleasantly diffuse, to play with your work, to be independent of time and space, than to conform to the stern condition of the stage and fight with stupidity before and behind the curtain.

Mr. Howells as a Poet

Harry Thurston Peck*

Mr. Howells is so universally admitted to hold the primacy among living American men of letters as to make his appearance in a new field of effort an event of peculiar interest. That he should turn to poetry is particularly certain to excite both curiosity and comment, for in many ways his theory of art is one that finds its most natural exemplification in prose, eschewing as it does the ideal and holding fast to the obvious and the actual. These productions of his, therefore, conceived in poetical form, have an unexpectedness about them that will inevitably lead to their being read with a sensation not unmingled with surprise.

The first and strongest impression that one gets from the perusal of this volume is an impression of intense sadness. A profound melancholy pervades every one of the short poems that are here collected. There is scarcely a line that sounds the note of carelessness and joy; and when the major chord is struck, it only gives additional intensity to the minor that invariably succeeds. This melancholy, this pervasive sadness, one cannot quite call pessimism, for it does not spring from a pessimistic spirit. True pessimism is seldom dissociated from cynicism, and is by no means inconsistent with a tone of gaiety. The standpoint of the real pessimist is that which is indicated in the famous saying, "There's nothing good and there's nothing true, and it doesn't signify." Mr. Howells, too, holds apparently that there is nothing good and nothing true, but to him it signifies very much indeed. It wrings his heart and afflicts his whole being with a sense of pain and of disappointment. The lines in which his feeling finds expression describe the mind of one who has hoped much and met nothing but disillusion; of one whose nerves are overstrained, whose spirit is sickened, and whose very soul is sorrowful and despairing. Life is one great failure—a mystery whose

*Reprinted from *Bookman*, 2 (February 1896), 525–27.

veil is quite impenetrable, and which, if one could penetrate it, would doubtless show us only forms more fearful and anguish still more intense.

[QUOTES POEMS:
"HEREDITY"; "TO-MORROW"; "CALVARY"]

And in another poem, which we cannot take space to quote in full, Mr. Howells gives his whole view of life—a hurried meaningless rout, amid which man is a bewildered guest, one who was not asked to come, who has never seen his host or had from him a word of welcome; but who, as he stands gazing on the foolish scene about him, hears from time to time a ghastly shriek as some one is hurried away to be seen no more. Each page bears witness to a like emotion, an emotion almost of disgust at the cross-purposes and senseless folly of all that men see and hope and do. The *Weltschmerz*, the *taedium vitae*, casts a grey light over every line.

It is all very strong writing. As literature it ranks very high. Does it rank equally high as poetry? Let those who can claim to speak with some degree of authority give an answer to this question. For our part, we do not think that these impressions of life gain much from the metrical form in which they appear. Without it, published as short prose impressions, like some of Mr. Hamlin Garland's, they would, we think, be equally effective; for their excellence from a literary point of view depends wholly upon their possession of the qualities that are peculiarly conspicuous in all of Mr. Howells's work. A marvellously keen eye for detail, a strong grasp upon the characteristic features of what he wishes us to see, an unerring instinct in language, and an exquisite sense of word-values—all these are present in his verse, but yet no more so than in his prose. . . .

Works of William Dean Howells—(1860-96)

Marrion Wilcox*

I

To some of those who write it happens that (imaginatively, and yet convincingly) they see themselves as though in the future—say, one

*Reprinted from *Harper's Weekly*, 40 (4 July 1896), 655–56.

hundred years from the date of the vision; and that they then find themselves much shrunken, so that they are not larger than a volume or two, or at most a little row of volumes. And yet, far from missing the corporeal part that they were wont to measure and weigh with such interest, they have a sense of comfort and of rest. There, on the shelf, is room enough, and in a "set" of books they feel commodiously housed, perhaps for the first time. And what entertainment they perceive in those who march up to them, and, without introduction, pat them on the back and commend them; or in those who perhaps are *not* complimentary—although these critics, being a hundred years or so younger than the subject of their criticism, might therefore express their estimate somewhat modestly: at the very worst. "That quaint old Asterisk!" or "*Rare* old Blank!" Then the apparent author has been wholly lost, and only the essential part—the real author—survives; and then is realized the futility of criticism which weighs and measures, comparing one author with another or with the others, and confidently saying, "This is the greater," or even "This is the most eminent literary person of his time and nation." But the real author is imponderable.

This caution occurred to me when, I confess, I was on the point of speaking of Mr. Howells in the terms of some such comparison. The fault I detect was about to become my own. Surely it was an inexact doctrine that Matthew Arnold formulated when, in his preface to an edition of Wordsworth's poems, he declared that a poet is to be ranked according to the quantity or amount of thought on life that one discovers in his works; but it is such a familiar doctrine that it has its use, and using a little of it will not do much harm.

II

Mr. Howells's earliest literary effort, or rather the first of which I have any knowledge, was a word picture of a winter day—such as winter days are in southern Ohio: the light snow almost disappearing at noon, but growing crisp again towards evening; the meeting and blending of two seasons in the course of twelve hours, as though the darkness only were winter and the light were summer. This composition was published in a newspaper when the author was fourteen years of age, and I think that in the choice of subject it must have reflected the influence of his father, who was a lover and close observer of nature. The boy's unguided impulse, I feel quite sure, would have been to write a story—a study of the life of a man, which is by so much the most interesting subject for literary treatment that sometimes one thinks it is the only interesting topic. And this may be said without disparagement of women, for the life of a woman is the story of one or more men. It is curious to note in Mr. Howells's later writings that when he goes back in memory to the same period and the same scenes the old influence is reasserted, and he straightway begins—unconsciously, no doubt—to give more space to scenery than is his custom. A fortunate result of the association of ideas this may well be called; we owe some very charming pictures to it. I may cite the following passage, which is somewhere in *My Year in a Log Cabin*:

> The woods were full of squirrels, which especially abounded in the wood pastures, as we called the lovely dells where the greater part of the timber was thinned out to let the cattle range and graze. They were of all sorts—gray, and black, and even big red fox-squirrels, a variety I now suppose extinct. When the spring opened we hunted them in the poplar woods, whither they resorted in countless numbers for the sweetness in the cups of the tulip-tree blossoms.
>
> I recall with a thrill one memorable morning in such woods— early, after an overnight rain, when the vistas hung full of a delicate mist that the sun pierced to kindle a million fires in the drops still pendulous from leaf and twig. I can smell the tulip blossoms and the odor of the tree bark yet, and the fresh, strong fragrance of the leafy mould under my bare feet: and I can hear the rush of the squirrels on the bark of the trunks, or the swish of their long, plunging leaps from bough to bough in the air-tops. I hope we came away without any of them.

In 1860 *Poems of Two Friends* appeared—the friends thus associated being the subject of this little sketch and John J. Piatt. Mr. Howells finished his *Life of Abraham Lincoln* in the same year. Then six years passed before the next book was published—*Venetian Life*. His *Italian Journeys* came in 1867; *Suburban Sketches* and *No Love Lost, a Poem of Travel*, in 1868; three years later *Their Wedding Journey*, and *A Chance Acquaintance* in 1873. Already the writer and his audience (a large audience) had come to understand each other thoroughly—to know what to give and what to expect. "I have spent the night reading *A Chance Acquaintance*," said Tourguénief, "and now I should like to visit a country where there are girls like the heroine." In other words, the characters represented in these earlier books convinced the reader of their reality; but Mr. Howells had not begun to think of himself as a "realist." His acceptance of the actual thing for use in his art—the types of character he observed, and their normal motives as he understood them—has an exceedingly simple explanation; he is appreciative and he is courageous. Other American writers, unresponsive to the vital interest of their surroundings, held fast to the English literary tradition; they insisted upon finding in their environment the approved literary ingredients. When they did not find them (and of course this was the rule) they invented. That, as I understand it, is the obnoxious part of "romanticism"; it is unpatriotic, untruthful; its product distorted and tinted images of American life, as viewed through literary spectacles, false in outline, false in spirit or coloring, yet without claiming the lawful freedom of romance. To Mr. Howells, because he was appreciative, this American life seemed the most attractive and the most worthy subject of study for an American artist; and because he was courageous his own method was shaped in faithful correspondence with his convictions. He also, and not less than the others, had been trained in the English tradition; he was of a reading family, and from the first had seen life through just such literary spectacles; but for his part he would have no more of them: he threw away *his* pair long before he thought of asking others to do the same, and without giving a name to his theory or making profession of a new literary faith. The campaigning for realism came later, as we shall see.

A Foregone Conclusion was published in 1874; in the following year Out of the Question and the Life of Rutherford B. Hayes; then A Counterfeit Presentment and some of the volumes of Choice Biographies (which Mr. Howells edited, with essays) came in 1877, and in 1878 The Lady of the Aroostook and the concluding volumes of the Choice Biographies. At intervals of two years (1880–82) the public acquired The Undiscovered Country and A Fearful Responsibility, and Other Tales; then followed, in 1883, Dr. Breen's Practice and A Modern Instance; in 1884, A Woman's Reason; in 1885 Three Villages, Tuscan Cities, and The Rise of Silas Lapham; in 1886 A Little Girl among the Old Masters, The Minister's Charge, and Indian Summer; in 1887 Modern Italian Poets and April Hopes.

The last-mentioned work, Mr. Howells says, was the first he wrote with the distinct consciousness that he was writing as a realist, and I think there is internal evidence of this consciousness, its people are so closely studied, and all details of manner, dress, expression, and gesture, as well as motive and environment, are so conscientiously reported. An unfair example, which shows not the normal but the extreme application of a theory, is this description of Alice Pasmer from the second chapter:

> Mrs. Pasmer looked at her daughter, but she stood as passive in the transaction as the elder Mavering. She was taller than her mother, and, as she waited, her supple figure described that fine lateral curve which one sees in some Louis Quinze portraits; this effect was enhanced by the fashion of her dress of pale sage green, with a wide stripe or sash of white dropping down the front from her delicate waist. The same simple combination of colors was carried up into her hat, which surmounted darker hair than Mrs. Pasmer's, and a complexion of wholesome pallor; her eyes were gray and grave, with black brows, and her face, which was rather narrow, had a pleasing irregularity in the sharp jut of the nose; in profile, the parting of the red lips showed well back into the cheek.

Annie Kilburn followed in 1888, and in the same year the *Library of Universal Adventure* was issued under Mr. Howells's editorial supervision. *A Hazard of New Fortunes, The Sleeping-Car, and Other Farces,* and *The Mouse-Trap, and Other Farces,* were published in 1889; *The Shadow of a Dream,* pre-eminent for literary quality and witty dialogue, in 1890; *An Imperative Duty* in 1891—that searching examination of the negro problem in its social aspect, with the pitiful figure of a beautiful girl whose voice "sounded *black.*" Sharply contrasting with this, in the same year, came *A Boy's Town, The Albany Depot,* and *Criticism and Fiction.* Overt realism in this last, roundly stated, elegantly reasoned. We carried the argument about with us in our minds—for that matter, we took the convenient little volume in our pockets; we discussed realism and romanticism when we met, restating and misstating, writing about both. I know that one of the commonest errors of the year was the assertion that Mr. Howells had a quarrel with Romance. Not a bit of it. He wanted to see the novel and the romance kept apart and distinct. No man more ready than he to do honor to the latter in its own sphere; but the former professed to be a faithful picture of real life, and he called for good faith in the discharge of this obligation; he protested against that anomalous thing, a romantic novel—against "romanticism."

A story of a defaulting treasurer, a handsome, clerical-looking, self-respecting thief, *The Quality of Mercy,* a syndicated serial story in many newspapers, appeared in 1892, and before the close of the year *The Letter of Introduction, A Little Swiss Sojourn,* and the volume of stories for children, entitled *Christmas Every Day.* A year later *The Unexpected Guests* arrived, *The World of Chance* essayed its fortunes in HARPER'S MONTHLY, and as a comely volume, *The Year in a Log Cabin* was recalled, and *The Coast of Bohemia* was rather harmlessly skirted: the young person is not impressed with the indispensableness of skillful navigation along that treacherous shore.

In June, 1894, when his first romance, *A Traveler from Altruria,* was about to appear in book form, Mr. Howells told me that during its publication as a serial he got more letters about it than about any other story he had written in many and many a year—"letters from all over the country and from all kinds of people." I think that some of the books one likes impose silence, while others have a tendency to make the reader communicative, and that *A Traveler from Altruria* belongs to the latter class. The Altrurian's doctrine, which is almost appealing in its frank good-will and its confidence that human nature is not altogether selfish, is an answer to grave questions that had arisen in the author's own mind: it is offered as a partial solution of problems which he found confronting himself, compelling attention, refusing to be curtly dismissed. They made their demand—these questions and problems—when Mr. Howells was writing *Silas Lapham.* His affairs prospering, his work marching as well as heart could wish, suddenly, and without apparent cause, the status seemed wholly wrong. His own expression, in speaking with me about that time, was, "The bottom dropped out!" A still more recent volume—the volume of poems entitled *Stops of Various Quills*—contains much of the same questioning. The poems are brief and gravely beautiful or finely epigrammatic things; and all assuredly unfeigned. If I had just denied the validity of certain comparisons I should like to say that there is nothing more modern, more searching than "Calvary":

> If He could doubt on His triumphant cross,
> How much more I, in the defeat and loss
> Of seeing all my selfish dreams fulfilled,
> Of having lived the very life I willed,
> Of being all that I desired to be?
> My God, my God! Why hast Thou forsaken me?

There remain only four titles: *My Literary Passions*, of last year; *The Day of their Wedding* and *A Parting and a Meeting*, of this year; and, in the present issue of the WEEKLY, "The Landlord at Lion's Head."

It is a very distinguished company of books; better than any mortal could do it, *they* introduce the new-comer.

III

An eminent German critic has said that the best thing he knows about America is the fact that books with the fine quality that he discovers in our author have a good sale in the author's own country.

The best thing I know about America is that it is impossible to imagine an American so unintentionally offensive as that German. But in any case of doubt, when the question has been raised whether this thing or that is characteristic of American life, where would you apply for information? If the question comes up now, there are few students who will not first think of Howells's works, and consult them with the highest confidence in the value of their evidence on this point. And when such questions shall be proposed in the future, will there be any other body of information by a single hand comparable with this, in respect to American life at the end of the nineteenth century? Are there other pictures of our times as faithful? Has another observer's regard embraced so many social phases?—although, it must be confessed, the survey is not absolutely complete, for there is not a bit of social impurity, immorality. And all of this "thought on life" (to recur to Matthew Arnold's phrase), instead of being offered as a mass, thrown formlessly into some dull, repulsive volume, has been beautifully grouped, invested with literary charm; and fortunately the best part of the series may be still to

come. I think the readers of this new story will find it in some respects
the best. And its author's zest is undiminished, and he is young enough
to plant trees.

Mr. Howells's Views

Anonymous*

Mr. Howells's new volume of essays is the report of a patient observer of existence concerning a few of the things he has seen and heard
during his progress down the years. Such a report, if delivered in sincerity, is always interesting, even when he who writes it is not skilled
in the writer's craft; for, if it furnishes no fresh revelation as to the ends
of existence, it at least discloses to us the intimate quality of a man's
mind. It is hardly necessary to say that in "Impressions and Opinions"[1]
will be found notable literary excellences superadded to the personal
revelation. To say that Mr. Howells writes well, is as superfluous as to
mention that the sky is blue. It is not possible to have any quarrel with
the manner of his essays, which in itself is calculated to give the reader
an immense amount of enjoyment—as much, at least, as the spirit in
which some of them are written will give him pain. In its subjective
aspect, the book is a revelation of moods rather than of principles, and
the moods which it discloses are at variance with one another.

The volume opens with an affectionate study of "The Country
Printer." The article is based upon the writer's early memories of a
printing office on the Western Reserve of Ohio before the war, and, incidentally, does justice to the sturdy qualities of mind and spirit which
characterized that New England colony. The sketch is a valuable contribution both to the social history of the region and to the annals of
the evolution of journalism. Next follows the "Police Report," first published years ago in *The Atlantic*. It is a record of two mornings spent
in a Boston police court. In point of characterization it is a marvellous
bit of unflinching realism, but the predominant note is that of a long-
suffering, gentle, humorous sympathy with human nature, no matter how
degraded its manifestations. This is followed by a humorous bit upon
the subject of dreams, and then come four essays which are the result
of observation about town in New York, and a paper dealing with the
closing of a summer hotel. The articles whose inspiration is New York
form an impressive and significant group, but it must be confessed that
the adventures of the author's mind in contact with the streets of the

*Reprinted from the *Critic*, NS 27 (2 January 1897), 5.

metropolis make reading which is depressing in the extreme. Mr. Howells does not love his New York. Given a social reformer without hope: complicate his humanitarian instincts with a strong aesthetic bias: set him down in any large American city, and he will be far from happy. The only place that could possibly hurt him more than New York is Chicago. If he has a fluent pen, he will make other people unhappy, too, but neither their sufferings nor his can be pronounced healthy, for they are purposeless. Mr. Howells sees no remedies for society, and apparently depairs of any. If he were a self-conscious French writer, these four essays would have been grouped by themselves under some title which could be adequately translated into "The Sensations of a Sick Soul," and we should have said: "This man suffers from *mal du ciel*. He is a victim to the passion for perfection in others. For him, no happiness on this side of Paradise."

In truth, Mr. Howells extracts misery from many things. A Broadway cable car, a rich woman in a victoria, a poor woman sitting in the park, a beggar in the street, a stretch of vacant lots, the jagged sky-line of Fifth Avenue, all cause him profound wretchedness. He finds the homes of the rich and of the poor almost equally squalid and disheartening, and the spectacle of the man who is eating in a restaurant, visible from the street, is only less melancholy than that of the man who is hungering outside. His nerves have been laid bare, and the slightest stimulus sets them quivering with pain. To the pleasurable stimulus which may also be legitimately derived from the spectacle of the streets, they apparently never respond. The tone of the essays is weary, and would be querulous were it a shade less mild. We miss the cordial, charming sympathy with all the phenomena of life so lavishly displayed in the opening sketches of the volume. The writer has lost heart. He is near the end of his patience with our formula of living. The city is a heavier load than he can carry.

Without doubt, the world is bad, but those who remind us of this fact are bound in justice to tell us that it had been worse, and that most wise men agree that it is getting better. Without doubt, New York has its repulsive aspects, but at least London and Paris are not free from them. Mr. Howells ought to tell us that he is not comparing the American metropolis with other earthly capitals, but rather with the New Jerusalem, the city of God come down out of heaven. But the New Jerusalem is more efficacious to salvation when we think of it as an ideal to be attained, than when we use it as a standard of comparison. The former attitude toward it means hope; the latter, despair. The social reformer who chooses despair for his portion discards at once his armor and his sword, and the artist who makes the same choice of a standpoint is in no better case. On the whole, the reader turns away from Mr. Howells's impressions of our civilization, doubting their insight and sanity. They are too bad to be true, and have, as all such impressions must, a certain malign, narcotic influence, difficult to describe and ill to feel.

1. Correct title, *Impressions and Experiences*.

Human Beings in New England

John D. Barry*

There are many readers who say of Mr. Howells that they liked his first novels, but lost interest in his work after he became realistic. The opinion, so lightly given, is seen upon examination to have been as lightly formed, for it is plain from the very beginning of Mr. Howells' career as novelist that he was bent on reproducing life as he saw it, that consciously or unconsciously he avoided the old conventions and the old exaggerations of novel-writing. It may be that he did not formulate his theory of realism till he had written several books; yet the scrupulous care with which the characters and their environment were woven from nature showed that the germ of realism was already in his mind.

It is true, however, that there is a difference between the Howells of "A Foregone Conclusion" and the Howells of *The Landlord at Lion's Head*. In both these works are the same adherence to the truth, the same fineness of observation, the same exquisite style—for Mr. Howells, unlike most writers, began with a style apparently perfectly developed; yet the second reveals the matured mind, the sobered thought, and—it is hard to say it—the pessimistic outlook. From long experience, from long searching into the recesses of the human heart, Mr. Howells has become saddened, and the revelations of his later novels betray the reason. The struggle between evil and good, ending so often with the triumph of evil—this is the spectacle that so perplexes and so fascinates him that it finds constant expression in his literature. In other words, during the past few years his work has deepened, has approached more closely the springs of human action.

In *The Landlord at Lion's Head* Mr. Howells has returned to the New England which he knows so well. Indeed, his absolute intimacy with the life there, his vivid power of reproducing it, contradicts Mr. Henry James' recently expressed opinion that the literary artist should write only of the impressions received in childhood and early youth. When Mr. Howells became familiar with New England he was a man of nearly thirty. But he had sprung from New England stock, and he fitted into the life of Boston as if he had always belonged to it. Perhaps

*Reprinted from *Book Buyer*, NS 14 (July 1897), 598–600.

his early years in Ohio enabled him to see New England with a clearer vision than he could have turned upon it if it had always been before his eyes. At any rate, in writing of New England life, he invariably gives the impression of having an absolute understanding of it, if not always an absolute sympathy with it. In the opening chapters of his latest novel the understanding is plainly there, together with a most beautiful and tender sympathy, translating the wild grandeur of the New England mountains into the fine simplicity of prose that Mr. Howells can make so effective and so convincing. In their way, Mr. Howells has done nothing finer than those chapters; they remind one of the beautiful picture of the Harvard Class Day which he has given in "April Hopes." The rustic figures introduced belong to the landscape, are, in a sense, a part of it. With swift, sure strokes they are outlined, and their identity is at once established. The first presentation of the hero, Jefferson Durgin, as a young bully delighting in the torture of a little girl, strikes the keynote of the character. Indeed, so accurate and so subtle are all the touches in these chapters that the attention of the reader is absorbed in spite of the slow movement of the narrative. It is plain from the beginning that Mr. Howells is lingering fondly over the life of his people and that in his mind the story is of minor importance.

The episodes in the book centre about the career of Jefferson Durgin, and they are a natural—indeed, Mr. Howells makes you feel—an inevitable development from the boy's character. With great minuteness the change is indicated from unsophisticated cubdom to the selfish shrewdness of youth, and the beginning of Durgin's career as an undergraduate at Harvard College marks the opening of the real drama. Here Mr. Howells is on ground where he has won many a triumph, for Cambridge is merely a district in the great field of social Boston, which he has often so mercilessly probed. There is this difference, however: not only does he give the Boston side of Durgin's career, but he does what no novelist has ever done before, he presents an absolutely true study of a phase of the social life at Harvard College about which very little is known by the world in general. Durgin, whose mother has brought him up on the profits of her boarding-house in the mountains, whose training has left him without polish, whose ideas of life, in spite of a certain vigorous intelligence, are the ideas of a man of vulgar instincts, meets a shallow-minded, vain, and flirtatious young woman in Boston society, Bessie Lynde, who amuses herself with him. Half-flattered, half-cynical, knowing the contempt she must feel for him as one wholly out of her world, and in spite of the fact that he is already engaged to the country girl he has known all his life, Cynthia Whitwell, he allows himself to be attracted into what ends finally in a brief engagement. His consequent loss of self-respect, his confession to Cynthia, whom he really cares for as much as he can care for anyone, the thrashing he receives from Bessie Lynde's brother, the opportunity that comes to him for vengeance—all these episodes enable Mr. Howells to display the many sides of an intensely human and interesting character; some of them, moreover, are so dramatic that, presented with the author's sturdy directness and unswerving restraint, they give the narrative moments in which the interest is extraordinarily concentrated. The insistence, however, is always on character, and in the case of the unheroic hero it is worth noting that Mr. Howells is uniformly just to him, that the evil never obscures the good. Perhaps for subtlety the young Boston girl deserves to be placed beside Durgin, and a more ruthless representation of feminine coquetry could hardly have been given. On the other hand, Mr. Howells has in Cynthia Whitwell introduced the most lovable of all the women he has ever drawn. Her patience with Durgin before and during and after their engagement, her simplicity, her seriousness, and her poise, are delineated with exquisite sympathy and truth; and in her father, with his rustic philosophy and his affectionate adherence to the *planchette*, Mr. Howells has produced a figure that deserves to rank among the greatest of his characterizations.

1898-1907

Mr. Howells' Socialism

Anonymous*

... The services that this distinguished author has rendered to the Socialist movement call for the warmest eulogy on the part of every propagandist of the cause. He has made his art the instrument of a great purpose. His "Annie Kilburn"; his "A Hazard of New Fortunes"; his "The World of Chance," wherein the alleged "laws of business" are considered to be merely accidental and undeterminable sequences; his "A Traveller from Altruria," the most definite and comprehensive expression of his social ideals, and his "Letters of an Altrurian Traveller," describing from the viewpoint of a Socialist the characteristics of the plutocratic city of New York, have set many thousands of minds forward on the right path.

A realist in fiction, he has not, like one branch of the school of realism, descended to the depicting of the darker and more vicious attributes of certain abnormal types of humankind, nor like another branch of that school, painted merely the superficial emotions and activities of better types; he has pictured for us our own time, the struggle of mankind one against another and against all others, in the fierce battle for bread; he has urged the obligation of brotherhood upon all of us, and has shown us the goal of practicable, attainable Utopia. At the head of American litterateurs, he has not temporized with nor glossed over, nor praised the false sentiments and beliefs which pass current for wisdom and morality among the selfish and unthinking, though he well may have known that acquiescence therein would be to his material advantage; he has, on the contrary, used his tremendous power toward the shattering of these intrenched falsities, and has striven to awaken in his readers the spirit of the new ideals. Particular abuses were sought to be corrected by Dickens, Thackeray and George Eliot. But the social purpose

*Reprinted from *American Fabian*, 4 (February 1898), 1–2.

of these writers is far below the splendid aim of Howells, who attacks the whole economic framework of modern society.

"What are the prospects for Socialism in America?" was asked.

"As to that, who can say? One sees the movement advancing all about him, and yet it may be years before its ascendancy. On the other hand, it may be but a short time. A slight episode may change history. A turn here or a turn there, and we may find our national headlong on the road to the ideal commonwealth."

So much for the social views and public character of Mr. Howells. As for the man himself, we cannot do better than to quote from a recent essay of Prof. Harry Thurston Peck: "Every one who knows his work can feel how fine a nature lies behind it, how much love of truth and justice, how much charity, how much devotion to all that is best and noblest; and every one who knows the man himself can tell of his unassuming kindliness, of his generosity to young writers who have still their spurs to win, and of all the traits that make his character so winning and so truly typical of the high minded American gentleman."

Mr. Howells on the Platform

Gerald Stanley Lee*

Every author has a theory, of course (especially if he is an Englishman), that no one can get him to lecture. The indefatigable Major Pond, who haunts the Atlantic, as everyone knows, in season and out of season, with a spy-glass in his hand, scanning the horizon for authors who venture abroad, apparently takes exception to this theory. It may be that he realizes in a general way that an author must have theories, and that his theory about himself is the hardest one of all to do anything with. But whether it is an infinite faith in patience, or in hard cash (or in patience if enough hard cash is put with it), it is certainly getting to be true, judging from events at least, that the entire problem of literature in England,—the problem of how to keep English literature at work producing itself, is getting to be the problem of How to Keep the English Author from Meeting Major Pond. This would seem (looked at from the outside) a moderately simple problem in a world with as wide a margin as this, but the fact remains—a fact of common observation—that the only English author coming to America, who has found the Atlantic large enough to dodge Major Pond in, is J. M. Barrie.

Nor is the situation in any wise different with our authors in the

*Reprinted from the *Critic*, NS 32 (November 1899), 1029–30.

United States. The facilities for a famous man's turning out, for his going around the lecture platform, are getting to be so scarce in the United States to-day, that the American public can be depended upon to assume, for all practical purposes at least, that all it has to do, is to appoint a committee, hire a hall, and send in an order for any author it happens to want, and he will be delivered in the proper place, C. O. D., as a matter of course, at the appointed time.

Under these conditions, while there is plenty of reason for gratitude, there is very little reason for surprise in the news that comes to us, that the last stronghold of bashfulness in American letters has capitulated to Major Pond, and that W. D. Howells is to go on a tour of fifty lectures in the leading cities of the United States. Aside from hearing him, the pleasantest thing about Mr. Howells doing this, is that he never has done it before. A man who can keep still must have something to say, and even if he has not (a wild hypothesis with Mr. Howells), it goes without saying, that if a man can be found in this American land of ours who can keep still for thirty or forty years (whether by Major Pond or anyone else), it must be esteemed a blessed privilege by us all, to be able to buy seats, to be allowed to go and sit in large audiences and have one good look at him before we die. It is to be hoped that parents will take their children with them. There is no telling when Major Pond will be able to find such a man again.

But it is not Mr. Howells's main distinction that he has kept still for thirty or forty years, nor is it merely his silence that gives such grace and fitness to his speaking now. We want to hear Mr. Howells in America to-day because he particularly belongs to us and because we particularly belong to him and because we are both proud of it. Judged from the ordinary standard of advertising and reputation-pushing that obtains to-day, it certainly must be admitted that Mr. Howells, though he created Silas Lapham and loved him, has never allowed Silas Lapham to brag about him. His work has never been pushed like the Persis Brand. He has stolen his public. There is nothing striking or picturesque or showy in his entire career. There never has seemed to be any one occasion rather than another that could be picked out, to make a parade in his honor. To people from the outside who come to us, we give dinners and make speeches. We make them make speeches. We cannot help it. Neither can they. It does not take very many of us to do it, and it is soon over and everybody bears up as well as he can, but we never celebrate Mr. Howells. He is part of our literary climate. We breathe Howells—most of us. It never occurs to people to hold an Anniversary for Oxygen. We probably would—if enough of it were taken away, but as long as we have it with us, we get all we can. It is our only way of appreciating it. The things that belong to us, that are really a part of us, in any great and vital and beautiful sense, are the things that we take for granted.

It never occurs to anyone to attempt a Parade in honor of the American Climate. It would make a very pretty procession no doubt, but no one makes a start. There never seems to be any particular occasion for it. It is a question whether anything elemental can ever lend itself to being celebrated. It can only be lived in. We cannot reduce Mr. Howells to the celebrating stage. We cannot get him far enough off. We cannot untangle him from ourselves. His art belongs to us. Our common American lives are the warp and woof of all that he has wrought. In his large and sane and noiseless way he may be said to have done more for the self-respect of American fiction than any other living man. Under these circumstances it is no small occasion—the announcement that we are to be permitted, in any general sense, to hear his voice on the lecture platform. There is something about Mr. Howells that makes a public—his own particular public—almost blush not to be as modest as he is himself. Going to hear him lecture is as near a celebration as we can get. We know him too well.

Many of us would find it interesting to follow Mr. Howells about from one hall to another. We would find it still more interesting to watch Mr. Howells, who is always a spectator and an artist, follow himself about. He will be cheered by seeing the Rev. Mr. Sewall and Lemuel Barker in the front row in some places, sitting unconscious side by side. Mrs. Corey will be there. Mr. Corey will want to know what it was like when she gets home. Mrs. Pasmer will not fail to say something delightfully not to the point. Bartley Hubbard will write it up, and all the Silas Laphams in the East and West will go home wondering how it is that a gentle, quiet, unnoticing-looking little man like this should understand them so much better than they understand themselves.

The Latest Novels
of Howells and James

Harriet Preston Waters*

Time was when to receive a package containing new books both by William Dean Howells and Henry James would have been a delightful and even exciting event. Such time was in the last century and ominously near a generation ago. It was in the eighteen-seventies that we had A Foregone Conclusion from Mr. Howells's pen, and Roderick Hudson and The American from that of Mr. James. These tales mark the highest achievement in fiction of both writers; while their later imaginative work

*Atlantic Monthly, 91 (January 1903), 77–79.

has been both so large in quantity, and, upon the whole, so even in quality, that it may very well be considered collectively and as fairly enough represented by The Kentons and The Wings of the Dove. Mr. James has indeed given us, during the same time, a good deal of acute and penetrating if rather finical criticism; while Mr. Howells, though so erratic in his judgments, or rather, as he himself would say, "not a bit good" critic, has yet published reams and tomes of pleasant writing about other people's books. But criticism, except of the great lonely classics, which, after all, are above it, is necessarily the most ephemeral kind of writing, and it is as novelists that our distinguished countrymen are mainly known and will be, for a longer or shorter time, remembered.

There are headlong followers of Mr. Howells, who revere him as a sociologist and will indignantly protest against any discrimination in favor of his earlier and more purely artistic work, as against that which is informed by a more palpable purpose. While it was yet a novel thing to apply to the miscellaneous phenomena of American life what one must, I suppose, call the realistic method, great things in the way of our edification, if not of our entertainment, were expected from such exhaustive studies of comparatively mean subjects as A Modern Instance, The Rise of Silas Lapham, and a less popular story which has always seemed to me better than either, The Quality of Mercy. It is customary nowadays to speak of Mr. Howells as a disciple of Tolstoï; and certainly he has blown the loud and melancholy trumpet of the Russian seer with a kind of passionate assiduity. But I think the prevailing impression does our countryman a little injustice; and that, though so single-hearted a follower after the great leader has arisen, he was also, to some extent, a pioneer. His first essay in the new manner, A Modern Instance, appeared in 1882, when Tolstoï was barely known outside of Russia, save by one brief but powerful sketch in which all his genius was implicit, The Cossacks, translated, I think, from the original, and published in America by the late Eugene Schuyler. It was in 1884 that the Vicomte de Vogüé began writing in the Revue des Deux Mondes, from the vantage ground of his personal familiarity with things Russian, and with a sympathetic eloquence all his own, of the Muscovite romance, as a genus,—and most impressively of that monumental work, Guerre et Paix. Now the whole question of Realism versus Romanticism in fiction— that is to say, whether the novelist shall aim at representing human things exactly as they are, or more or less as they might be—is too vast a one for the present place and the present writer. I have indeed my own ideas about it; but the point at present is that our two most considerable American novelists since Hawthorne—who was already ten years dead when they were in the heyday of their promise—did both, to some extent, although in different ways, belie their native bent by adopting what was then the new fashion; and while each has been, and still is in some sort, a power in English letters, both have unquestionably disappointed the most brilliant of the hopes at one time entertained of them.

It will not, I think, be disputed that the charm of Mr. Howells, as a writer, was always, to an unusual degree, a personal one. The man was ever more interesting than his theme or his thesis, and infinitely more amusing. His playful wit, so whimsical and yet so natural, hiding often under a mask of gentle irony the quiver of an all but unmanageable tenderness, his gift of cunning observations, his tone, at once candid and demure, his honest, if queer convictions, and deep illogical earnest-ness,—all these things contribute to a mental make-up, a little more feminine than masculine perhaps, but very distinguished, and irresistibly attractive. And in nothing that he has written is this winning personal factor more conspicuous than it is, by moments, in the truly vapid story of The Kentons. The plodding narrative is mercifully lightened by num-bers of those flattering asides in which the author goes far toward be-guiling his reader's better judgment, by laughing with him, *sous cape*, at the foibles and absurdities of his own slight characters:—

"He put this temptation from him, and was in the enjoyment of a comfortable self-righteousness, when it returned in twofold power," etc.

"He found Boyne" (the precocious young moralist) "averse even to serious conversation," etc.

"He reflected that women are never impersonal,—or the sons of women, for that matter."

"In that pied flock, where every shade and dapple of doubt, fore-gathered in the misgiving of a blessed immortality," etc.

The last quotation shows how capable Mr. Howells originally was of a nobler and more potent form of satire than he often cares to employ. But subtract the element of personal amenity from the book before us, and what remains? A tale so thin and pointless, describing with tedious particularity the languid interaction of a half dozen so utterly insignifi-cant puppets, that is has absolutely nothing to recommend it but the author's name and charm. What can ever matter, either to morals or to art, the honestly prosperous parents of the Kenton household, who were so well in the stuffy little library of their Ohio home, where "momma" knitted while "poppa" read aloud, and who are so drearily lost in the greater world? And if not they, even less their vastly inferior offspring;— the shadowy, neurotic, and erotic elder daughter, the prematurely sage and preëminently silly boy (who is, however, the best character in the book), and the insufferable younger girl? Beside these, we have the clerical buffoon, with his veneered gentility and self-satisfied impiety,— the vulgar Trannel, and the repulsive Buttridge! The latter is the proper mate of Judge Grant's terrible Selma; and the longer I consider the matter, the more doubtful seems to me the propriety—I had almost said the decency—of giving such types the publicity of print at all. Types they may be, but normal and complete human beings they are not. They are the scum and spawn of a yeasty deep,—the monstrous offspring of barbarous and illicit social relations. They are necessarily short-lived, and, it is to be hoped, sterile; and if let alone would probably perish with the transitory conditions that gave them birth. To make of their deformities a dime side show at our noisy National Fair is, to say the least of it, not nice. To pursue them intently—to approach their sad case with paraphernalia of literary preparation—is like riding in pink, and with winding of horns, to a hunt of cockroaches! . . .

Mr. Howells' Philosophy and "The Son of Royal Langbrith"

E.S. Chamberlayne*

Mr. Howells has attained the distinction which some few living writers in each generation share with the phenomena of nature, the distinction of being criticised, even, if you will, of being roundly abused, as the weather is, for example, and of being, at the same time, artistically almost as indispensable, almost as much taken for granted, as the weather itself. . . . Mr. Howells has become one of the chief elements in our American literary weather. One may say at once that one doesn't like the climate—which makes it obviously open to one to move—but so long as one lives, intellectually, in America it is essential to a certain very desirable quality of mind that one accept Mr. Howells, with all his limitations, in the same philosophical spirit in which one meets the trifling infelicities of our peculiar American climate.

And in recent years he has given us nothing that so well repays a critical acceptance as the vision of himself that appears in his latest novel. In 'The Son of Royal Langbrith,' he has produced, perhaps without intention, a tragedy. . . .

It may be Mr. Howells's misfortune—it is certainly his charm—that his attitude toward life is rarely quite his reader's attitude, is perhaps rarely the attitude of his countrymen, of his contemporaries. And for this, however roughly it may occasionally rub his sensibilities, we must be selfishly grateful. For, though we in America still are, and may always be, too immature in a literary sense, to view life as he views it, we are far from wishing him to view it as we do. It is not in the least necessary to agree with Mr. Howells—or, so far as that goes, of course, with any

Poet Lore, 16 (Autumn 1905), 144–51.

man—in order thoroughly to like him. We do thoroughly like him, and, if one may venture to guess, this is perhaps just because we so little agree with him.

. . . . Lapham was so typically an American of the better sort that we take it a little hard he should not still stand for us in his representative capacity, as so related to one of these 'younger sets.' But we do not take it hard that Mr. Howells in this earlier work has given us so clear a vision of his literary personality. America can very well endure the loss of the finest product of Lapham's million, the modern American girl—we have her, as it is, in such abundance—but the America of today, and more, one fancies, the America of tomorrow, could ill endure the loss to its letters of this expression of the strong, kind, sane spirit we all admire.

And some of us again, I fear, as we finish the tragic story of Dr. Anther in this later novel, will feel constrained to disagree with Mr. Howells about that admirable old New England village doctor. We want to feel that life would have treated him more kindly than Mr. Howells has treated him.

The middle-aged doctor in 'The Son of Royal Langbrith' loves a widow who lacks the courage to tell her son that his father was a scoundrel, and so to win for herself the young man's sanction for the second marriage that, as it is, the boy's ignorant worship of his father's memory would make a sacrilege. The ostensible problem of the tale is the ethical question whether the truth should be told about the man who is believed in the village to have been a worthy character, the question whether, from largely selfish motives, one should ever set in motion moral forces that might prove, however slightly or subtly, of evil effect. The problem is treated as only Mr. Howells could treat it, and Dr. Anther's conclusion that he is not justified in bending the weak will of the woman he loves to compass the end they both desire becomes, with some reservations, the reader's own.

The ethical problem is satisfactorily solved; but there appears to be still a question unanswered. And it is in the answer to this question that one finds the heart of Mr. Howells's philosophy. Dr. Anther is the hero of the novel. The widow's son, with his blind worship of his unworthy father, is merely one of the implements fate has used to thwart the Doctor's love. The real problem seems only to be fairly stated when this first and superficial question has been settled. For the real problem, the question toward which the current of the story has been setting from the first, is the old, old question of the human will in its relation to destiny. What shall be a man's attitude toward the Power that thwarts his will? Anther is not a great personage. There is no glitter and tinsel about him, very little even of cleverness and worldly knowledge in his composition; though Mr. Howells has seen him a slightly clearer, more refined intelligence than Lapham required for his career. But the world-old tragedy is as truly stated in this prosaic, middle-aged man with his love for a weak and simple woman as in any dramatic philosopher or poet of the past. For none of the vital things of life is primarily a matter of expression. No man, were he poet or clown, ever found speech that would rightly express his love; and the tragedy of life is as real in the private of the Guard, crushed and dying in the ditch, as in the emperor, riding off into the night with the bitterness of Waterloo upon his heart. Men of duller vision have rebuked Mr. Howells for not giving his problems a broader, more vivid statement; as though love and life, purpose and failure and death were matters of mere expression and somehow lost their essence when not stated in courtly phrases.

It is not, however, the particular expression he has here chosen that so arrests attention. The life he pictures is much like that of his other novels. The New England villagers and the young Harvard men seem as true, as like to life, as thoroughly natural, in a word, as any of the long line of those that have come before them. There is even discernible in the impalpable medium in which they move a kind of scent—one would not like to call it a fragrance—as though the moral essence of long generations of Puritan consciences, slowly drying and hardening, had permeated the atmosphere, as in some localities one detects, faint and delicate and by no means disagreeable, the distant suggestion of dried and salted cod. The casual reader may esteem the Doctor's love story but slightly; and, indeed, if the casual reader be young—as she is likely to be—she may even fancy that the undisciplined Harvard student, with his own little love affair, is the center of interest. But the story is the story of Dr. Anther; and we follow with appreciation the vision of his struggle, as he gropes, dumb and blind, amid the shadows of desire—as, in degree, we all must do—until he wins his way to the one right course that fate has allotted him. And yet, there is in the novel something more engrossing than even this view of Anther's tragedy. It is, in a word, just the expression, in this new form, of the view that Mr. Howells takes artistically, of all that is tragic.

Perhaps a man's personality never anywhere gets quite so clear a statement as in his attitude toward the tragedy of life.... Hawthorne,... one might fancy, sought the tragedy of life because, dreaming, moody, long shut unnaturally within himself, only the tragic in life could furnish objective forms of the shadows that had gathered in the disused chambers of his soul. Mr. Howells turns to the tragic, if at all, as in this recent novel, with an air of reluctance, as though under compulsion of his exacting literary conscience.... Life, for him, holds tragedies, of course; but they are so, one sees, only because men fail of the right view of life. For what is bitterness in them may be transmitted into serenity and peace, into even joy and happiness of a kind, if one but has this secret.

And in 'The Son of Royal Langbrith' Dr. Anther has the ill fortune to receive this secret from Mr. Howells.

Dr. Anther, in a word, wins peace, not as we all may in the kind embrace of Time, which gave us birth, but at once—on the spot, as one may say—by the simple expedient of abandoning, not alone the woman he loves, but his love as well. His sudden tranquillity comes to one with the effect of a shock. And if, in the end, the atmosphere of the story is one of gloom, it is an atmosphere born less of the Doctor's death than of the deeper tragedy of the death of his love. For his love dies with the birth of his peace; he may not realize it, it is open to question whether Mr. Howells realized it, but it dies as surely, almost as dramatically, as the Doctor himself does.

For it is not in love to abandon its object without suffering. Peace comes with time, not with renunciation. To love, in such a case as this, is inevitably to suffer. And what, indeed, one asks, is suffering, what unendurable thing it is, that it should be escaped at such a cost? After all, love is the stuff that life is made of. Philosophy and the calm serenity of age are doubtless well in their way; but their way is not the way of youth. And youth, as it happens, is the abiding element of life. The world never grows old. Men are always at the beginning. Through the ages they have been pushing their slow way into the shadows of the Unknown. The way looks long in the retrospect. But the Mystery they search is boundless, and they stand today where they stood yesterday, where they will stand tomorrow, where, in effect, they will always stand, at the threshold of life. It is idle for age to tell them it has found the way of peace, has discovered an escape from suffering. Who wishes to escape? Not youth, surely. Not love. What does youth reck of suffering? And love—love is not love without suffering. There are many finer things in life than peace. Oh, if one comes to that, there are many finer things in life than the wisdom and serenity of age. There are, for example, the blunders and the follies of youth, the blind stuggles of ignorance and weakness, the inevitable failure of the dreams of love and their eternal rebirth. These things are finer, for it is upon these that the structure of human life, like the ocean coral, is slowly reared.

It is the failing of common men to view life only in its relation to themselves; they fail to see life whole and themselves as only factors. The child wonders for what purpose curious bugs and insects are created. And men look upon trees and plants and animals only as ministering in some way to themselves. It never occurs to them that an oak, for instance, or a toy spaniel, may exist primarily for itself. It is only the artist who sees all life as so existing; for it is only beauty that translates these alien forms of being into terms that men can comprehend. Science and philosophy fail in this, for they are bounded by reason; and the mystery of the spirit that is in all life is never revealed to the mind alone. No mere intellectual effort will ever bring us into the heart of another personality. Love will do it for the individual; and art, closer always to love than philosophy, will do it for the race. Men of a certain temper view woman as always something relative to man; they see her as the loved mistress or as wife and mother, but in all other ways they see her as only a kind of inferior man. But the true literary artist never compares her; he lets her stand alone and be herself. He shows to cruder, duller minds the vision of her beauty; and common men, touched by this vision, may know her, if they will, as she is.

It is the same with many of the common things of life; they lie so close about us that we never think of looking at them as other than related to ourselves. We see the life of the average person in terms of the life we live, or of the life we aspire to live, and so turn from it. And when an artist with so fine a feeling as Mr. Howells takes these seemingly inferior forms of life and reveals their essential truth and beauty, he does us a service that we cannot appreciate too highly. For art, after all, is far more true, far more enduring, than any philosophy of life.

In fact, though Mr. Howells's philosophy is so sane and kind and sure an element in his work, it is his artistic vision that makes the stronger appeal. We see this in the conclusion of the present story. Mrs. Langbrith, as he sees her, is perhaps as weak a woman as any he has shown us, just as Dr. Anther is one of his finest, strongest men. But Mr. Howells whispers no philosophical secret to the woman in her distress; he leaves her to life and to her woman's nature. And these deal with her far more kindly, leave her more consistent with herself, leave her, in a word, by her very suffering and grief, closer to the reader's sympathies than her lover's dearly bought tranquillity leaves him. She has been weak, throughout the story, where he is strong, weak in will, weak perhaps in mind; but in the end she shows some evidence of the woman's strength that has been latent in her, shows at least the woman's power to love and to suffer. And the reader knows that this, however crude her expression of it, is as fine a thing as the man's strength he has been earlier asked to view.

It is easy to say that Mr. Howells would make a deeper appeal if his artistic vision of life were less obscured by the rosy clouds of his philosophy. But that is merely saying that if he were not Mr. Howells he would obviously be someone else. And, in truth, we do not want him other than he is. The American climate has various admittable infelicities, but on the whole it suits the American temper. And more than that, it bears its part—perhaps no small one—in forming this temper, of which in a modest way we sometimes boast. We grumble about our climate now and then, but our fault finding is itself of the whimsical American kind which only foreigners ever make the blunder of taking seriously. It is, after all, our climate and no one's else; we may say of it what we will. But let no alien raise a voice against it. It must not be touched with ungentle hand; it is something essentially American and therefore not to be profaned. And so the younger generation makes rather free with Mr. Howells, as the way of younger generations mostly is. They recognize certain infelicities in his work; but he, too, suits their temper, else he could not have had so large, though of course so unacknowledged, a share in forming it. But let no man who is not, artistically, his country-man raise a voice against him. He is not to be profaned by alien touch. He is ours and no one's else. For he, too, in what is faulty, as in what is finest, truest, best, is essentially American.

William Dean Howells

Samuel Langhorne Clemens*

Is it true that the sun of a man's mentality touches noon at forty and then begins to wane toward setting? Dr. Osler is charged with saying so. Maybe he said it, maybe he didn't; I don't know which it is. But if he said it, and if it is true, I can point him to a case which proves his rule. Proves it by being an exception to it. To this place I nominate Mr. Howells.

I read his *Venetian Days*[1] about forty years ago. I compare it with his paper on Machiavelli in a late number of *Harper*, and I cannot find that his English has suffered any impairment. For forty years his English has been to me a continual delight and astonishment. In the sustained exhibition of certain great qualities—clearness, compression, verbal exactness, and unforced and seemingly unconscious felicity of phrasing—he is, in my belief, without his peer in the English-writing world. *Sustained.* I intrench myself behind that protecting word. There are others who exhibit those great qualities as greatly as does he, but only by intervalled distributions of rich moonlight, with stretches of veiled and dimmer landscape between; whereas Howells's moon sails cloudless skies all night and all the nights.

In the matter of verbal exactness Mr. Howells has no superior, I suppose. He seems to be almost always able to find that elusive and shifty grain of gold, the *right word*. Others have to put up with approximations, more or less frequently; he has better luck. To me, the others are miners working with the gold pan—of necessity some of the gold washes over and escapes; whereas, in my fancy, he is quicksilver raiding down a riffle—no grain of the metal stands much chance of eluding

*Reprinted from *Harper's Monthly*, 113 (July 1906), 221–25.

him. A powerful agent is the right word: it lights the reader's way and makes it plain; a close approximation to it will answer, and much travelling is done in a well-enough fashion by its help, but we do not welcome it and applaud it and rejoice in it as we do when *the* right one blazes out on us. Whenever we come down upon one of those intensely right words in a book or a newspaper the resulting effect is physical as well as spiritual, and electrically prompt: it tingles exquisitely around through the walls of the mouth and tastes as tart and crisp and good as the autumn-butter that creams the sumac-berry. One has no time to examine the word and vote upon its rank and standing, the automatic recognition of its supremacy is so immediate. There is a plenty of acceptable literature which deals largely in approximations, but it may be likened to a fine landscape seen through the rain; the right word would dismiss the rain, then you would see it better. It doesn't rain when Howells is at work.

And where does he get the easy and effortless flow of his speech? and its cadenced and undulating rhythm? and its architectural felicities of construction, its graces of expression, its pemmican quality of compression, and all that? Born to him, no doubt. All in shining good order in the beginning, all extraordinary; and all just as shining, just as extraordinary to-day, after forty years of diligent wear and tear and use. He passed his fortieth year long and long ago; but I think his English of to-day—his perfect English, I wish to say—can throw down the gloves before his English of that antique time and not be afraid.

I will go back to the paper on Machiavelli now, and ask the reader to examine this passage from it which I append. I do not mean, examine it in a bird's-eye way; I mean search it, study it. And, of course, read it aloud. I may be wrong, still it is my conviction that one cannot get out of finely wrought literature all that is in it by reading it mutely:

> Mr. Dyer is rather of the opinion, first luminously suggested by Macaulay, that Machiavelli was in earnest, but must not be judged as a political moralist of our time and race would be judged. He thinks that Machiavelli was in earnest, as none but an idealist can be, and he is the first to imagine him an idealist immersed in realities, who involuntarily transmutes the events under his eye into something like the visionary issues of reverie. The Machiavelli whom he depicts does not cease to be politically a republican and socially a just man because he holds up an atrocious despot like Caesar Borgia as a mirror for rulers. What Machiavelli beheld round him in Italy was a civic disorder in which there was oppression without statecraft, and revolt without patriotism. When a miscreant like Borgia appeared upon the scene and reduced both tyrants and rebels to an apparent quiescence, he might very well seem to such a dreamer the savior of society whom

a certain sort of dreamers are always looking for. Machiavelli was no less honest when he honored the diabolical force of Caesar Borgia than Carlyle was when at different times he extolled the strong man who destroys liberty in creating order. But Carlyle has only just ceased to be mistaken for a reformer, while it is still Machiavelli's hard fate to be so trammelled in his material that his name stands for whatever is most malevolent and perfidious in human nature.

You see how easy and flowing it is; how unvexed by ruggednesses, clumsinesses, broken metres; how simple and—so far as you or I can make out—unstudied; how clear, how limpid, how understandable, how unconfused by cross-currents, eddies, undertows; how seemingly unadorned, yet is all adornment, like the lily-of-the-valley; and how compressed, how compact, without a complacency-signal hung out anywhere to call attention to it.

There are thirty-four lines in the quoted passage. After reading it several times aloud, one perceives that a good deal of matter is crowded into that small space. I think it is a model of compactness. When I take its materials apart and work them over and put them together in my way I find I cannot crowd the result back into the same hole, there not being room enough. I find it a case of a woman packing a man's trunk; he can get the things out, but he can't ever get them back again.

The proffered paragraph is a just and fair sample; the rest of the article is as compact as it is; there are no waste words. The sample is just in other ways: limpid, fluent, graceful, and rhythmical as it is, it holds no superiority in these respects over the rest of the essay. Also, the choice phrasing noticeable in the sample is not lonely; there is a plenty of its kin distributed through the other paragraphs. This is claiming much when that kin must face the challenge of a phrase like the one in the middle sentence: "an idealist immersed in realities, who involuntarily transmutes the events under his eye into something like the visionary issues of reverie." With a hundred words to do it with, the literary artisan could catch that airy thought and tie it down and reduce it to a concrete condition, visible, substantial, understandable and all right, like a cabbage; but the artist does it with twenty, and the result is a flower.

The quoted phrase, like a thousand others that have come from the same source, has the quality of certain scraps of verse which take hold of us and stay in our memories, we do not understand why, at first: all the words being the right words, none of them is conspicuous, therefore we wonder what it is about them that makes their message take hold.

> The mossy marbles rest
> On the lips that he has prest
> In their bloom,

And the names he loved to hear
Have been carved for many a year
On the tomb.

It is like a dreamy strain of moving music, with no sharp notes in it. The words are all "right" words, and all the same size. We do not notice it at first. We get the effect, it goes straight home to us, but we do not know why. It is when the right words are conspicuous that they thunder—

The glory that was Greece and the grandeur that was Rome!

When I go back from Howells old to Howells young I find him arranging and clustering English words well, but not any better than now. He is not more felicitous in concreting abstractions now, than he was in translating, then, the visions of the eye of flesh into words that reproduce their forms and colors:

In Venetian streets they give the fallen snow no rest. It is at once shovelled into the canals by hundreds of half-naked *facchini*; and now in St. Mark's Place the music of innumerable shovels smote upon my ear; and I saw the shivering legion of poverty as it engaged the elements in a struggle for the possession of the Piazza. But the snow continued to fall, and through the twilight of the descending flakes all this toil and encounter looked like that weary kind of effort in dreams, when the most determined industry seems only to renew the task. The lofty crest of the bell-tower was hidden in the folds of falling snow, and I could no longer see the golden angel upon its summit. But looked at across the Piazza, the beautiful outline of St. Mark's Church was perfectly pencilled in the air, and the shifting threads of the snowfall were woven into a spell of novel enchantment around the structure that always seemed to me too exquisite in its fantastic loveliness to be anything but the creation of magic. The tender snow had compassionated the beautiful edifice for all the wrongs of time, and so hid the stains and ugliness of decay that it looked as if just from the hand of the builder—or, better said, just from the brain of the architect. There was marvellous freshness in the colors of the mosaics in the great arches of the façade, and all that gracious harmony into which the temple rises, of marble scrolls and leafy exuberance airily supporting the statues of the saints, was a hundred times etherealized by the purity and whiteness of the drifting flakes. The snow lay lightly on the golden globes that tremble like peacock-crests above the vast domes, and plumed them with softest white; it robed the saints in ermine; and it danced over all its work, as if exulting in its beauty—beauty which filled me with subtle, selfish yearning to keep such evanescent loveliness for the little-while-longer of my whole life, and with despair to think that even the poor lifeless shadow of it could never be fairly reflected in picture or poem.

Through the wavering snowfall, the Saint Theodore upon one of the granite pillars of the Piazzetta did not show so grim as his wont is, and the winged lion on the other might have been a winged lamb, so gentle and mild he looked by the tender light of the storm. The towers of the island churches loomed faint and far away in the dimness; the sailors in the rigging of the ships that lay in the Basin wrought like phantoms among the shrouds; the gondolas stole in and out of the opaque distance more noiselessly and dreamily than ever; and a silence, almost palpable, lay upon the mutest city in the world.

The spirit of Venice is there: of a city where Age and Decay, fagged with distributing damage and repulsiveness among the other cities of the planet in accordance with the policy and business of their profession, come for rest and play between seasons, and treat themselves to the luxury and relaxation of sinking the shop and inventing and squandering charms all about, instead of abolishing such as they find, as is their habit when not on vacation.

In the working season they do business in Boston sometimes, and a character in *The Undiscovered Country* takes accurate note of pathetic effects wrought by them upon the aspects of a street of once dignified and elegant homes whose occupants have moved away and left them a prey to neglect and gradual ruin and progressive degradation; a descent which reaches bottom at last, when the street becomes a roost for humble professionals of the faith-cure and fortune-telling sort.

What a queer, melancholy house, what a queer, melancholy street! I don't think I was ever in a street before where quite so many professional ladies, with English surnames, preferred Madam to Mrs. on their door-plates. And the poor old place has such a desperately conscious air of going to the deuce. Every house seems to wince as you go by, and button itself up to the chin for fear you should find out it had no shirt on,—so to speak. I don't know what's the reason, but these material tokens of a social decay afflict me terribly: a tipsy woman isn't dreadfuler than a haggard old house, that's once been a home, in a street like this.

Mr. Howells's pictures are not mere stiff, hard, accurate photographs; they are photographs with feeling in them and sentiment, photographs taken in a dream, one might say.

As concerns his humor, I will not try to say anything, yet I would try if I had the words that might approximately reach up to its high place. I do not think any one else can play with humorous fancies so gracefully and delicately and deliciously as he does, nor has so many to play with, nor can come so near making them look as if they were doing the playing themselves and he was not aware that they were at it. For they are unobtrusive, and quiet in their ways, and well conducted. His is a humor which flows softly all around about and over and through the mesh of the page, pervasive, refreshing, health-giving, and makes no more show and no more noise than does the circulation of the blood.

There is another thing which is contentingly noticeable in Mr. Howells's books. That is his "stage directions"—those artifices which authors employ to throw a kind of human naturalness around a scene and a conversation, and help the reader to see the one and get at meanings in the other which might not be perceived if intrusted unexplained to the bare words of the talk. Some authors overdo the stage directions, they elaborate them quite beyond necessity; they spend so much time and take up so much room in telling us how a person said a thing and how he looked and acted when he said it that we get tired and vexed and wish he hadn't said it at all. Other authors' directions are brief enough, but it is seldom that the brevity contains either wit or information. Writers of this school go in rags, in the matter of stage directions; the majority of them have nothing in stock but a cigar, a laugh, a blush, and a bursting into tears. In their poverty they work these sorry things to the bone. They say:

". . . . replied Alfred, flipping the ash from his cigar." (This explains nothing; it only wastes space.)

". . . . responded Richard, with a laugh." (There was nothing to laugh about; there never is. The writer puts it in from habit—automatically; he is paying no attention to his work, or he would see that there is nothing to laugh at; often, when a remark is unusually and poignantly flat and silly, he tries to deceive the reader by enlarging the stage direction and making Richard break into "frenzies of uncontrollable laughter." This makes the reader sad.)

". . . . murmured Gladys, blushing." This poor old shop-worn blush is a tiresome thing. We get so we would rather Gladys would fall out of the book and break her neck than do it again. She is always doing it, and usually irrelevantly. Whenever it is her turn to murmur she hangs out her blush; it is the only thing she's got. In a little while we hate her, just as we do Richard.

". . . . repeated Evelyn, bursting into tears." This kind keep a book damp all the time. They can't say a thing without crying. They cry so much about nothing that by and by when they have something to cry *about* they have gone dry; they sob, and fetch nothing; we are not moved. We are only glad.

They gravel me, these stale and overworked stage directions, these carbon films that got burnt out long ago and cannot now carry any faintest thread of light. It would be well if they could be relieved from duty and flung out in the literary back yard to rot and disappear along with the discarded and forgotten "steeds" and "halidomes" and similar stage-properties once so dear to our grandfathers. But I am friendly to Mr. Howells's stage directions; more friendly to them than to any one else's, I think. They are done with a competent and discriminating art, and are faithful to the requirements of a stage direction's proper and lawful office, which is to inform. Sometimes they convey a scene and its conditions so well that I believe I could see the scent and get the spirit and meaning of the accompanying dialogue if some one would read merely the stage directions to me and leave out the talk. For instance, a scene like this, from *The Undiscovered Country*:

"....and she laid her arms with a beseeching gesture on her father's shoulder."

"....she answered, following his gesture with a glance."

"....she said, laughing nervously."

"....she asked, turning swiftly upon him that strange, searching glance."

"....she answered, vaguely."

"....she reluctantly admitted."

"....but her voice died wearily away, and she stood looking into his face with puzzled entreaty."

Mr. Howells does not repeat his forms, and does not need to; he can invent fresh ones without limit. It is mainly the repetition over and over again, by the third-rates, of worn and commonplace and juiceless forms that makes their novels such a weariness and vexation to us, I think. We do not mind one or two deliveries of their wares, but as we turn the pages over and keep on meeting them we presently get tired of them and wish they would do other things for a change:

"....replied Alfred, flipping the ash from his cigar."

"....responded Richard, with a laugh."

"....murmured Gladys, blushing."

"....repeated Evelyn, bursting into tears."

"....replied the Earl, flipping the ash from his cigar."

"....responded the undertaker, with a laugh."

"....murmured the chambermaid, blushing."

"....repeated the burglar, bursting into tears."

"....replied the conductor, flipping the ash from his cigar."

"....responded Arkwright, with a laugh."

"....murmured the chief of police, blushing."

"....repeated the housecat, bursting into tears."

And so on and so on; till at last it ceases to excite. I always notice stage directions, because they fret me and keep me trying to get out of their way just as the automobiles do. At first; then by and by they become monotonous and I get run over.

Mr. Howells has done much work, and the spirit of it is as beautiful as the make of it. I have held him in admiration and affection so many years that I know by the number of those years that he is old now; but his heart isn't, nor his pen; and years do not count. Let him have plenty of them: there is profit in them for us.

Notes

1. Not *Venetian Days* but *Venetian Life*, of course.

Mr. Howells at Work at Seventy-Two

Van Wyck Brooks*

Mr. William Dean Howells has never surprised anybody, thrilled anybody, shocked anybody. His career and his works alike seem devoid of inspired moments. He has never written a bad sentence, never struck a false note. To great numbers of people, he is simply "uninteresting." Nevertheless, there is a curious paradox in his position. The very people who would be first to call his work mediocre are those who instinctively recognize in him a unique distinction. He is, in fact, a very great and very choice artist—"one of the chief honors of our literature," Lowell called him. His light is the light of common day. He has pictured nothing remote, fantastic, tragic. It is only rare minds who are impressed by common things. Ordinary people are not interested in ferry-boats and office-desks and knitting-needles, and yet these are really the true, immediate, actual things that make up life. Mr. Howells is interested in these things, and, therefore, his audience is small. But it is picked, and constant.

In the light of this, I found a deep significance in his answers to a few of the questions I asked him, in the study where he had cordially agreed to receive me.

"Do you ever find that you have lost yourself in your work, that your characters get the better of you, that your own feelings become entangled?" I asked.

"Never," he replied. "The essence of achievement is to keep outside, to be entirely dispassionate, as a sculptor must be, moulding his clay. And this is true also, I think, of all good acting. Harrigan, the actor, once told me that the character he was playing was like a mirror held up before him. A good actor never for a moment identifies himself with his part."

In his opinion, was this true also of novelists who dealt with crude and powerful emotions, with moments of tragedy which, after all, do

*Reprinted from *World's Work*, 18 (May 1909), 11547–49.

occur in life? I asked him if Dickens did not occasionally allow his own feelings to intermingle with those of his characters.

"Dickens," he replied, "was essentially a cold man. He was a born actor, and his effects were those of an actor. He was never really touched himself. There is an element of claptrap in many of his highly emotional scenes."

I asked him if he found some places more congenial for his work than others—if he found New York congenial.

"You often wonder," he replied, "why a certain great industry grows up in a place which appears to have no special elements contributing to it. It is the man who does it all." And again he said, "You cannot write yourself out. What the schoolmasters tell you about writing too much or too little is all stuff. You do according to your nature."

"Do you find that interruptions disturb you and break in upon the vividness of the scene?"

"I am an old hand," he replied. "You must remember that you are talking to an old man. I have been writing for fifty years. I am not broken up by things as I used to be—the fibre isn't as brittle as it was."

Mr. Howells is, in fact, a man without a "method." He goes into his little study after breakfast, and sits down at a very clean, plain writing-table, and writes. It is a habit of half a century—if you can call anything a habit which represents the work of a perpetually fresh, sensitive, spontaneous mind. It is a mind which has held itself in mastery over all its creations, a little too fastidious to be eccentric. Is there not in this, perhaps, the explanation of a certain lack of force, a lack of that which compels readers and its characteristic of the supreme novelist as well as of those who have a great popularity for the moment? True as his novels are, a unique mirror of all the common things of life, one rebels against them, as one rebels against the common things themselves. One feels that in standing away from his characters to mass them properly, he has focused them all in a group very far away, so that all appear the same size, and all under middle height. It is not that men and women are infallible—the day of the perfect hero is past—but men are very far from being pale, and there are not nearly as many young girls who giggle in real life as in Mr. Howells's books. When you are prepared to admire some admirable and strong man, like *Hughes* in "The World of Chance," you feel that Mr. Howells, in making doubly sure that he has the character firmly in hand and at a distance sufficient to survey him behind and before, has crushed him into insignificance and pushed him almost out of sight. The penalty is that one does not long remember the individual characters or the individual books.

No, it is the impression of the whole that one remembers, the average of this enormously wide, serene, fresh panorama of human life.

Holding, as he does, the panoramic theory of the novel, Mr. Howells very justly pays small heed to plots. To make a work of art, it is necessary to take a piece out of life and round it off; and, so long as the piece is perfectly rounded off and complete in itself, so long as the chosen group of characters are perfectly proportioned in relation to one another, he holds that there is no need to introduce an artificial chain of action. I asked him if he planned a novel out completely in advance—if he made a scenario.

"Hardly at all," he answered. "I start with an idea. For example, in the "Ragged Lady" I began with the idea of a girl who had a genius for society, a delightful social creature. I know the story is to come out in a certain way, but I don't know at all how."

There was another point about the "Ragged Lady." He told me that he had gone out a good deal in the American society at Florence, and I was interested to know how in this novel he could draw a picture of a small society and reproduce the total impression without drawing upon the original characters who composed it. I did not easily see how he could make an entirely imagined set of characters produce exactly the same whole effect as the real society.

But that was easily explained, he said. "New York is an organism, each person is an organism—yet still the whole is an organism. The whole remains while the individuals change. You take something from the air and something from the personnel—a sort of composite. You put one character on another and you get a likeness, a likeness of the whole—and then you dissolve the composite into an entirely new set of individuals. In 'Indian Summer,' I obtained a group of four or five people in this way."

I asked him in which, as a man of letters, he took most delight, his fiction or his travels and criticism.

"Oh, fiction, fiction," he replied, with a good deal of warmth. "Writing novels is a kind of work in which you do not satisfy yourself entirely, but nothing could more nearly satisfy an honest man. I have never been really pleased with any of my criticism. Here and there would be a piece of luck—that is all."

It was a pleasure to him, however, to have introduced to the American public such a novelist as Leonard Merrick, who is already, he said, "not quite unknown" here. He compared him with Robert Herrick, "the best of our younger novelists," in the quality of his public. "They both have the confidence and security of all the truest critics, but their reputations are not grouped—they have no whole effect with the public."

And then he spoke of the greatest influence in his life—that of Tolstoy. "I read Tolstoy first in 1886," he said. "But as a writer I have not been influenced by him—my work has no trace of his influence."

I had been speaking of the "Kreutzer Sonata," and he said, "I have been told that the 'Kreutzer Sonata' was suggested to Tolstoy by my own story of the Shaker celibates in 'The Undiscovered Country.' But I don't, of course, know that this is true. It is not of any consequence, anyway." Are there not persons, however, to whom, as a literary fact or a literary surmise, it is of considerable consequence?

A little bookcase stood beside the writing-table, and, as he opened the glass doors, I saw that it contained his own books, row after row of them, in every sort of binding and in many editions—there were hardly any books beside. It was wonderful to see them all and to think of them as fifty years' achievement—the work of a man whose first books are read as eagerly as his last and will be read when he himself is gone. In a way it was like standing in the room with a classic; for the nature of Mr. Howells's reputation, in whatever degree it has strength and power, is that of a classic—moderate, steady, and perennial. There were French and German translations of his works, and paper-covered hammock sets, worn, old brown-covered copies of "Venetian Life," the first books of half a century ago, and luxurious editions which he handled with a certain bashfulness. And, as I turned to go, he showed me a little photograph of the palace on the Grand Canal with its tiny balcony where, as consul at Venice, he would stand and look out at sunset in those early days.

They were the days in which he was a friend of Longfellow, of Lowell and Holmes, of Emerson and Hawthorne. "That boy will know how to write if he goes on," wrote Lowell in 1868, "and then we old fellows will have to look about us." One thinks of him, indeed, as in some sort the successor of these men. There is a tradition that centres in him, and its flavor is native and American. Gracious, mild, and tranquil, he is at the same time shrewd, plain, and full of humor.

In his seventy-third year, Mr. Howells is of an age with Swinburne and Mark Twain. It is in comparing him with the former of these great writers, however preposterous in other ways the comparison might be, that one feels how little his power has depended upon the qualities of youth and how little it can be impaired by age. One never thinks of him as an old man, perhaps because one thinks of him as a man who has always been mature.

After a long silence, broken now and then by essays of travel and criticism, Mr. Howells is to publish another novel, and its name will be "The Children of the Summer."

1912-1920

William Dean Howells at 75:
Tributes from Eminent Americans
to Our Foremost Man of Letters

William Stanley Braithwaite*

William Stanley Braithwaite, the famous Black literary editor of Boston's supreme newspaper, wrote, leading off, that Howells was "the sole surviving figure of importance who links our own day to the fast receding period of the New England group. And through and out of the mated East and West of our national culture, typified in his own genius, he has been the herald taking our responsiveness to the light of contemporary Continental literature." There was something provincial in soliciting tributes from John D. Long, quondam Secretary of the Navy, Henry Van Dyke, or J. Berg Esenwein. But writers of permanent value and valid insight participated.

Mary Wilkins Freeman was subtitled as writing on "The Permanency of Mr. Howells."

I remember when I was a child, playing hide and seek (I think they used to call that innocent infantile game Hide and Seek), I discovered that the very best hiding place was in plain sight. I used to stand in full evidence, say at a house corner and all my little mates would race back and forth past me, hunting in good hiding-places, according to their notions, and not realizing that a hiding-place is not a hiding-place, and may serve a double purpose, by concealing itself as well as its inhabitant.

Well, in thinking about Mr. William Dean Howells, I have been wondering if he has not succeeded during recent years in doing just what I did in that childish game. Eager hunters after good literature have raced after it, searching hither and yon, in native and foreign byways and hedges, in cellars, and behind stumps and trees. Best sellers have flamed out of such places, and speedily became ashes,

*Reprinted from *Boston Evening Transcript*, 24 February 1912, p. 2.

215

and all the time William Dean Howells has stood shining calmly in his Place in plain sight. He has remained. He arrived years ago and he has never left. Others have pushed and been pushed between himself and the mental vision of the public, but he was there in his steadfast place when the pushers and the pushed were spoken of no more.

William Dean Howells, in more than one sense, has remained. He has never left his own country. He is our great American Author. He has never gone nugget-hunting in foreign fields. America would not be America without its incomparable asset of this Artist who is loyal. America, crude, and aggressively sophisticated, new, and daring the feats of wisdom of the aged, meek and devil-may-care, is His Country, and he has stood fast in its service, with his great brain directing his faithful pen. He has kindled and kept burning a light of knowledge which will never die, for the benefit of his own Country-men, to their credit at home and abroad. We have had a few whose originators have themselves passed beyond our ken, but their works remain. We have a few great living men who are content with the content of true greatness, to stand behind it and think little of them-selves in comparison.

They are the torch-bearers obscured by the guiding flames of their own fortunes, satisfied to be so, even satisfied that their guiding lights are missed for the sake of false ones, confident in the certainty of a return.

To say that we are all proud of William Dean Howells is to say too little. We are more than proud, we live because of his life. A great author is one of the props in the history of a great nation. We cannot proffer him glory, which he already has. We can add nothing to his fame, which will endure for the generation. But we can awake to a new realization of his greatness. Upon his seventy-fifth birthday we can look upon him and his work as if for the first time. We can, we who know, and have always known, his true value, regard him, as with the eyes of children, with a wonder of surprise and appreciation. The truly great is forever new, possessing inviolable youth. That quality we can recognize and be dazzled by the light of that one genius as if for the first time. In that way we can offer a birthday gift to William Dean Howells which he can accept from his own countrymen and know there is no duplicate. All American readers and authors love and revere this great author, and we offer him upon his seventy-fifth birthday a renewal of our love and reverence, which means much more to us than the original, and may mean more to him.

Mary E. Wilkins Freeman

Robert Herrick wrote:

A WARM CHAMPION OF THE TRUTH

Mr. Howells has the rare good fortune of enjoying the triumph of those ideals in literature which he has championed by critical word and even more by fine example all his long life. He has believed fervently in the worth of truth in art, as well as in life—the unremitting effort to perceive and record realities which has been the fundamental aim of all important literature. The half-century of his experience has reached all the way from the Victorian realists to Wells and Bennett and Galsworthy, spanning a swamp of silly pseudo-romance wherein the raw appetite of a newly awakened and uncultivated audience regaled themselves. Mr. Howells, more than any other American certainly, has educated his own people to appreciate and understand the newer masters of imaginative realism who indisputably hold the stage today both in England and America. And all this dreary time, when the popular tastes seemed ever to be astray searching for some false god to worship, Mr. Howells has cheered on the lesser workers in the field—the younger and unknown writers—with his unstinted, generous praise and eager sympathy. It is an encouraging reflection, therefore, his career affords—that the permanency and the real importance of a writer's achievement, even in his own lifetime, are not measured always by the numbers of his audience. While others have garnered their harvests from the populace—and gone down to deserved oblivion—Mr. Howells has written himself ineffaceably into the record of American literature.

Robert Herrick

Yet perhaps most significantly for us in our times, Braithwaite chose to reserve for climax a tribute by what may still be the best of Afro-American minds. It ran:

As a Friend of the Colored Man

In the composite picture which William Dean Howells, as his life work, has painted of America, he has not hesitated to be truthful and to include the most significant thing in the land, the black man. With lie and twistings most Americans seek to ignore the mighty and portentous shadow of ten growing millions, or if it insists on darkening the landscape, to label it as joke or crime. But Howells in his "Imperative Duty" faced our national foolishness and shuffling and evasion. Here was a white girl engaged to a white man who discovers herself to be "black." The problem looks before her as tremendous, awful. The world wavers. She peers beyond the veil and shudders and then—tells her story frankly, marries her man and goes her way as thousands have done and are doing.

It was Howells, too, that discovered Dunbar. We have had a score of artists and poets in black America, but few critics dared call them so. Most of them, therefore, starved, or, like Timrod, passed as white. Howells dared take Dunbar by the hand and say to the world, not simply here is a black artist, but here is an artist who happens to be black. Not only that, but as an artist Dunbar had studied black folk and realized the soul of this most artistic of all races. "I said," wrote Howells, "that a race which had come to this effect in any member of it, had attained civilization in him, and I permitted myself the imaginative prophecy that the hostilities and the prejudices which had so long constrained his race were destined to vanish in the arts; that these were to be the final proof that God had made of one blood all nations of men. I thought his merits positive and not comparative; and I held that if his black poems had been written by a white man, I should not have found them less admirable. I accepted them as an evidence of the essential unity of the human race, which does not think or feel black in one and white in another, but humanly in all."

Finally, when, on the centenary of Lincoln's birth, a band of earnest men said: We must finish the work of Negro emancipation and break the spiritual bonds that still enslave this people, William Dean Howells was among the first to sign the call. From this call came the National Association for the Advancement of Colored People and the "Crisis Magazine."

W. E. Burghardt Du Bois

The 75th Birthday Dinner:
In Honor of Mr. Howells

Anonymous*

A dinner in honor of the seventy-fifth birthday of William Dean Howells was given by Colonel George Harvey at Sherry's, New York, on March 2d. A reception was held at half-past six o'clock, and more than four hundred men and women prominent in letters congratulated Mr. Howells and wished him many added years. Practically every literary celebrity in the United States was present—never before in America have so many literary people been gathered under one roof; and Presi-

*Reprinted from *Harper's Weekly*, 56 (9 March 1912), II, pp. 27–34.

dent Taft came over from Washington to do honor to the venerable author.

Mr. Howells sat at Colonel Harvey's right hand and President Taft at his left. The dinner was served at fifty small tables. President Taft, Hamilton W. Mabie, Winston Churchill, Basil King, William Allen White, Augustus Thomas, and James Barnes spoke, in addition to the guest of honor and his host.

Colonel Harvey's Prefatory Remarks

Colonel Harvey spoke as follows in greeting and introduction:

The first realization that springs from a glance at your birthday party, sir, is that of your own amazing versatility. One needs only to recall the titles of your books to paint the picture. The unique gathering itself, for example, might be designated with exactitude as "A Modern Instance." You find yourself primarily among "Literary Friends and Acquaintance." Behold, sir, with gratification and delight the "Heroines of Fiction" and rest assured that not one is "A Counterfeit Presentment."

The mere presence of so many wives without their husbands and *vice versa* affords a vivid reminder of "No Love Lost." Before the evening closes it is quite within the range of possibility that we shall hear "Stories of Ohio." For myself I freely admit that I am assuming "A Fearful Responsibility" and I plead for the full exercise of "The Quality of Mercy." You yourself will be confronted presently by "An Imperative Duty," while on your right, if you but turn your head you will perceive "A Little Girl Among the Masters"—between two of them, if I may be permitted to say as much. And so we might continue almost indefinitely, even, I dare say, to the point of finding somewhere in the room "A Pair of Patient Lovers."

No less varied than your literary product has been your work, and here again you breathe an atmosphere of congeniality. You have edited newspapers. Our most famous journalists are here. You have published a book or two. Behold, sir, our greatest publishers. You have set type. In that by-gone occupation I claim companionship before the time when inventive ingenuity transformed an art into a science. You are a novelist, a poet and a dramatist. A novelist, a poet, and a dramatist shall address you.

But, sir, never forget that you began your splendid career as a native of Ohio. As such it was inevitable that public office should not only pursue, but overtake you, as in truth it did, to the joy of mankind, since it landed you in your beloved Venice. As a statesman, then, a statesman from Ohio, if you please, you naturally crave the delight of sympathetic comradeship upon an occasion such as this. That void, sir, shall be filled to overflowing. Indeed, I may be so bold as to declare unhesitatingly that he who links arms with you to-night as a public servant is not only a native of Ohio, but is, with one exception, the most distinguished native of Ohio now living.

The delegates who framed the Federal Constitution decreed at first as follows:

"The executive power of the United States shall be vested in a single person. His style shall be 'President of the United States' and his title shall be 'His Excellency.'"

Subsequently they dropped the "title," but they kept the "style." Hence the word "stylish," meaning handsome in person and gracious in demeanor. Yet another cognomen was proposed and, indeed, is frequently used to this very day. That is "Chief Magistrate." It is an appellation which personally I have always liked and which I should surely elect as peculiarly fitting in this particular instance. What are the attributes of a great Chief Magistrate? Pliny, Plutarch, Aristotle, Montaigne—all agree. He must be a wise man; he must be a brave man; he must be a kindly man; he must be a patient man; above all, he must be a just man. Such an one, sir, it is the exceptional blessing of our beloved country now to possess—the embodiment, in truth, of sagacity, of moral courage, of benignity, of leniency, of justice.

There is yet another attribute held in high esteem by the philosopher who guided the Medicis. "The good and wise prince," he writes, "should be a lover and protector of men of letters." That sentiment surely we can all indorse. It completes the list of essential qualities. By his presence to-night, sir, our Chief Magistrate is proved in the last analysis as one who keeps the faith.

But obedience to the letter, no less than to the spirit of our fundamental law, requires recognition of the "style" designated by the Constitution. And, much as we may prefer the other, truly it is not so bad.

I have the honor, sir and ladies and gentlemen, to present the President of the United States.

President Taft's Speech

President Taft spoke as follows:

I have traveled from Washington here to do honor to the greatest living American writer and novelist. I have done this because of the personal debt I feel for the pleasure he has given me in what he has written, in the pictures of American life and society and character he has painted, and with which I have had sufficient familiarity to know the truth and delicacy of his touch. Neither the rhythm, nor the emphasis, nor the shading of his meaning has robbed his style of the lucidity and clearness that delight a common mind like mine, and his delightful and kindly humor that leaves a flower in one's memory has created a feeling of affection for the author that prompts an expression like this.

Easily at the head of the living literary men of the nation, Mr. Howells is entitled, on the celebration of his seventy-fifth birthday, to this tribute of respect.

Like Shakespeare, like Burns, like Lincoln, Mr. Howells is not a university man, but he began his literary education on a country newspaper at a time of life when others begin to prepare for an academic training, and he has continued that education to this present period of youthful old age.

I perhaps may say outside of the record that on the occasion of my graduation from Yale in 1881 Mr. Howells received the honorary degree of doctor of laws. I was very nervous as I went up to receive my degree, and Mr. Howells spoke some comforting words to me. That was more than thirty years ago, but compliments don't wear out.

Born in Ohio, in a "Boy's Town" on the beautiful river, he formed what was there an unusual ambition to succeed as a man of letters, and he began at the very bottom rung of the ladder by learning to set type. By his *Campaign Life of Lincoln* he earned enough to enable him to take that charming wedding journey in which those of us that love old Quebec and the lower St. Lawrence and Saguenay often have followed him; and then, with the additional compensation for his political work, he became consul in Venice in the four years of Mr. Lincoln's term. What business there was of a consular character between the United States and the old mistress of the Adriatic he doubtless properly performed, but *The Venetian Life* which grew in that soil of patronage was a beautiful flower which makes us patient with the system that contributed much to the literary preparation of men like Hawthorne and Howells.

Mr. Howells is not a writer whose periods of inspiration are fitful and occasional, but he has educated and prepared himself to do literary work, as men work in other professions, making his mind and imagination respond to the regular demand of duty. On the other hand, unlike Trollope, who worked like a machine, finishing so many pages a day and showing in his work the evidences of haste and mechanical striving, all that has come from Mr. Howells's pen is beautifully wrought out, with no suggestion of hurry or the oil of the machine.

Mr. Howells, in his long and useful life, has been content to live in literature. He has attempted to play a part in no other sphere. By taste, by ability, by imagination, by the genius of taking pains, he finds himself now five years beyond the age of the psalmist, representing the best and highest of American literature. Everything that he has written sustains the highest standard of social purity and aspiration, of refinement and morality, and of wholesome ideals, and he has added to American literature a treasure of literary excellence the enjoyment of which will make coming generations grateful.

Address of Winston Churchill

Winston Churchill spoke as follows:

When I was in Boston the other day I ran across two of the most distinguished of our New England writers and each of them spoke of this dinner. Each of them gave me three reasons for coming here tonight, and I venture to say it is the same reason which has brought every man and woman to this distinguished gathering—affection, respect, and admiration for William Dean Howells.

I cannot but think it is somewhat presumptuous for me to speak of him, since my acquaintance with him has been chiefly confined to his writings. I am so seldom out of New Hampshire that I regret to say I have missed a personal relationship, the value of which is universally acknowledged by those whose privilege it has been to profit by it.

It is interesting in these modern days when the shuttle is moving with such bewildering rapidity, when the threads unconsciously woven into our lives are so numerous and seemingly so tangled, to pause and attempt to discover the pattern which any particular individual has traced upon the cloth. For we are all weaving patterns into the lives of others and often these of more importance than we shall ever divine.

So when I was asked to say a few words here this evening I tried to analyze with some definiteness just what Mr. Howells meant to me. And I find that, first of all, the sight of his name in print has come more and more to suggest a quality of great value in America to-day, honest workmanship. The fertility of our native inventive genius, as well as the temptations offered by the perplexing variety and novelty of the life passing before our eyes, threaten continually to carry us away, incite us to record as many aspects as we can, in our brief existence, of a new and shifting civilization. Mr. Howells stands not only for the conception—the thing itself, but also—what I think more important—how the thing is done.

And secondly, he stands for another quality which (it is becoming increasingly apparent) must be a part of the equipment of the serious and responsible modern novelist—a consistent philosophy—viewpoint of life. It may not be our good fortune to achieve one so early as Mr. Howells did his own and our philosophy may not necessarily be his. But I believe if we hope ultimately to count that we must develop a viewpoint.

Again, he stands for something which should earn for him the gratitude of all men of letters, that purity of the English language of which we are in America in a large sense the trustees, and at a time when it is threatened and assailed by an insidious multitude of polyglot corruptions.

Perhaps not the least of the debts which literature owes him is that he has kept himself clean against the pollution of American letters by the muddy tide of commercialism, of materialism, which has swept over our country and which is leaving its stain, I am sorry to say, on other dignified professions besides our own.

I cannot wish him friends, for he has them in abundance. And he is filled with honors. But I do wish him, and heartily, many more years as the dean of American letters, as the guardian of the dignity and freedom of our literature.

Mr. Mabie's Speech

Hamilton W. Mabie said:

There is a pretty legend about a gentleman of Naples who fought thirteen duels to sustain his contention that Ariosto was a greater poet than Tasso. As he lay dying, after the thirteenth duel, he expressed his sincere regret that now he should never be able to read the work of either poet! I am not in that position, for I have read Mr. Howells from my youth up; and if he objects to this phrase I will modify it by saying, from my comparative youth up. He has said that the man who introduces you always says those things about you which you secretly believe to be true. This is one of those happy phrases which belong to the fiction side of his writing, for every one knows that a more modest man, nor a more retiring one, never put pen to paper. To-night we are invading his privacy; and I, for one, have such respect for privacy that I am not willing to be a party even to a friendly invasion. I shall not speak of Mr. Howells, therefore, but an imaginary person who was born in Ohio at the right time in the last century. You remember that some Far-Western wit once said that Ohio was settled by people who started to go West and lost their nerve. But Ohio has long been a nursery of statesmen, and of writers as well.

Let us imagine that this person of whom I speak began in the composing-room of a newspaper; and that, instead of learning first in a didactic way the art of writing, his fingers came to know the feel of the type; and he came to know through observation the very stuff of which the life around him was made. Here, then, we have a man over whom the classic tradition did not cast its spell in his youth, who studied the rudiments of life and the rudiments of art at the same moment, and whose career attests the vitality of this earliest unity of interests.

Ohio defines one of the few localities on this continent which has atmosphere. In that State one sees on early spring days or late autumn afternoons a landscape suffused with that mysterious quality which we call atmosphere; in which the hard outlines, without losing their reality, take on a poetic suggestiveness; and one sees the landscape not in a dream, but brooded over by the sky. If one is a boy in such a country, he will learn early and intimately that the sky must be studied from the earth, and that the earth can never be seen without the sky. If he is fortunately endowed, he will become an observer; but he will not divorce the power of seeing from that higher vision, which is not of the eye, but of the mind.

A year ago they were telling a story in Florence of two American women meeting on the Ponte Vecchio. One said to the other, "Is this Florence or Venice?" And the other said, "What day of the week is it?" "Wednesday," replied the first. "Then," said the second, "it is Venice."

Let us imagine this young man transferred from Ohio to Venice; from the young world to the very old; from the country of to-day and to-morrow to the city of the splendid past.

Here, then, one would imagine the young American, born with taste, with the instinct for knowledge which means culture, might have been overborne by a wealth of associations and swept from his footing in the realities of the modern world. But, if this youth had been asked, he probably would have said, as Mr. Howells once said, "It does not make any difference how long one lives in Venice, at the end it is still a dream." But what a beautiful dream it was! How it enriched the imagination and tempered the observation of this young writer! With what sensitiveness he caught the elusive charm which issues from the lagoon! Keenly sensitive to the glory of the past and intensely American, the shadow of Austrian oppression rested upon him; and, as in Mr. Howells's case, he felt deeply the humiliation of the people to whom the Far East had once paid tribute, and whose civic life had been more magnificently dressed than that of any other people in the history of the world. Venice spoke not only to the imagination of this young writer; she was also the university in which he began the study of modern languages; for the modern spirit was so strong in him, and he was so distinctively a man of his time, that to know Italian and French and Spanish was more than an accomplishment: it was part of a training which not only affected his art, but broadened his sympathies and deepened the passion for humanity, which was one of his prime qualities.

Imagine this young American, steeped in the traditions of beauty and culture of the older world in its modern aspects, going back to his own country; young, ardent, generous, and thoroughly trained. It would seem inevitable that upon such a man should fall the responsibilities that had been borne by Lowell and Fields, and that the earliest and still the most distinctive literary periodical in the country should come under his supervision and should reflect his knowledge of the old and his quick and helpful sympathy with the new. It would have been a fortunate moment, for there were inspiring figures in the Cambridge of that day— men of marked and fascinating personality. If this young man could have met them with his ardor, he would have loved them. If he had written his recollections of them he would not have called them *My Reminiscences*, but *My Literary Passions*. It was a happy moment in other ways. One period of literary expression had passed; one epoch of national history had closed; the making of the nation was complete; a new chapter was opened; and, wherever this young man of rare talent, who felt the attraction of character and could read it with his imagination, turned, he found figures ready to his hand. Balzac had come at the right moment to transfer into the *Comedie Humaine* great sections of the social life of his time. Dickens and Thackeray owed as much to their sitters as Rembrandt to the men and women he painted. Hawthorne, with subtle and sensitive art, had portrayed the pure New England type. The hour was ready for this young man; and it fell to him to touch with a beautiful skill, with humor, and with integrity of observation the American life of his day.

Imagine how finely a man of this temper and training would touch the ideals, the personality, sensitive but vigorous, the unspoiled charm of purity and dignity of the American girl, born, perhaps, in Maine, and going to Europe for the first time. In the opening of the new era there were figures of a new type: men bustling to the front, untrained, but of powerful will and penetrating practical intelligence; and one can imagine this young writer drawn to the study of this type. One can imagine him writing a story like *The Rise of Silas Lapham*, which some of us count one of the original novels in our fiction; done with such art that one hesitates to call it a "human document" lest he should brush with a heavy hand the bloom of feeling which lies on the surface of it.

One can imagine this man, grown older, going to the metropolis, where life is not half so comfortable, but where it is intensely, almost overpoweringly interesting, and bringing the freshness of an unspoiled mind to this great mart, where some men pray and many speculate and all work out their destiny according to their natures. One can imagine him reporting *A Hazard of New Fortunes*.

And all this time side by side with this running stream of fiction, this student of life, this accomplished artist, would be seeing and thinking; and in essay and poem his gentle but open-eyed philosophy of life would find expression.

If, for instance, "The Easy Chair" were left by that master of the beautiful phrase, who wore through bitter controversy and the storm of war the white flower of a blameless life, one would turn involuntarily to a man so admirably trained for the kind of comment on life which Addison would have made if he had lived in the nineteenth century; or, shall we rather say, Steele, since here is a flexibility, a humor, a lightness of touch which belong to Steele rather than to Addison.

One can imagine such a career as this, lived in the public view and yet never sacrificing its privacy, making its appeal to a whole people, and yet never surrendering for a moment its convictions. A delicate art in- deed, but a very deep and beautiful feeling for all humankind; an in- stinctive and passionate love of liberty, an unassuming but dauntless courage. Would it be extraordinary that when such a career should reach its seventh decade we should find that the seeds of helpfulness sown by the way of unassuming sincerity and charm of manner had blossomed into a universal regard and affection, so that when the name was spoken there was always a note of something intimate and personal in the appreciation that followed?

If Mr. Howells were to have a birthday, and I should be honored with an invitation to say something about him and his work, I fancy I should have said many of these things, only I should have said them with more grace and eloquence because I should have said them of a person for whom I have a very great respect and a very warm affection. Very likely I should have ventured a little farther afield and recalled the course of literature in our time, I should have measured the distance of his point of view from that of the literature and the art which culmi- nated in the Superman; a superb, one-sided, and almost brutal enthrone- ment of the strong over the weak; the arrogant denial of all the great truths of the gospel of pity and helpfuless. Instead of this lonely path pursued by the soul that grows strong by its separation from its kind, its indifference to them and its exaltation of its own moods into universal law, I should have seen Mr. Howells, moved by the sorrows of humanity, passionately akin with them like Ruskin and Tolstoi, striking hands with his fellows. I should have seen within his work the steady light of a passionate desire for social justice, I should see him a man whose delicate art has enriched the palace of life with a tracery as fine as that which hides the strength of the Damascus blade; but never sitting at ease and looking out of the windows on the sorrows of the world.

And if I had looked at our own literature I think I should have found him striking a beautiful balance between the independence of judgment, the freshness of feeling, the democratic point of view of the New World, and the ripeness, the charm, and the refinement of the Old World; one who knew life and art and loved both, but cared most for life.

A Tribute from Kansas

William Allen White made these remarks:

What a blessed privilege it is to be one of the pioneers of a big historic movement and to live long enough to see the main army come up and camp where once angels feared to tread. Twenty-five years ago this country was in the midst of the greatest era of sheer materialism that it ever has known. As a nation we were crass. In the West we were booming. In the South we were seeing visions of a new prosperity; in the East we were thinking in States and cities and sections translated into millions.

In that day a kindly-mannered stoutish, mild-voiced, middle-aged man took his pen in hand and began to write about altruism. Comparatively few people in the country at that time knew or cared what altruism meant. Mr. Howells was to the vast majority of the reading public at that time a most interesting literary man with a curious theory of life. It was the day when any man who could write anything without using "whereas," "inasmuch as," "therefore," and "as follows" was regarded in America as one of "them damn literary fellers" and little attention was paid to him. If Mr. Howells cared to preach altruism, it was to the powers that were in those days as though he had promulgated a new theory of the dimensions. Doubtless a number of those who really knew what he was driving at were horrified, and shocked that apparently so sane a man as Mr. Howells seemed to be should begin to exhibit signs of mental decay so early. But even those who were shocked were alarmed only for Mr. Howells. They did not know that he was a sower going forth to sow.

For twenty-five years this sower has been scattering seeds. Some fell in good ground and now the earth is covered with the propaganda. Social justice is the one big dominant issue of all our politics. Business, religion, literature, art—all the relations of life are permeated with the idea of duty between men. And in this country no other single force during the past quarter of a century has so steadily stood for social and industrial righteousness as our dearly beloved friend. His hand holding the torch of light never has wearied. His vision never has been dimmed. A gentle, brave pioneer soul he has been. To him the newly awakening social conscience of his country owes much, for to him all that is just and beautiful in our national life, all that is equitable and worthy in the new trend of our economic expression, is government—the many laws establishing justice between men that are being sustained by our Supreme Court—to him all these are but dreams that he has dreamed coming true. How sweet it must be to awaken from "a noble dream and find one's dream still there and that nothing is gone but his sleep"!

LETTERS FROM ABROAD

Messages of congratulations to Mr. Howells had been received from writers of distinction both abroad and at home. Some of the letters follow:

From Arnold Bennett

GRAND HOTEL CALIFORNIE, CANNES,
15 February, 1912.

MY DEAR COLONEL HARVEY,—I hear with pain that you have taken advantage of my short temporary absence from the United States to arrange a dinner in honor of William Dean Howells. I suppose you were afraid that if he and I got together he might be found not disagreeing with those views on certain Victorian novelists which I have expressed once too often and which have procured my ruin in the esteem of all thoughtful Americans. I would have given much to be able to be present at this dinner, for there is no man of letters in the whole world whom I regard more highly than I regard your guest.

It may astonish you to learn that even thirty years ago—and more—HARPER's used to penetrate monthly into the savage wilderness of the Five Towns and that the first literary essays I ever read were those of W. D. Howells and Russell Lowell. (I preferred the former because they were more friendly, persuasive, and human.) Thus I was at a tender age more American than some Americans. My delight in W. D. Howells has never lessened; it has, indeed, increased in proportion as I have learned to appreciate the subtlety of his wit, the sure fineness of his taste, the immense sweep of his culture, and the force of his creative gift. Criticism, travel, novels, plays—for I am not one to forget on this august occasion that W. D. Howells is an admirable playwright—I have feasted on his output and stolen innumerable ideas therefrom since the period when I could only smoke in secret; and I propose to continue feasting as long as Mr. Howells provides the fare. May that be a very long time! It is rumored that the man is seventy-five years old. Incredible! Pick up almost any number of HARPER's and you will find evidence that he is not seventy-five, but about forty-four—a nice youthful age—and my own.

I have never met Mr. Howells. When I go to America he retires to Spain and when I come to France in search of him he has vanished to Timbuctoo. But I intend to meet him. And in the mean time I should like to express through you my profound admiration for him and, if I may be permitted, my grateful affection. I cannot raise my glass. But I can raise my pen, and I do to his health and long life and unabated activity. I feel very strongly about W. D. Howells. We of the Five Towns are always least articulate when we feel most strongly and I realize that I have not said what I wanted to say. But W. D. Howells will forgive me.

Yours sincerely,

(Signed) ARNOLD BENNETT.

Thomas Hardy Sends Greetings

MAX GATE, DORCHESTER, *February 16, 1912.*

DEAR MR. HOWELLS,—It is with a movement of surprise that I recognize your being on the point of celebrating your seventy-fifth birthday. If you are at all the same man as he who kindly came to see me at my London flat about a year and a half ago, and revived a friendship of I should think thirty years' standing, you have no cause to complain of the clawing of time's "crouch."

The experience and outlook of some of us may lead us to shuffle past such anniversaries with as little recognition of them as possible; but you have no need to fall into such shabby habits. I do not remember that a single word except of praise—always well deserved—has ever been uttered on your many labors in the field of American literature. You have, too, always beheld the truth that poetry is the heart of literature, done much to counteract the suicidal opinion held, I am told, by young contemporary journalists, that the times have so advanced as to render poetry nowadays a negligible tract of letters.

I hope you will long continue to fill the "Easy Chair" of the MAGA-ZINE to the edification of its readers, and am,

Yours ever sincerely,

(Signed) THOMAS HARDY.

LETTERS FROM AMERICAN AUTHORS

G. W. Cable's Praise

BILOXI, MISSISSIPPI, *February 23, 1912.*

MY DEAR MR. HARVEY,—I cannot limit myself to ordinary form in expressing my regret that your invitation to meet Mr. Howells and participate in the celebration of his seventy-fifth birthday finds me at so great a distance from my home and from New York that I am compelled to forego the honor.

For half a lifetime I have regarded Mr. Howells with the highest admiration and grateful affection. To my mind, no other writer has equally enriched the treasury of American literature or so ennobled its standards of art and use. From the beginning of his career to the present hour the purity, grace, and dignity of style in all his work, its refined, powerful, and life-like portraiture of character, its adventurous yet faultless moral ideals, the catholicity of his tastes and views, his compelling wit and inevitably well-placed satire, so convincing by its gentleness, his critical acumen and generosity, and his combined virility and human kindness have given him an easy supremacy which the charms of his personal character fitly adorn.

His birthday at seventy-five, revealing him with his pen still in hand and all his gifts in full play, truly calls for, and must elicit, universal rejoicing. With warmest thanks and every good wish, I am ever,

Yours truly,

G. W. CABLE.

A Letter to Mr. Howells

Henry James*

It is made known to me that they are soon to feast in New York the newest and freshest of the splendid birthdays to which you keep treating us, and that your many friends will meet round you to rejoice in it and reaffirm their allegiance. I shall not be there, to my sorrow; and, though this is inevitable, I yet want to be missed, peculiarly and monstrously missed, so that these words shall be a public apology for my absence: read by you, if you like and can stand it, but, better still, read *to* you and, in fact, straight *at* you by whoever will be so kind and so loud and so distinct. For I doubt, you see, whether any of your toasters and acclaimers have anything like my ground and title for being with you at such an hour. There can scarce be one, I think, to-day who has known you from so far back, who has kept so close to you for so long, and who has such fine old reasons—so old, yet so well preserved—to feel your virtue and sound your praise. My debt to you began well-nigh half a century ago in the most personal way possible, and then kept growing and growing with your own admirable growth—but always rooted in the early intimate benefit. This benefit was that you held out your open editorial hand to me at the time I began to write—and I allude especially to the summer of 1866—with a frankness and sweetness of hospitality that was really the making of me, the making of the confidence that required help and sympathy and that I should otherwise, I think, have strayed and stumbled about a long time without acquiring. You showed me the way and opened me the door; you wrote to me and confessed yourself struck with me—I have never forgotten the beautiful thrill of *that.* You published me at once—and paid me, above all, with a dazzling promptitude; magnificently, I felt, and so that nothing since has ever quite come up to it. More than this even, you cheered me on with a sympathy that was in itself an inspiration. I mean that you talked to me and listened to me—ever so patiently and genially and suggestively conversed and consorted with me. This won me to you irresis-

*Reprinted from *North American Review*, 195 (April 1912), 558–62.

tibly and made you the most interesting person I knew—lost as I was in the charming sense that my best friend was an editor, and an almost insatiable editor, and that such a delicious being as that was a kind of property of my own. Yet how didn't that interest still quicken and spread when I became aware that—with such attention as you could spare from us, for I recognized my fellow-beneficiaries—you had started to cultivate *your* great garden as well; the tract of virgin soil that, beginning as a cluster of bright, fresh, sunny, and savory patches close about the house, as it were, was to become that vast goodly pleasaunce of art and observation, of appreciation and creation, in which you have labored, without a break or a lapse, to this day, and in which you have grown so grand a show of—well, really of everything. Your liberal visits to *my* plot and your free-handed purchases there were still greater events when I began to see you handle, yourself, with such ease the key to our rich and inexhaustible mystery. Then the question of what you would make of your own powers began to be even more interesting than the question of what you would make of mine—all the more, I confess, as you had ended by settling this one so happily. My confidence in myself, which you had so helped me to, gave way to a fascinated impression of your own spread and growth, for you broke out so insistently and variously that it was a charm to watch and an excitement to follow you. The only drawback that I remember suffering from was that *I*, your original debtor, couldn't print or publish or pay you—which would have been a sort of ideal of *re*payment and of enhanced credit; you could take care of yourself so beautifully and I could (unless by some occasional happy chance or rare favor) scarce so much as glance at your proofs or have a glimpse of your "endings." I could only read you, full-blown and finished, always so beautifully finished—and see, with the rest of the world, how you were doing it again and again.

That, then, was what I had with time to settle down to—the common attitude of seeing you do it again and again; keep on doing it, with your heroic consistency and your noble, genial abundance, during all the years that have seen so many apparitions come and go, so many vain flourishes attempted and achieved, so many little fortunes made and unmade, so many weaker inspirations betrayed and spent. Having myself to practise meaner economies, I have admired from period to period your so ample and liberal flow; wondered at your secret for doing positively a little—what do I say, a little? I mean a magnificent deal!—of Everything. I seem to myself to have faltered and languished, to have missed more occasions than I have grasped, while you have piled up your monument just by remaining at your post. For you to have had the advantage, after all, of breathing an air that has suited and nourished you; of sitting up to your neck, as I may say—or at least up to your waist—amid the sources of your inspiration. There and so you were at your post; there and so the spell could ever work for you, there and so your relation to all your material grow closer and stronger, your perception penetrate, your authority accumulate. They make a great array, a literature in themselves, your studies of American life so acute, so direct, so disinterested, so preoccupied but with the fine truth of the case; and the more attaching to me always for their referring themselves to a time and an order when we knew together what American life *was*—or thought we did, deluded though we may have been! I don't pretend to measure the effect or to sound the depths, if they be not the shallows, of the huge wholesale importations and so-called assimilations of this later time; I only feel and speak for those conditions in which, as "quiet observers," as careful painters, as sincere artists, we would still in our native, our human and social element, know more or less where we were and feel more or less what he had hold of. You knew and felt these things better than I; you had learned them earlier and more intimately, and it was impossible, I think, to be in more instinctive and more informed possession of the general truth of your subject than you happily found yourself. The *real* affair of the American case and character, as it met your view and brushed your sensibility, that was what inspired and attached you, and, heedless of foolish flurries from other quarters, of all wild or weak slashings of the air and wavings in the void, you gave yourself to it with an incorruptible faith. You saw your field with a rare lucidity: you say all it had to give in the way of the romance of the real and the interest and the thrill and the charm of the common, as one may put it; the character and the comedy, the point, the pathos, the tragedy, the particular homegrown humanity under your eyes and your hand and with which the life all about you was closely interknitted. Your hand reached out to these things with a fondness that was in itself a literary gift and played with them as the artist only and always can play: freely, quaintly, incalculably, with all the assurance of his fancy and his irony, and yet with that fine taste for the truth and the pity and the meaning of the matter which keeps the temper of observation both sharp and sweet. To observe by such an instinct and by such reflection is to find work to one's hands and a challenge in every bush; and as the familiar American scene thus bristled about you, so year by year your vision more and more justly responded and swarmed. You put forth *A Modern Instance*, and *The Rise of Silas Lapham*, and *A Hazard of New Fortunes*, and *The Landlord at Lion's Head*, and *The Kentons* (that perfectly classic illustration of your spirit and your form) after having put forth in perhaps lighter-fingered prelude *A Foregone Conclusion*, and *The Undiscovered Country*, and *The Lady of the Aroostook*, and *The Minister's Charge*—to make of a long list too short a one; with the effect again and again of a feeling for the human relation, as the social climate of our country qualifies, intensifies, generally conditions and colors it, which, married in perfect felicity to the expression you found for its service, constituted the originality that we want to fasten upon you as with silver nails to-night. Stroke by stroke and book by book your work was to become for this exquisite notation of our whole democratic light and shade and give and take in the highest degree *documentary*, so that none other, through all your fine long season, could approach it in value and amplitude. None, let me say, too, was to approach it in essential distinction; for you had grown master, by insidious practices best known to yourself, of a method so easy and so natural, so marked with the personal element of your humor and the play, not less personal, of your sympathy, that the critic kept coming on its secret connection with the grace of letters much as Fenimore Cooper's Leatherstocking—so knowing to be able to do it!—comes in the forest on the subtle tracks of Indian braves. However, these things take us far, and what I wished mainly to put on record is my sense of that unfailing, testifying truth in you which will keep you from ever being neglected. The critical intelligence—if any such fitful and discredited light may still be conceived as within our sphere—has not at all begun to render you its tribute. The more inquiringly and perceivingly it shall still be projected upon the American life we used to know, the more it shall be moved by the analytic and historic spirit, the more indispensable, the more a vessel of light, will you be found. It's a great thing to have used one's genius and done one's work with such quiet and robust consistency that they fall by their own weight into that happy service. You may remember perhaps, and I like to recall, how the great and admirable Taine, in one of the fine excursions of his French curiosity, greeted you as a precious painter and a sovereign witness. But his appreciation, I want you to believe with me, will yet be carried much further, and then—though you may have argued yourself happy, in your generous way and with your incurable optimism, even while noting yourself not understood—your really beautiful time will come. Nothing so much as feeling that he may himself perhaps help a little to bring it on can give pleasure to yours all faithfully,

Henry James

A National Contribution

Edith Wyatt*

On a wet, December evening, after everybody else had gone to bed, I once picked up a book and began to read. The whole house was still. I was dissatisfied with my thoughts not only of myself, but "on man, on nature, and on human life"—too dissatisfied either to face the difficulties that distressed me or to dismiss them.

I read for two hours a familiar novel of Mr. William Dean Howells, *The Son of Royal Langbrith*. This is the page at which I began.

> —the doctor asked, "What do you think of the man who takes the life of another's soul—destroys his soul? It was a woman's expression." The judge smiled intelligently. "I should imagine. But I should doubt whether it could be done. Do you want to engage me for the defense?

For the rest of the two hours I lived the days of Dr. Anther in the town of Saxmills. I lived the tissue of the existence of Hawberk, the opium victim whose soul was being destroyed, and of his daughter who comforted his nightmares, and of the men and women there whose fates were still affected by the evil exploitations of Royal Langbrith, now long dead. As Hawberk I struggled gradually to recovery. I sat with Dr. Anther in his office and talked to him of Langbrith, my dead enemy.

> I've seen the time when I wanted to go into the cemetery and dig him up and burn him, but I don't know as I do now. What do you say, Doct' Anther? Let bygones be bygones, as the fellow said about his old debts when he started in to make new ones? Still it does gravel me—

Our library lamp had begun to go out. I was myself again. As it winked and gulped and I blew it out to darkness, I could see that upstairs they had thoughtfully left the hall gas burning for me; and that, since it was late, and they would probably wake up when I put it out, I ought to go to bed. I went, filled with the thought of the wonder of the actual world and the adventures of its myriad souls, souls so magnificent, so funny, so tragic, so miraculous, each in his own way on his journey unlike that of any other soul.

I had known before that "life like a dome of many-colored glass stains the white radiance of eternity." But I had forgotten it, until the repose and charm of a work of art revealed the truth to me. Now that the multitudinous, differentiations of life had been suggested to me, I was able to look as through a crystal at my difficulties. Whatever

North American Review, 196 (September 1912), 339–52.

they had been, I could have looked at them with a clearer mind, and as after a clarifying recreation.

It is for this I read fiction—for its imaginative realization of life, for its creative power. A book is no better to me than a dungeon, a party telephone, or any other formal accepted method of preventing genuine, human intercourse, unless I can live freely in its pages, unless I can emerge from the convincing truth of its world, back into my own ways, as from some sparkling sea-change into something rich and strange.

I turn to fiction to be metamorphosed, and literally for my re-creation. Of course I know there are other ways of reading novels.

> Who shall meet them at these altars—who shall light them to that shrine?
> Velvet-footed who shall guide them to the goal?
> Unto each his voice and vision, unto each his spoor and sign—

People read novels as differently as they dance and dress and eat. Many, far from liking a thorough metamorphosis, feel a species of alarm before a work of fiction unless it has the quality of unreality. These readers prefer in a novel some rather violent presentment of which they are to be reassured as to its illusory character. They are with superficial, but without essential, difference the immemorial audience of Shakespeare's humorous outline, who must be continually told that the stage-lion is really Snug the joiner, and that the composition truly is child's play.

Others enjoy in the art of fiction only the reproduction of certain conventional literary effects. Their pleasure in reading is not in walking into the picture, but in looking to see whether it repeats some pattern they had delighted in before.

I love to walk into the picture. I love to read "dreaming true." I love to read myself awake in fresh fields and pastures new and to walk through them, letting down the bars on one unknown incarnation of existence after another. I wish a novel to maintain the old connotation of its name, and far from painting again a conventional and twice-told or hundred-times-told composition to give me a *Weltanschauung* which is new. I ask of a novelist not that he should convince me of the un-life-likeness of his fable, nor that he should repeat a pattern in writing, but that he should add an authoritative and original design, should evoke for the world his own peculiar and fresh impression of life—that he should contribute.

The genius of Mr. Howells contributes a great gallery of these impressions, an exhibition of social story heretofore untold, of country and city scenes, of human souls and characters in a variety and scope, which makes them, for readers who have the passion for dreaming true, a constant admiration, a beloved enjoyment, and what can only be described as a solid satisfaction. . . .

Innumerable authors can call spirits from the vasty deep of American life without ever making them come. Doubtless it is because he uses the right words to bring them that they answer Mr. Howells's summons, in such numbers and variety. Judges and traveling-men and lawyers and doctors and dressmakers and spiritualists and society leaders and farmers and cabin-boys and playwrights and inventors and agitators and convicts and clubmen and millionaires and boarding-house keepers and journalists and Shakeresses—men and women and children of all sorts and conditions.

They rise before you with the delicacy and right individuality of human friends. The society women are not social strugglers bound up in the possession of their poodles and tiaras, but the sensible and distinguished Mrs. Bowen of the Italian-American consular circles and the humorous limited and graceful Nannie Corey of Boston. The dressmakers can speak in natural accents and without pins in their mouths; and you can like them and love them and look forward with delight to spending the afternoon with them. The former old farmer, Deacon Latham, talks to you, not of crops, but of whether his granddaughter is going to be homesick with her aunt in Venice. The clubmen are visible at instants when they are not tipping the waiter. You know one of them, Mr. Otis Binning, for instance, an elderly bachelor, far better than as though you had seen him hailing cabs and tipping waiters interminably, by one paragraph of a letter of his, written to a relative in Boston after he has been in New York two months:

> The literary superstition concerning us elderly fellows is (or used to be in the good, old Thackeray times) that we are always thinking of our first loves, and are going about rather droopingly on account of them. My own experience is that we are doing nothing of the kind. We are the only cheerful people in the world, and so long as we keep single we are impartially impassioned of almost every interesting type of woman we meet. I find the greatest pleasure in bestowing my affections right and left, and I enjoy a delightful surprise in finding them hold out in spite of my lavish use of them. If I totted up the number of my loves, young and old, since I came here early in December, Leperello's list would be nothing to it.

Mr. Howells's millionaires and agitators are men besides being millionaires and agitators. The vivid and moving tale of Dryfoos, the speculator and owner of the land where natural gas-wells are discovered; the portrait of Silas Lapham against the riches of his mineral-paint industry are of the profoundest force and wisdom of Mr. Howells's art. They are absolute. Of the same quality is the tragic figure of Lindau— the veteran German-American Socialist and translator, who has lost his hand in the Civil War. . . .

Among all his portraits none are more arresting than Mr. Howells's presentations of speculative American natures—Dr. Boynton, Fulkerson, Colville, Mr. Waters, Wanhope, Hewson, March—perhaps there is a touch of the love of speculation in all his American men. Indeed, it sometimes seems as though the passion for speculation, whether exemplified by men shouting in the pit, in the Board of Trade, or by the tendency to say "I guess," or by William James's "Will to Believe," or San Francisco's generous determination to give Ruef a chance in civic life after his prison term, were characteristic of almost all kinds of American men—their most deep-seated, national characteristic, and producing at once their meanest acts and their greatest. The trait is wonderfully revealed in *The Quality of Mercy, The Son of Royal Langbrith, The Undiscovered Country, A Hazard of New Fortunes.* Sometimes it is indicated with the perfection of irony. . . .

Sometimes the passion for speculation is conveyed with an ineffable emotion and beauty that lie too deep for tears, as in the death of Dr. Boynton.

Again, the charm of a fancied plan for the sake of the glamour of chance is perfectly evoked, as it shines in a boy's heart, in *The Flight of Pony Baker*—told with a warmth, a funniness, a justice to the soul of a child, which make you feel that every boy on earth needs to be understood as delicately as Howells understands Pony Baker, and ought to be as responsibly cherished.

In general I believe that cosmopolitanism and international understanding are better served by the novelist who discovers to the world the natures of his own countrymen as they develop in their own land, than by the novelist who contributes his guess about the inhabitants of other countries. Of course, Mr. Henry James, distinguished genius in surmise, his reverence and absoluteness in "making out" the texture of the spirits of the men and women of other countries, as well as of his own, are a complete exception. His endowment and career in this kind are not only supreme and peerless; I think they are unique. Thackeray's Florac and Mr. Howells's Lindau and his wonderful delineation of an Austrian officer in *A Fearful Responsibility*, Mr. Galsworthy's Louis Ferrand, and Arnold Bennett's French aeronaut in *The Old Wives' Tale*, all seem compact of essential truth. One can call to mind many a solitary and occasional figure and even group, in literature, created and presented with verity by a novelist of an alien nation. But in general I believe the great and authoritative tale a writer has to tell the world will be the tale of life in his own land. Whatever else he may say, Daudet tells the tale of the boastful, the fatuous and irresistible Midi unless he tells the tale of the worldly sparkle and the worldly tragedy of Paris. Whatever else he may say, Turgénief tells the tale of the brooding sadness and oppression of liberty-loving Russia. Whatever else he may say, Howells tells the tale of the speculative soul of America. The "French" novels, the "Russian" novels, the "American" novels of these writers are not "views" of these countries caught through the fancy nor upon a railroad journey, nor assembled from popular reports; they are knowledge of these nations learned through the penetration and imaginings of enriching years of life.

I believe there is no way in which a novel *has* to be made. Or, if there is, it certainly should be opposed for its arbitrariness, in the interest of truth. But the novel in whose pages I dream true most fully is generally made, or rather grows, from the natural actions of its men and women, instead of having its movement worked from outside, as it were, by the determination and ingenuity of the author. I know that in the English of "criticism," or maybe it is the English of advertising, the words "novel of action" are ordinarily used to mean "novel of mechanism"; and that a gay book where the characters are manipulated smartly from spot to spot to suit a skilful plan of the author, as in a marionette theater or a game of chess, is called a "novel of action"; and a novel like *The Old Wives' Tale* or *Fathers and Sons* or *The Quality of Mercy,* where the men and women are not pawns or marionettes, but figures of flesh and blood, and are not mechanically manipulated, but act, is never called a "novel of action." So that when one employs the word "action" to indicate in fiction anything else but sword-play, one must qualify the term. I admire Mr. Howells's books because they are made of the *natural* actions of men and women, succeeding and struggling and failing and cheating and hating and loving and parting and marrying and dying. I admire a story of the burning hopes and desires of idealistic youth, like *The Apprenticeship of Lemuel Barker*; and the absurd and tragic episode of his arrest and his night and day in the police-station are among the most dramatic situations I have ever seen in any novel. I admire a story of the misunderstanding of different generations; and the scene where Dryfoos stands by his son's coffin in *A Hazard of New Fortunes* is one of the most intense scenes I have ever lived in on a printed page. I admire a story of passion and jealousy and infidelity like *A Modern Instance*; and a story of crime and of human forgiveness and the punishments of the heart and of the law like *The Quality of Mercy*; and a story of the freshest romance of love, like *The Lady of the Aroostook.* All the score and more of Mr. Howells's novels present the movement of human nature with the arresting and convincing clearness of realization, with abiding fictive power.

Whatever scene or situation Mr. Howells imprints has always the air of being an integral part of the whole wide world. You are not oppressed as you sometimes are in the presence of some other scenes and situations in literature—by a starved sense of the violent fictive isolation of some "set" of people, who seem to be cut off from all healthful nourishment from the common springs of the various, actual life of the globe.

These social scenes and situations are as various and heretofore untold as Mr. Howells's characters—the public masked ball Mrs. Bowen, Imogen, and Colville attend in Florence; the shooting of Conrad Dryfoos in the car riot; the dedication of the library at Saxmills to the hypocritical exploiter of his townsmen, by his victims; Marcia Hubbard's meeting on the Boston afternoon street, with the girl her husband has wronged; the snow battle in *Fennel and Rue*—many other aspects and deeds of life, newly observed and lucidly revealed.

Among all these scenes I chance to like best those that breathe the charm and scent of tangled outdoor places. That ragged sharp-branched look of the roads and woods, even of settled country, in America, that look which is somehow of the very essence of a rough sweetness and homeliness, gives me an indescribable and peculiar delight such as one finds in a change of weather or the honk of a wild duck. . . .

It is so, that every creative book breathes to the reader dreaming true a special vision of existence. It is so, that each of Mr. Howells's novels says by its presence, something about life which none of its drama alone, nor its scene alone, nor its narrative, nor its characters can tell. It is, I think, the souls in a novel which make its soul. Only art or the living presence may evoke the soul. It is not by speaking of them you know the souls of Mr. Howells's men and women, which are the finest evocations of his art; nor know the soul of each of his novels, but only by reading them.

While each of Mr. Howells's novels sings its own melody, it keeps the time of "the ragged rhythm of life." The incongruous contrasts, the familiar queernesses and illogicality of mortal circumstances—the quality in the fates that makes one almost able to rely upon their being irrational and unexpected in their determination—weave that seizing rhythm through all Mr. Howells's fiction. . . .

The objection has been made to Mr. Howells's poetry, as to other work of his, that it is sad. Such a criticism, in the character of an object, seems to me inept. For if expression does not recognize sadness, how can it give comfort? I will go further than this and say that I believe that not only is there no comfort for sadness in the expression which implies an ignoring of loss or an ignoring of injustice or of hardship upon earth, but that the completest mercy of mirth itself remains unknown to him who never ate his bread with tears.

In his editorial writing, too, in social criticism and literary criticism, in biography and autobiography, as in his novels and poems, I am cheered by the fact that Mr. Howells is not of those who consider, like Dickens's people at the picnic, that "whatever is the matter we ought always to dance." I am reassured because he has no alarming credulous confidence that all that is in American institutions is right; and reassured because his national interest has none of that fatalistic depressing "patriotism" contained in the phrase, "My country, right or wrong," of which Mr. Chesterton remarks that it is as though one should say, "My mother, drunk or sober." This pessimistic species of "patriotism" seems especially undesirable in a critic.

For if the tones of novels, of plays, of poems present, for the reader who reads dreaming true, the inner life, the moods of some changed existence, it would seem to be the function of those other arts in letters which may be loosely called criticism—editorial and biographical writing, travels and reviews—less to assert a devotion to the errors of one's nation than to open a window for the reader upon its ideas and affairs as a part of the ideas and affairs of the whole world.

In this field Mr. Howells has offered to his readers a view of more scope than that displayed by any other of our men of letters I can call to mind. It was he who, as Mr. William Allen White has pointed out, expressed the idea of altruism to America in a day when that principle was chiefly regarded here simply as "a curious theory." It was he who, as Mr. Frank Harris has pointed out, spoke for freedom of belief and against the murder of the Chicago anarchists, in a day when the whole mind of the American public was as closed, as darkened and insane a bedlam on the subject as the mind of Massachusetts once had been upon the subject of the practical necessity of burning witches.

It has been Mr. Howells in a very great degree who has helped America to know, by his acumen and by the generosity and warmth of his appreciation, the power and genius of the great Russians Turgénief and Tolstoi, the drama of Ibsen and Björnsen, the dreaming glamour of Du Maurier, since so widely worshiped and apparently so widely forgotten, the thrilling supernaturalism of Hauptmann, the enchanting light on life that falls from the fresh and spiritual tales of the Spanish Valdés and the Italian Verga. His enlightening survey of the ideas of the world reaches not only around us and before us, but back to the true romance and immortal irony of Cervantes and the wisdom of Machiavelli.

Letters is of all others the social art. By social I mean communicative, intended for every one. A marked gift of Mr. Howells, as a critic, is his talent of geniality, that ambassadorial grace of a man of the world, which is also the grace of genuine democracy and makes the reader feel in the presence of a thrilling, new idea, or a distinguished, relative piece of literature as though this were one's natural sphere.

In his service to the great cause of good reading, reading for the realization of what is before the reader, reading for the free and inspiring reception of new truth, Mr. Howells's career as a critic has been of incalculable value to all American letters. By a psychological process very comprehensible, the sort of fiction-reader who likes to be subconsciously assured that the stage-lion is only Snug the joiner, and that the bloodshed, violence, and oppression he is reading about are not as they are in nature but are all child's play—by a very facile turn of thought this sort of reader is apt, when he sees a real lion brought upon the stage by a truthful journalist or reviewer or publisher, to soothe himself by thinking there is nothing to the lion, and he is artificial; apt to soothe himself about some honest factual account of suffering, of poverty or oppression on our earth, by thinking it must be just an illusory story—without reality. The worst effect of the opiate manner of reading fiction is that it unavoidably begets an opiate manner both of reading and of facing fact. Still more than for the writers and the readers of fiction, Mr. Howells's constant stand for the clear discriminations of the truth is of value for the writers and the readers of facts supporting the whole press, the book, the periodical, the newspaper press—all the readers and writers who are or ought to be concerned with the candid presentation of contemporary history.

The clear discriminations of truth in public expression are especially necessary for our own country where all confusion of verity is certain to become worse confounded from the circumstance that its people are more heterogeneous, of more various traditions and races and tongues, than those of any other one land.

In his life-long service for the realization of truth, both as a constructive critic and as a creative artist, Mr. Howells has, I think, made for his nation an immortal contribution to the cause of social sympathy and genuine common understanding which is the great end of all letters.

Who can come away from the sincerity of his pages without a sense of the profound poetry of realization, the poetry of knowing life? Who can come away without the belief that nothing else is so vital and so thrilling an adventure as to know one's own life, in one's own place on this actual earth of one's own day and generation?

For whatever our uncertainty, our dream, or faith about the eternities before us and behind us, we have by the proof of our senses this miraculous existence here. In this we know that the greater and deeper achievement of truth bestowed upon us by each generation is all that has helped us to more free enjoyment and fairness, all that has helped us to understand our fellow-mortals more generously and more rightly on our mysterious journey, and to warm and sustain one another more richly from the unknown fire of life kindled in us in the beginning. No names are more honored nor more loved than those which stand for the greater and deeper achievement of truth.

One cannot give thanks exactly for their contribution, for thanks are too little and too personal a thing to give, besides being rather unnatural. One's feeling for the things one cares about is less the sense of thanks than simply one of happiness. It is more with that sense than with any other that one thinks about the beautiful and continuing career of a constant truth-teller, the beloved and honored name of William Dean Howells.

Howells

John A. Macy*

. . . . Nature made him witty, genial, sympathetic, observant, and endowed him with an infallible ear for the rhythms of English prose. To read any of the beautiful pages of "Venetian Life" (the book in which he is nearest to being a poet, for in those days romance and youth were still a generous current in his soul)—then to read "The Flight of Pony Baker," a delicious boy's book which proves that he was incorrigibly young at sixty-five—then to read any of his twenty novels— is to get an impression of a man of rare and diversified gifts born to be one of the great interpreters of human life. But something happened to him—he was stricken by the Dead Hand in Literature. There was in his vicinity no live literature to sustain him, to keep him in a state of courageous contemporaneity with the world about him. He fell back on the past; and even the seven or eight modern European literatures with which he is familiar are, as he speaks of them, remote, romantic, misty. He writes of Tolstoy as he writes of Jane Austen or Dante. He became the Dean of American Letters, and there was no one else on the Faculty. Huckleberry Finn ran away from school and did not go near college until Yale and Oxford played a joke under cover of the academic twilight and gave him gorgeous red gowns; Mr. Howells was very early Europeanized and Bostonized, and his Ohio outlook on life was dimmed by the fogs of tradition.

It was the letter of old Europe and old Boston, not the spirit, that assailed and clouded him. He read French fiction and admired its shapelessness, yet he caught little more from its intensity and candour than a virginal New England schoolmistress might have received. He is as innocent (and charmingly so) as his own Lydia Blood. He read Tolstoy, and he makes the amazing statement that Tolstoy had a great influence on him. One would hear with no less surprise that Hawthorne was profoundly influenced by Swift or that Jane Austen felt that she had been made over by Rabelais. There is not one trace of the

*Reprinted from *The Spirit of American Literature* (New York, 1913), 278–95.

influence of Tolstoy, of Tolstoy's body of thought, soul, purpose, method, power, on any page of Mr. Howells that I have read. Tolstoy's terrific sense of life does not ripple the surface of Mr. Howells's placid unemotional work. And his essay on Tolstoy is sentimental, feminine and unimpressive.

Some one (was it Mr. George Moore?) has said that Mr. Henry James went to Paris and read Turgenev and that Mr. Howells stayed home and read Mr. James. This is malicious and probably not true as a matter of biographical fact. But it is aimed near the critical truth. The realistic novel grew up naturally from historic roots in France and in Russia. It was nurtured by a veracity of mind and a social freedom, utterly alien to the hypocrisy and the superficial optimism of America. Mr. Howells and Mr. James, alert to fine achievement, admired this great Slavic and Gallic performance and they seem to have said: "Go to! realism is the real thing; we will be realists." They thus accepted the self-imposed limitations of realism, but they could not accept its profound privilege of telling the truth. America would not perhaps have tarred and feathered a man honest and intrepid enough to write as Balzac, Flaubert, Tolstoy, Dostoievski wrote, but it would not have permitted him to be Dean. Mr. Howells's realism is like a French play adapted for our stage; the point of the original is missed, and we wonder, as we watch the Frohmanized translation, how Frenchmen can be so dull. To take the method of realism without its substance, without its integrity to the bolder passions, results in a work precise in form and excellently finished, but narrow in outlook and shallow. Hamlet and the King's crime are both left out.

Mr. Howells, with no American but Mr. James to invigorate him by contest or support him by intelligent coöperation, got into a *cul-de-sac*; it looked like the way to a new country, but the way was barred. As a critic, he became the lone argumentative voice of a realism which he could not practise; he could not in his novels illustrate his conviction, or make clear what the issue is.

The issue may be stated roughly as follows: Fiction is a poetic limitation of biography. It makes the magnificent assumption that its characters are real people and proceeds to tell a part of their lives. In order to maintain this primary assumption, it must do one of two things: either it must make events so entertaining that no one cares to question the reality of the people (as when Achilles slays Hector or Dido pines for Aeneas); or it must make the people so real, so verisimilar, that no one dares to question their reality. Romance does the first of these two things; the kiss of the fairy prince is so delicious that no one asks whether there ever was a fairy prince. Realism does the other thing. It says that its people are true and are interesting because they are true. Truth cannot go wrong; it must hold the attention of intelligent minds, and as for unintelligent minds, they may devote themselves to bridge-whist and comic operas. But having thrown down the gauntlet to falsehood and unlife-like invention, Realism immediately puts itself under obligation to deal with the whole truth so far as artistic proportions allow; it cannot slink behind timid suppressions and reservations and still hope to win in its contest with Romance. It cannot play with its left hand tied behind its back. To the reader of fatuous romance, Realism says: "Life is more interesting than that; read this; it is about life." And it must offer something really richer and more interesting; it must offer Tolstoy or Balzac.

What if it offers "A Modern Instance?" It loses its case at once. Instead of demonstrating that life is interesting, that the commonplace is uncommonly interesting if you get under it and understand it, "A Modern Instance" demonstrates with fine precision that life is not interesting to the people that live it and that commonplace is just as commonplace as the romantic had always supposed it to be. Living people, common or extraordinary, have passions. "A Modern Instance" is passionless. The people in it, with the exception of Squire Gaylord, are not so profoundly moved that the reader catches the contagion of *their* feelings and *their* interests. Mr. Howells's realism, proclaiming the identity of life and literature (and his critical essays proclaim the same truth many times and in admirable manner) leaves the great things in life out. If there were no more passion in the world than Mr. Howells recognizes and portrays, about eighty million of us Americans would never have been born, and, once born, half of us would have died of ennui.

Mr. Howells says somewhere that he cares only for the thing, common or uncommon, that reveals its intrinsic poetry. That is a right attitude, but it is not the attitude of Mr. Howells's novels, for he is not a poet, as Meredith and Hardy and Flaubert are poets. He strips life not only of its false romance but of its true romance. True realism imaginatively understands the romantic feelings of people in ordinary daylight circumstances. A sworn champion of theatric and juvenile romance, like Stevenson, does not need to be argued into liking the great realists, Fielding or Balzac; he takes to them naturally because they are rich and humane, because they too are men of fancy and see that life is full of terrific tragedies and adventurous comedies. Mr. Howells, narrow in his convictions and timid in his handling of the very passions which make great realistic novels, tilts his lance against Stevenson and other men of exuberant fancy and thinks he is fighting the battle of honest fiction. He is not, and the net result of his critical writings and his novels is to turn the battle against himself. Seldom in his books does he come to grips with a terrible motive or heart-tearing ecstasy—and people have those motives and those ecstasies in real life. . . .

Is he not, after all, a feminine, delicate, slightly romantic genius, theoretically convinced that realism is "the thing," but not equipped with the skill and experience to practise it? . . . . His knowledge of things and people is as restricted as that of the New York *Nation* or the *Saturday Review.* Life may be a tempest in a teapot. If it is, Mr. Howells is one of its finest and most faithful recorders. But he puts the emphasis on the teapot and not on the tempest, which is hardly consonant with his often restated, almost militant declaration that literature is life. He sees things from a distance; he is a sketcher, a very delicate farceur, a war correspondent who has never been in range of the bullets.

The foregoing negations oversay themselves, unless it is understood that Mr. Howells takes literature with tragic seriousness and that he handles other authors in a very strict and schoolmasterly fashion; so that he is fairly to be judged by his own severe standards of what is worth while in fiction. In his book "My Literary Passions" ("passions" there is the only case in all his work of a misused word), and in his pronouncements from "The Easy Chair" and other seats of critical judgment he has been plain and direct, for all his mild manners and unapproachable tact, in his abuse of some very great writers. Moreover, the negations that are here somewhat awkwardly set down are valid, only on the hypothesis that we are discussing a man of genius, a man worth discussing, and are trying to say why an important, capable novelist is not a great one. Within his limits he is a perfect artist. His slender comedies are without a blemish. He never wrote a bad page, never wrote a sentence that any one else could make better. . . .

If in his many books Mr. Howells has not had a great deal to say that is significant, he has said everything he meant in an unimprovable manner. There are secondary writers who have no influence on our thinking, whose wisdom is not profound, whose ideas we do not vividly recall, for example Addison, Hawthorne, Pater. But any one with a sense of literary craftsmanship can read them with pleasure, reread them with increasing admiration. Such a writer is Howells. Even when his story is not quite compelling, his writing fascinates; it is a joy to watch him manoeuvre the English language. . . .

Mr. Howells's books are of such even excellence that perhaps none is unquestionably best, but one vote is cast herewith for "The Kentons." There Mr. Howells is getting back home. He knows the Ohio state of mind; at least—since there may be no Ohio state of mind—he knows that one Ohio family, and it is an excellent family, in itself as a collection of human beings and in its artistic entity as a novelist's creation. Bittridge is a sort of middle-western Bartley Hubbard, but he is much better drawn than the other journalistic bounder. As for the girls, they are a little more warmly and humanely handled than some of the other young people whose love affairs Mr. Howells has graciously sketched.

The suffering of the elder daughter is quite poignant and moving. On the whole Mr. Howells's treatment of young people in love is refreshing in a world full of novels the chief object of which is to get a man and a girl eagerly into each other's arms on the last page; there is a slight acidity in his management of youthful matings which makes for sanity and never becomes so sharp as to be unkindly or at the least cynical. The grand passions, sexual or other, he does not draw and seldom attempts to draw; therefore he has never written a great novel.

Contemporary Novelists:
William Dean Howells

Helen Thomas Follett and Wilson Follett*

I

William Dean Howells is quite the most American thing we have produced. Almost all that one can profitably say of him distributes itself about his central magnetizing fact. Of the lessons he has taught us, no other seems half so important as the supreme value of having a home, a definitely local habitation, not to tear one's self away from, to sigh for, to idealize through a mist of melancholy and *Weltschmerz*, but simply and solely to live in, to live for. This part of his doctrine, more than any other, has the noble force of an eternal verity preached with striking timeliness. It is in itself the special crown of Mr. Howells, the open secret of his democratic grandeur; and it wins double emphasis because it had to be urged against the sterile aesthetic cosmopolitanism of the eighteen-eighties. Both his historical importance and, one may confidently hope, his permanence are affirmed by his anchorage in a provincialism as remote from mere provinciality as from the opposite extreme of cosmopolitanism—the 'wise provincialism' of Royce's *Philosophy of Loyalty.*

Moreover, the work of Mr. Howells, the most soundly representative expression of America as a spirit, is also the most broadly representative of America as a civilization. It falls in the era of the great transitions of our national life, the confusion of shifting ideals and mislaid ideas which led to the most American thing we have ever done—our specialization of everything. The war is over, and Howells comes back from his Venetian consulship to watch the phenomena of reconstruction, the

*Reprinted from *Atlantic Monthly,* 119 (March 1917), 362–72.

emergence of a more centralized political system, and the dawn of a new unity. Agriculture grows relatively less important, manufacturing relatively more so; and thereupon begins the flux of young men and women from village to city, from farm to factory and office, and the consequent specialization of multitudes of lives. In industry, the epoch of individual enterprise merges into that of great combinations and corporate monopolies; business too becomes specialized. As commerce gains respectability, idleness becomes dubious and finally odious; and the result is a cleavage between generations in many a patrician family, the parents clinging to an old ideal of the leisured ornamental life, the sons drawn by a new ideal of useful prestige.

When the new aristocracy of vigor has supplanted the old aristocracy of cultivation, there arises the new cultivation, through efficiency. The laboring class, disproportionately augmented by immigration, develops a self-consciousness; its problems become insistent and terrible. In the professions, the general practitioner of an elder time turns into the specialist. Journalism and advertising—the quintessentially modern professions—begin to have their day. Among women, too, a ferment is at work: they swarm through doors once closed, they begin to know something, subtle changes take place in the home, marriage itself hears questions asked of it and knows that sooner or later it must answer them. Dogmatic theology is sharply challenged when the physical sciences reconceive the world, and the social sciences the people in it. The sense of an organic unity replaces that of an organized unity—and the world begins to wonder what purpose it serves, what it can possibly *mean*. Casting about, it begins to think it sees a purpose in unity itself. And through the confusion there crystallizes slowly the dream of a real society in which the common interests shall overthrow the conflicting ones. In a score of ways the America of 1875 was at the crossroads. And William Dean Howells was the man who was there with her to see everything. He saw—and he understood.

All these tendencies and forces—the recital of them may be tedious, but it is certainly indispensable—are charted in the fiction of Mr. Howells, with an amplitude and a fidelity applied elsewhere, as in the novels of Trollope, to much narrower sectors of life, but never before in English to all the important phases in the life of a whole nation. It is as lavish as anything since Balzac, and it is focal. Howells is master of village and town, farm and city, New England and the Middle West; he is at home in factory and lumber-camp; he knows artisan and idler, preacher and teacher, the scientist, the journalist, the commercial traveler, the *nouveaux-riches* and their débutante daughter, the country squire, the oldest inhabitant, the village scapegrace and the village fool, the doctor and the lawyer; he misses nothing as a review written by his greatest American contemporary once phrased it, of 'the real, the natural, the colloquial, the moderate, the optimistic, the domestic, and the democratic.'

And he has through all this, in addition to the notion of where we are, the vision of where we are going. His novels convey the impression of greater lapses of time than any one of them actually records, because each one of them is an inquiry into something that is about to become something else. *The Rise of Silas Lapham,* our first and best analysis of the self-made man and of the social implications of his money, is a tragedy whose significance reaches nearly the whole of self-made America. Written at the nexus of so many tendencies and interests, the novel remains to-day as poignantly contemporary as ever, a drama of transitions not yet more than half accomplished. We clamor still for 'the great American novel'? Why, we have been reading it these thirty years and more.

II

A comment of thirty years ago, written by one of the most unflattering of critics, has at least the merit of confirming, from a hostile and derogatory point of view, this fact of Mr. Howells's provincialism. 'Henry James,' said Mr. George Moore in *Confessions of a Young Man,* 'went to France and read Tourguénieff. W. D. Howells stayed at home and read Henry James. . . . I have no doubt that at one time of his life Henry James said, I will write the moral history of America, as Tourguénieff wrote the moral history of Russia—he borrowed at first-hand, understanding what he was borrowing. W. D. Howells borrowed at second-hand, and without understanding what he was borrowing.'

These remarks, whether or not we can agree to find in them something more important than their author intended to put there, leave something to be desired as accounts of literal fact. It should be evident now, for example, even if it was not in 1887, that it was Mr. Howells, rather than Henry James, who consciously set out to write the moral history of America. Also, Mr. Howells knew at first-hand, not only his Tourguénieff and his James, but Galdós and Valdés as well. If his critical interest was never quite so intensive in its workings as Henry James's, it was certainly much more eclectic. Its boundaries in 1887 did in fact touch everything that we now recognize as having been at that time important in Continental fiction and drama, with the single exception of Meredith, who seems, lamentably, to have meant nothing to Howells. Many readers and some critics could still learn a good deal about Balzac and Zola, about Dostoïevski and Tolstoï, from what Mr. Howells wrote about them more than a quarter of a century ago.

But one of the principal effects of his excursions among Italian,

Spanish, Russian, and French realists was greatly to intensify his appreciation of Miss Wilkins, Miss Jewett, Mrs. Cooke, Miss Murfree, and Mr. Cable—American realists whose worth, like his own, is all in their provincialism; whose breadth is, as he says, 'vertical instead of lateral.' If his fiction withholds the cheap tribute of imitation, it is doubly rich in its recognition of the inimitable. His way of learning from Tourguénieff was not to copy Tourguénieff, but to be as American as Tourguénieff was Russian. In the profoundest spiritual and moral sense, he did stay at home; but neither physically nor intellectually can he be said to have done so. He not only understood just what he might have borrowed, whether from Continental fiction or British: he understood it too well to borrow it at all.

The alleged resemblance between Howells and Henry James is a subject which has been irritatingly overelaborated by criticism. What resemblance there is is so superficial, and leaves room for differences so fundamental, that it becomes a point for criticism of Mr. Howells's critics rather than of Mr. Howells himself. But so many have conspired, both before and since George Moore, to make sure that neither great man shall be named without the other, that it is actually more invidious to ignore the point than to treat it.

To make an end of the matter, one may say that the similarities are most important where there is least hint of any debt,—that is, where each author is writing of the New England he knows—and that where there *is* the hint of a debt, the similarity is purely verbal and almost too insignificant to bother with. However strange it may seem, it is true that Mr. Howells, whose style has for fifty years remained limpid and lacustrine, shows after 1895 an unconscious infiltration of the abused 'third manner' of Henry James. *Miss Bellard's Inspiration*, a tenuously delicate bit of high comedy, includes among its pretty sophisticated trifles some persiflage of the Henry James idiom—for example, the parting comment by Mr. Crombie, 'Well, I suppose she did n't want a reason, if she had an inspiration.'

But this sort of thing is of slight avail, is in fact positively silly, when one is dealing broadly with the question of 'influences.' While Henry James withdraws further and further from the America we know, into the queer world of his own intensely self-conscious art, Howells remains as objective, as regional, and as little self-conscious as an artist can be. It is utterly true that, in the sense we have described, he stayed at home; but the compliment is to America, not to a brother author.

There is assuredly nothing in all this to disturb our account of that provincialism which is the nourishing root of his greatness. Morally, it is the whole story. If we speak, as here we have had to for a moment, of lighter and lesser things,—aesthetics, comparative literature, the transmission of influences,—we have to revise the account only so far as to say that Mr. Howells, if he did not stay at home, *went* home. We find him going everywhere but to go back again; enjoying one after another his Continental journeys of the mind and of the body, as turnings of the road; never forgetting that great sprawled-out provincial modern Rome to which, he knew, whatever road he happened to be on must at length lead back; finding beauty, the beauty of self-fulfillment, in each successive reunion between the America he had left and the American he was.

Concretely, his books of travel, his various *Italian Journeys* and *London Films*, are better and truer records because there is no affectation in them of being anywhere except 'abroad.' Provincialism, like religion, is a surrender of something for the sake of something else that means more. If you are at home everywhere, you have lost the meaning of home. Mr. Howells prefers to give up being at home everywhere, in order to see Europe through naïve yet shrewd 'Yankee' eyes, very much in the mood of

> You have curious things to eat,
> I am fed on proper meat;
> You must dwell beyond the foam,
> But I am safe and live at home.

The result is that his most casual sketches of Italy, Spain, and England are not less American than *A Boy's Town* and *The Lady of Aroostook* —which are as American as Abraham Lincoln.

III

In speaking of the sacrifices with which Mr. Howells, like any one, must pay for a sound and wise provincialism, we have in mind first of all the penalty inherent in any choice, the mutual exclusion of opposites. It is in the nature of things that you cannot be at the same time cosmopolitan and provincial: you can have everything or you can have something which shall mean everything to you, but not both. This is the inevitable penalty. And it is well for the artist who has the courage or the sublime innocence to pay it, as we see proved in the unpretentious successes of such authors as Trollope and Jane Austen. If we require proof that it is *not* well for the artist who lacks the courage or the innocence, we need seek it no further back than the pretentious failures of the Celtic Renaissance—a movement which had its headquarters in France and its impulse from a cosmopolitan aestheticism, and which was everything else before it was Celtic. We are safe, then, while we laud Mr. Howells for giving up everything, and acquiring nothing, which could have made him less definitively cisatlantic.

But there is another kind of penalty, incidental and secondary, not at all in the nature of things, which Mr. Howells also elected to pay, with damage to his work and even some risk to its lasting qualities. Seemingly in pure national self-assertiveness and a kind of fierce pride in heaping up the measure of his self-denials, he refused some things which he might fully as well have had. These minor refusals of his are made in all conscience, indeed with the finest recklessness; but they unquestionably blemish his work as that of a rounded artist, while adding nothing to its value as a national institution. If the future should disprove his theory that truth to fact is everything; if it should show that care for treatment counts for more than he supposed it could, his greatness will have been impaired, and none the less surely because through his own deliberate renunciations.

One is happy to note, first, that he was constantly threatening some sacrifices which he never made, and that his work as critic abounds in precepts the consequences of which he refused to incur in his own practice. He despises care for style, and says that style becomes less and less important to fiction: yet he writes a style finer on the whole than Hardy's, since it is just as objective, just as clear, much more full of high lights and undertones, and less metallically cold. He damns with faintest praise the necessary technical means of art; he seems to imply that the artist can draw the pattern of his facts, as well as the facts themselves, from life; his account of Jane Austen would lead one to suppose that the sum of her process was to look about and jot down what she saw; in short, he develops a theory of the relation between literature and life that would result, if anyone literally practiced it, in novels with masses of subject-matter but no subject at all. 'Out of this way of thinking and feeling about these two great things, about Literature and Life,' there has indeed 'arisen a confusion as to which is which'—a confusion which has become in the last decade one of the least promising symptoms of the novel. And Mr. Howells seems to welcome the confusion when he says, 'It is quite imaginable that when the great mass of readers, now sunk in the foolish joys of mere fable, shall be lifted to an interest in the meaning of things through the faithful portrayal of life in fiction, then fiction the most faithful may be superseded by a still more faithful form of contemporaneous history.'

Yet here again Mr. Howells follows infirm doctrine with sound practice: his own novels enjoy all the advantages of the definite issue carefully extracted from life and then displayed before the reader as having relevance to some unified critical purpose. To young authors he says, 'Do not trouble yourselves about standards and ideals.' Himself, he follows a better precept: 'Neither arts, nor letters, nor sciences, except as they somehow, clearly or obscurely, tend to make the race better and kinder, are to be regarded as serious interests'—a dictum which is unintelligible unless it provides art with a *rationale*. The creative artist is made as much by what he *wants* as by what he knows; and what he wants involves, of course, the whole question of how he is to get it. It is strange that Mr. Howells, who never desired fiction to be less than a criticism of life, should so often have ignored this truism in his critical writings and so unfailingly have used it in his fiction.

Neither in the style nor in the architecture of his novels, then, does he suffer the logical consequences of what is narrowly provincial in his theory. But in one deficiency of treatment, the enormous excess of conversation over everything else, his stories do suffer from his contempt of design. He appears, as Henry James wrote long ago, 'increasingly to hold composition too cheap'; he neglects 'the effect that comes from alternation, distribution, relief.' The dialogue especially needs to be 'distributed, interspaced with narrative and pictorial matter.' It is not that there is too much of the dialogue, which is uniformly of the first excellence, but that there is too little else. Mr. Howells is at his very best when he is giving his subject wrapped in interpretation of character and manners. He makes a woman speak 'with that awe of her daughter and her judgments which is one of the pathetic idiosyncrasies of a certain class of American mothers.' He speaks of the deplored 'infidelity' of a New Hampshire village squire as a time-honored local institution, 'something that would hardly have been changed, if possible, by a popular vote.' He is subtle in his notation of such realities as 'the two sorts of deference respectively due to the law and the church,' and 'the country habit of making no comment in response to what was not a question.' These touches are treatment, presentation at its finest, 'the golden blocks themselves of the structure'; and when Mr. Howells dispossesses them in favor of talk and still more talk, he deprives us of that which he can more abundantly afford to give than we can afford to be without.

IV

Unless one is in the heroic mood to require that the writer of fiction supply a full measure of everything one happens to like, one need not be greatly disturbed by the several details about Mr. Howells that one simply cannot understand. Why does it happen that, with all his coldness to technique, he instinctively warms to the most careful technicians, from Jane Austen to Hardy and Henry James? Why, against that same coldness, should he reject Thackeray because Thackeray pleased to 'stand about in his scene, talking it over with his hands in his pockets, interrupting the action, and spoiling the illusion in which alone the truth of art resides'—a minor technical quiblet if ever there was one?

Why should he denounce Scott for 'acquiescence in the division of men into noble and ignoble, patrician and plebeian, sovereign and subject, as if it were the law of God,' without allowance for the fact that Scott often makes his plebeians nobler than his patricians, the subject more of a man than the sovereign? Why, above all, should he belittle Dickens because of the occasional caricature of people and the romantic distortion of facts, and not see that Dickens was *on the whole* a valiant fighter in the cause of realism against an effete romanticism, precisely as Mr. Howells himself was?

The only explanation of these sophisms is that Mr. Howells loves truth—by which he nearly always means actuality—so much that the most trivial violation of it affronts all his sensibilities. Let an author, especially a British author, tell more truth than anything else, let him further truth in intercourse and sternly rebuke whatever tends to defeat it: all this goes for naught, if in a moment of deference to some innocent romantic fashion now discredited, he is caught dodging realities. Why, the fellow cherishes 'shadows and illusions,' he is 'very drolly sentimental and feeble'; Mr. Howells will have none of him. We can think of hardly any other critic of equal repute who has allowed so little that he disliked to overrule so much that he would have liked if he could have taken the trouble to see it. This is an explanation, of a limping sort; but it does not materially reduce the deficit chargeable to Mr. Howells as critic.

What does materially reduce it is, of course, his historical position and influence. Preaching realism and democracy at a time when the novel, under the sanction of Stevenson and Anthony Hope Hawkins, was trying as hard as it could to get back to Scott and Dumas, he was in the position of a man who must shout if he is to make the unwilling crowd listen, and even so can make them hear but one thing. Most of Mr. Howells's criticism, despite its urbane moderateness of tone, is essentially controversial. He was decrying a fashion which he hated as spurious and silly; his own message was the ugliness of whatever denies or shirks reality, and his exaggeration of that ugliness was simply the raising of his voice to overcome inattention. We do not think that he said what he did not mean, in order to be heard; but unconsciously he was carried away by his enthusiasm, as any small minority tends to be. The measure of his usefulness was the universal need of just that message, and his justification is its later universal acceptance. He fought the costume romance, and it is dead; he predicted the 'sociologic' novel, and it has come, to the exclusion of pretty nearly everything else.

In short, the author of *Criticism and Fiction* (1891) was one of the very few great modern men who have been deeply enough immersed in the stream of historical tendencies, and sensible enough of main currents in the life about them, really to understand and work for the future. He decried the romantic novel when it had most applause, in terms which show that he thought of it as already discredited. More characteristically, he decried a certain mawkish and very fashionable kind of sentimentalism—the sentimentalism of useless self-sacrifice made in a bad cause, on the theory that self-sacrifice is in itself a great enough good to be sought at the expense of everything else. Many readers will recall the instance in *Silas Lapham*: a girl's refusal to marry a man because her sister is madly in love with him, and the author's admonition (expressed, it happens, through a minister of the gospel) that it is better for two people to be happy and a third unhappy for a time than for all three to be permanently wretched. In both these particulars Howells is of the twentieth century more than of the nineteenth.

But even these are as nothing to his vision of what the future was to do for brotherhood among men, the increase of economic and social community, and the sense of 'living in the whole.' That sense, he saw, was what fiction must acquire unless it were altogether to lose step with the world; and in precept and practice he helped fiction acquire it. 'Men are more like than unlike one another,' he said; 'let us make them know one another better, that they may be all humbled and strengthened with a sense of their fraternity.' 'The work done in the past to the glorification of mere passion and power, to the deification of self, appears monstrous and hideous. . . . Art, indeed, is beginning to find out that if it does not make friends with Need it must perish.' And to Matthew Arnold's complaint that there was no 'distinction' in our national life, he justly and eloquently retorted:—

'Such beauty and such grandeur as we have is common beauty, common grandeur, or the beauty and grandeur in which the quality of solidarity so prevails that neither distinguishes itself to the disadvantage of anything else. It seems to me that these conditions invite the artist to the study and the appreciation of the common, and to the portrayal in every art of those finer and higher aspects which unite rather than sever humanity, if he would thrive in our new order of things. The talent that is robust enough to front the every-day world and catch the charm of its work-worn, care-worn, brave, kindly face, need not fear the encounter, though it seems terrible to the sort nurtured in the superstition of the romantic, the bizarre, the heroic, the distinguished, as the things alone worthy of painting or carving or writing. The arts must become democratic, and then we shall have the expression of America in art; and the reproach which Mr. Arnold was half right in making us shall have no justice in it any longer: we shall be "distinguished."' '

V

Because Mr. Howells's love of reality is more intense and consistent than that of any other important novelist we can think of,—and we have thumbed the list of others with some pains for the possible exception,— his realism is inexpressibly more vital than most realism. Of writers who explored the actualities because they distrusted or feared them, despised or did not know what to make of them, we have seen many, perhaps too many, since the turn of the century; but Mr. Howells is not of this company. No one has done him justice who has not seen that his love of life is his belief in life, and that it is to him quite literally a *faith*. By this we do not mean that he accepts everything as it is, proposing no improvements,—we have already seen how much courage he derives from the facts of social evolution,—but we do mean that he sees in life itself, ever struggling to articulate consciousness and beginning to operate all the forces that are necessary to a great society and a great art. For him, there is no need of a fiat to legislate order into society from without; nor does he go to the opposite extreme of giving up the hope of order. All things work together for good, because that is the nature of them—even of things not in themselves good.

Thus, for him, intimacy with the real stands in the room of more prerequisites to art, and is altogether more sufficient, than we commonly know it capable of. He is a generation further along in the chronology of art than such a realist as Gissing, with whom reality was a distressing makeshift for lost faith. Mr. Howells appears never to have cherished illusions. Partly because he brought over from his early work as journalist and editor a vivid sense that life was in itself enough, and more because he was born with the probing mind that will not believe without sight where it is possible to see, he picked his way serenely through the religious disturbances of the decades when even Huxley and Arnold were spending themselves in theological controversy. He reports the disturbances, indeed, but tolerantly, indulgently, as things milder than they seemed, more ephemeral, less real. Here again his faith took him forward beyond the stresses of his time; he looks back on struggles little more than begun.

This faith in the reality which is our daily life is strikingly exemplified in everything Mr. Howells has written about the phenomena of mysticism. It was only the other day that he gave us, after a long incubation, *The Leatherwood God*, his record of religious imposture in a small Ohio community of the early nineteenth century. It shall not be said here that he intended this story as a sly and subtle *exposé* of all religion through direct physical revelation: all that the evidence warrants is the assertion that he *may* so have intended it, and that if so he could not have done much more to sharpen its point. Clearly it expresses his contempt of the faith that demands a sign. And in Squire Matthew Braile, the shrewd and humorous 'infidel' of Leatherwood, we have not only a striking individual of one of Mr. Howells's most sympathetic types, but also the intellectual point of view of the book. 'Why,' says Braile, 'I don't see what you want of a miracle more than you've had already. The fact that your cow did n't come up last night, and Abel could n't find her in the woods-pasture this morning, is miracle enough to prove that Dylks is God. Besides, did n't he say it himself, and did n't Enraghty say it? . . . When a man stood up and snorted like a horse and said he was God, why didn't they believe him?' In all this quizzical irony did Mr. Howells mean to say, for hearing ears only, that Christianity is to him, not the water and the wine, the loaves and fishes, the empty tomb, the harps and crowns, but a rule of life which can neither be given nor taken away by any of these, and which is real whatever becomes of them?

We ask, not answer, the question. But it is worth while to note that the conjecture interlocks most adroitly with something Mr. Howells had written more than thirty-five years earlier—his analysis of spiritualism and its materializations in *The Undiscovered Country*. 'All other systems of belief, all other revelations of the unseen world, have supplied a rule of life, have been given for our *use* here. But this offers nothing but the barren fact that we live again. . . . It is as thoroughly godless as atheism itself, and no man can accept it upon any other man's word, because it has not yet shown its truth in the ameliorated life of men. . . . As long as it is used merely to establish the fact of a future life it will remain sterile. It will continue to be doubted, like a conjuror's trick, by all who have not seen it; and those who see it will afterwards come to discredit their own senses. The world has been mocked with something of the kind from the beginning; it's no new thing.'

The quoted words are Dr. Boynton's: who can doubt that the meaning is the meaning of Howells? He will have nothing to do with the mysticism which is only 'a materialism that asserts and affirms, and appeals for proof to purely physical phenomena.' Its sole effect is to drive him homeward to the plain every-day faithful and courageous actual. His philosophy is all in the cry of a foolish woman who has given a bolt of linsey-woolsey that the Leatherwood God may turn it into 'seamless raiment.' ' "Oh, I don't care for the miracle," she kept lamenting, "but what are my children going to wear this winter? Oh, what will *he* say to me!" It was her husband she meant.'

VI

The corollary of faith is peace. And the faith of Mr. Howells in the realities of life brings to him, throughout the inordinate business of his career,[1] a peace, a large serenity, that one instinctively thinks of in Scriptural phrases—'the peace that passeth understanding'; 'He that believeth shall not make haste.' We have seen how little friction and loss he suffered during years when the fading of supernaturalism brought a tragic unrest into nearly the whole Western world. Through those years while others fought, he enjoyed; and even when he fought, as sometimes one must for opinions worth holding, it was in the jolliest fighting mood, and with a good-nature as uncompromising as the opinions. If he had enemies to tackle, at least he was on the best of terms with himself. If it were not so, how should one account for the preponderance in him of humor, a tranquil attribute, over wit, a restive?

We would be at some pains to distinguish this deep composure of Mr. Howells from the merely vegetative contentment of which he is rather irresponsibly accused in several quarters. To words already quoted Mr. George Moore adds, in the mood of patronizing impishness which had then become his fixed mental posture: 'I see him [Mr. Howells] the happy father of a numerous family; the sun is shining, the girls and boys are playing on the lawn, they come trooping in to a high tea, and there is dancing in the evening. . . . He is . . . domestic; girls with white dresses and virginal looks, languid mammas, mild witticisms here, there, and everywhere; a couple of young men, one a little cynical, the other a little overshadowed by his love; a strong, bearded man of fifty in the background; in a word, a Tom Robertson comedy faintly spiced with American.' These are indeed the ingredients, this is a large part of the formula—and it is a large part of America, too.

What George Moore really meant was that Mr. Howells had not chosen to be turgidly frank about sex. To which the answer is that Mr. Howells had chosen *not* to be, for the good reason that America does not share the Continental obsession, and provides singularly little in sex to be turgidly frank about. Mr. Howells explains himself on this point in two chapters of *Criticism and Fiction*; and in *A Modern Instance*, which contains some of his most intimitably faithful tragicomedy of New England village life, he makes these observations upon the girl entertaining her suitor at midnight in a sleeping household: 'The situation, scarcely conceivable to another civilization, is so common in ours, where youth commands its fate and trusts solely to itself, that it may be said to be characteristic of the New England civilization wherever it keeps its simplicity. It was not stolen or clandestine; it would have interested every one, but would have shocked no one in the whole village if the whole village had known it; all that a girl's parents ordinarily exacted was that they should not be waked up.'

This is not the ignorant bliss; it is the *pax Americana* that leaves youth blessedly and uniquely free from the experience of guilty love,—

> . . . a heart high-sorrowful and cloy'd,
> A burning forehead, and a parching tongue.

No: the equableness of Mr. Howells is something other than the languor that aspires 'to sit in a corner tippling tea.' It consists of elements dynamic but under the control of knowledge and faith. Set a taut wire vibrating and touch it with the thumb-nail: it gives forth a jangling buzz. Mr. Howells's criticism of life is the wire left to vibrate harmoniously; there is nothing to disturb its free play in the vast quiet space of his charity, his faith, and his self-command. The Celtic rebelliousness which he inherited gives it *timbre* and poignancy but not discordance; and again and again the rarely beautiful overtones, such as that poor defrauded woman's cry for her lost labor, prove that it is taut, not slack.

And, finally, Mr. Howells proves his profound calm in his most American appreciation and retention of the ardors of youth. We cannot see that he wrote better about youth when he had it than latterly, with all his weight of years and honor; or that he knows the meaning of age better in his eightieth year than in his fortieth. In his philosophy, things must always be renewed if they are to live; the present must re-create itself out of the dead past, and be perpetually attaining perpetual youth. Language renews itself: 'No language is ever old on the lips of those who speak it.' Literature renews itself: 'Most classics are dead.' And life renews itself. When, in *The Son of Royal Langbrith*, Mr. Howells treats the problem of wealth got through the chicane of the father, and the serious question of the children's attitude toward it, he makes an end of the whole matter by letting the sleeping dog lie. 'It came to Anther again, as it had come before, that each generation exists to itself, and is so full of its own events that those of the past cannot be livingly transmitted to it; that it divinely refuses the burden which elder sins or sorrows would lay upon it, and that it must do this perhaps as a condition of bearing its own.'

There is more than a touch of this indomitable youth in the characters, the best of whom live on, no older now than when we last saw them. Rarely, they step, like Trollope's characters, from one book into another—and then they are doubly welcome, doubly alive.

This year of Howells's eightieth birthday is also the centenary of Jane Austen's death—fitly, because he has honored himself in honoring her, and because she too loved reality and made successful war, from her provincial citadel, on superstition, on mawkish sensibility, and on the tinsel romanticism of the fashion then current. The years in which she was quietly fulfilling her allotted task were, like this year, made terrible by war and the pouring out of blood; yet she pursued her way and kept her faith, in a quietude untroubled by the great stirrings of empire abroad.

It is to be feared that Mr. Howells has not known how to keep himself untroubled—for the world is smaller now, and crowded, and what hurts one hurts all. Our wish for him on New Year's Day, when these words are written, is that he may wring from this very fact, the community of pain, a confirmation of solidarity in the world, and a hope for its eventual triumph. If we could venture to wish him anything else, it would be that he might find somehow the way to keep on believing in America—his America of the soiled hands and the good heart.

Notes

1. Including, as readers of this article will like to remember, a fifteen years' connection with the *Atlantic*, of which he was editor-in-chief for ten years [authors' note].

The Dean

H. L. Mencken*

Americans, obsessed by the problem of conduct, usually judge their authors, not as artists, but as citizens, Christians, men. Edgar Allan Poe, I daresay, will never live down the fact that he was a periodical drunkard, and died in an alcoholic ward. Mark Twain, the incomparable artist, will probably never shake off Mark Twain, the after-dinner comedian, the flaunter of white dress clothes, the public character, the national wag. As for William Dean Howells, he gains rather than loses by this confusion of values, for, like the late Joseph H. Choate, he is almost the national ideal: an urbane and highly respectable old gentleman, a sitter on committees, an intimate of professors and the prophets of movements, a worthy vouched for by both the *Atlantic Monthly* and Alexander Harvey, a placid conformist. The result is his general acceptance as a member of the literary peerage, and of the rank of earl at least. For twenty years past his successive books have not been criticized, nor even adequately reviewed; they have been merely fawned over; the lady critics of the newspapers would no more question them than they would question Lincoln's Gettysburg speech, or Paul Elmer More, or their own virginity. The dean of American letters in point of years, and in point of published quantity, and in point of public prominence and influence, he has been gradually enveloped in a web of superstitious reverence, and it grates harshly to hear his actual achievement discussed in cold blood.

Nevertheless, all this merited respect for an industrious and inoffensive man is bound, soon or late, to yield to a critical examination of the artist within, and that examination, I fear, will have its bitter moments for those who naïvely accept the Howells legend. It will show, without doubt, a first-rate journeyman, a contriver of pretty things, a clever stylist—but it will also show a long row of uninspired and hollow books, with no more ideas in them than so many volumes of the *Ladies' Home Journal*, and no more deep and contagious feeling than so many reports of autopsies, and no more glow and gusto than so many tables of bond prices. The profound dread and agony of life, the surge of passion and aspiration, the grand crash and glitter of things, the tragedy that runs eternally under the surface—all this the critic of the future will seek in vain in Lr. Howells' elegant and shallow volumes. And seeking it in vain, he will probably dismiss all of them together with fewer words than he gives to "Huckleberry Finn." . . .*

Already, indeed, the Howells legend tends to become a mere legend, and empty of all genuine significance. Who actually reads the Howells novels? Who even remembers their names? "The Minister's Charge," "An Imperative Duty," "The Unexpected Guests," "Out of the Question," "No Love Lost"—these titles are already as meaningless as a roll of Sumerian kings. Perhaps "The Rise of Silas Lapham" survives—but go read it if you would tumble downstairs. The truth about Howells is that he really has nothing to say, for all the charm he gets into saying it. His psychology is superficial, amateurish, often nonsensical; his irony is scarcely more than a polite facetiousness; his characters simply refuse to live. No figure even remotely comparable to Norris' McTeague or Dreiser's Frank Cowperwood is to be encountered in his novels. He is quite unequal to any such evocation of the race-spirit, of the essential conflict of forces among us, of the peculiar drift and color of American life. The world he moves in is suburban, caged, flabby. He could no more have written the last chapters of "Lord Jim" than he could have written the Book of Mark.

The vacuity of his method is well revealed by one of the books of his old age, "The Leatherwood God." Its composition, we are told, spread over many years; its genesis was in the days of his full maturity. An examination of it shows nothing but a suave piling up of words, a vast accumulation of nothings. The central character, one Dylks, is a backwoods evangelist who acquires a belief in his own buncombe, and ends by announcing that he is God. The job before the author was obviously that of tracing the psychological steps whereby this mounte-

*The ellipses are Mencken's, and his text is entire.

bank proceeds to that conclusion; the fact, indeed, is recognized in the canned review, which says that the book is "a study of American religious psychology." But an inspection of the text shows that no such study is really in it. Dr. Howells does not *show* how Dylks came to believe himself God; he merely *says* that he did so. The whole discussion of the process, indeed, is confined to two pages—172 and 173—and is quite infantile in its inadequacy. Nor do we get anything approaching a revealing look into the heads of the other converts—the saleratus-sodden, hell-crazy, half-witted Methodists and Baptists of a remote Ohio settlement of seventy or eighty years ago. All we have is the casual statement that they are converted, and begin to offer Dylks their howls of devotion. And when, in the end, they go back to their original bosh, dethroning Dylks overnight and restoring the gaseous vertebrate of Calvin and Wesley—when this contrary process is recorded, it is accompanied by no more illumination. In brief, the story is not a "study" at all, whether psychological or otherwise, but simply an anecdote, and without either point or interest. Its virtues are all negative ones: it is short, it keeps on the track, it deals with a religious maniac and yet contrives to offer no offense to other religious maniacs. But on the positive side it merely skims the skin.

So in all of the other Howells novels that I know. Somehow, he seems blissfully ignorant that life is a serious business, and full of mystery; it is a sort of college town *Weltanschauung* that one finds in him; he is an Agnes Repplier in pantaloons. In one of the later stories, "New Leaf Mills," he makes a faltering gesture of recognition. Here, so to speak, one gets at least a sniff of the universal mystery; Howells seems about to grow profound at last. But the sniff is only a sniff. The tragedy, at the end, peters out. Compare the story to E. W. Howe's "The Story of a Country Town," which Howells himself has intelligently praised, and you will get some measure of his own failure. Howe sets much the same stage and deals with much the same people. His story is full of technical defects—for one thing, it is overladen with melodrama and sentimentality. But nevertheless it achieves the prime purpose of a work of the imagination: it grips and stirs the emotions, it implants a sense of something experienced. Such a book leaves scars; one is not quite the same after reading it. But it would be difficult to point to a Howells book that produces any such effect. If he actually tries, like Conrad, "to make you hear, to make you feel—before all, to make you *see*," then he fails almost completely. One often suspects, indeed, that he doesn't really feel or see himself. . . .

As a critic he belongs to a higher level, if only because of his eager curiosity, his gusto in novelty. His praise of Howe I have mentioned. He dealt valiant licks for other débutantes: Frank Norris, Edith

Wharton and William Vaughn Moody among them. He brought forward the Russians diligently and persuasively, albeit they left no mark upon his own manner. In his ingratiating way, back in the seventies and eighties, he made war upon the prevailing sentimentalities. But his history as a critic is full of errors and omissions. One finds him loosing a fanfare for W. B. Trites, the Philadelphia Zola, and praising Frank A. Munsey—and one finds him leaving the discovery of all the Shaws, George Moores, Dreisers, Synges, Galsworthys, Phillipses and George Ades to the Pollards, Meltzers and Hunekers. Busy in the sideshows, he didn't see the elephants go by. . . . Here temperamental defects handicapped him. Turn to his "My Mark Twain" and you will see what I mean. The Mark that is exhibited in this book is a Mark whose Himalayan outlines are discerned but hazily through a pink fog of Howells. There is a moral note in the tale—an obvious effort to palliate, to touch up, to excuse. The poor fellow, of course, was charming, and there was talent in him, but what a weakness he had for thinking aloud—and such shocking thoughts! What oaths in his speech! What awful cigars he smoked! How barbarous his contempt for the strict sonata form! It seems incredible, indeed, that two men so unlike should have found common denominators for a friendship lasting forty-four years. The one derived from Rabelais, Chaucer, the Elizabethans and Benvenuto—buccaneers of the literary high seas, loud laughers, law-breakers, giants of a lordlier day; the other came down from Jane Austen, Washington Irving and Hannah More. The one wrote English as Michelangelo hacked marble, broadly, brutally, magnificently; the other was a maker of pretty waxen groups. The one was utterly unconscious of the way he achieved his staggering effects; the other was the most toilsome, fastidious and self-conscious of craftsmen. . . .

What remains of Howells is his style. He invented a new harmony of "the old, old words." He destroyed the stately periods of the Poe tradition, and erected upon the ruins a complex and savory carelessness, full of naïvetés that were sophisticated to the last degree. He loosened the tightness of English, and let a blast of Elizabethan air into it. He achieved, for all his triviality, for all his narrowness of vision, a pungent and admirable style.

INDEX

Stedman, E.C., xv, 52
Steele, Richard, 225
Stendhal, 149
Sterne, Lawrence, 101
Stevenson, Robert Louis, 148, 167, 244, 253
Stowe, Harriet Beecher, 75
Swift, Jonathan, 242

Taft, William Howard, 219, 220-21
Taine, H., 233
Tarkington, Booth, xxi
Tennyson, 77, 137
Thackeray, W.M., xv-xvi, 31, 32, 35-36, 37, 42, 57, 100-01, 110, 115, 116, 150, 156, 159, 164-65, 175, 191, 225, 252
Thayer, William Roscoe, xi, xx, xxiii, xxiv, 147-56
Ticknor & Co., 90
Timrod, Henry, 218
Tolstoi, xii, xxiii, 59, 78-79, 100, 112, 141, 151-52, 157, 165-67, 211-12, 226, 240, 242-43, 244, 248
Trollope, Anthony, 31, 116, 221, 247, 250, 258
Turgenev, xii, 43, 59, 79, 84-86, 88, 179, 237, 240, 243, 248, 249

Valdés, A. Palacio, 107, 240, 248
Vedder, H.C., xxiv, 157-60
Venice, xii-xiii, 4-5, 17-18, 58, 62, 63, 130-32, 141, 221, 224, 236
Verga, Giovanni, 240
Vogüé, Emile de, 147-48, 195

Wallace, Lew, 139
Warner, Charles Dudley, xxiii, 31, 32, 93, 125-26
Washington, D.C., 57-58, 73-77, 220
Waters, Harriet P., xxix, 194-97
Wells, H.G., 217
Wharton, Edith, 261-62
White, William Allen, 219, 226-27, 240
Whitman, Walt, xxiii, 107, 122-25, 138
Whittier, J.G., 76-77, 138
Wilcox, Marrion, 177-83
Wilkins, Mary E., 144, 215-16, 249
Wordsworth, William, 3, 101, 125, 155, 178
World's Work, 209-12
Wyatt, Edith, xxx, 234-42

Zangwill, Israel, 148
Zola, Émile, xviii, xxiii, 43, 44, 53, 54, 59, 66, 79, 86, 114, 135, 148, 149, 150, 156, 166, 248